Reflective Teacher Education

SUNY Series, Teacher Preparation and Development
Alan R. Tom, Editor

Reflective Teacher Education

Cases and Critiques

Linda Valli,
Editor

STATE UNIVERSITY OF NEW YORK PRESS

Published by
State University of New York Press, Albany

© 1992 State University of New York

For information, address State University of New York
Press, State University Plaza, Albany, N.Y., 12246

Production by E. Moore
Marketing by Dana E. Yanulavich

Library of Congress Cataloging-in-Publication Data

Reflective teacher education : cases and critiques / Linda Valli,
    editor.
        p.   cm. — (SUNY series, Teacher preparation and development)
    Includes bibliographical references (p.   ) and index.
    ISBN 0-7914-1131-1 (alk. paper). — ISBN 0-7914-1132-X (pbk. :
alk. paper)
    1. Teachers—Training of—United States—Case studies. I. Valli,
Linda, 1947-   . II. Series: SUNY series in teacher preparation and
development.
LB1715.R35   1993
370'.71'0973—dc20   91-30789
                                                                          CIP

10 9 8 7 6 5 4 3 2

Contents

ALAN R. TOM

Foreword

Little more than five years ago, I was a participant in a symposium on "inquiry-oriented" teacher education at the annual meeting of the American Educational Research Association. In my presentation, published as "Inquiring into Inquiry-oriented Teacher Education," I created three dimensions for identifying and explicating the differences among existing rationales and approaches to inquiry-oriented teacher education. In preparing the paper, I had considerable difficulty deciding which approaches to teacher education should be included under the rubric of inquiry-oriented, and finally concluded that "the parameters for what counts as inquiry teacher education are fuzzy" (Tom, 1985, p. 36).

I believe that ours was the only AERA symposium in 1985 on inquiry-oriented teacher education, a not surprising development in that very few teacher education programs had an inquiry emphasis other than in student teaching and the supervision accompanying that student teaching. However, I do remember that the audience at the symposium was attentive to our presentations, and subsequent years have witnessed accelerating involvement by teacher educators in inquiry-oriented teaching, now commonly called reflective teaching, a label change probably attributable to Schön's influential book published in 1983.

While I did anticipate more attention to reflective teaching among teacher educators, I was completely unprepared for the explosion of interest that occurred in the late 1980s. I am amazed that a mere six years after our 1985 symposium Zeichner and Tabachnick (1991, p. 1) can state: "There is not a single teacher educator who would say that he or she is not concerned about preparing teachers who are reflective." As some evidence for this broad claim, I moderated another AERA symposium last year in which teacher educators representing such diverse perspectives as cognitive psychology, social reconstructionism, and narrative inquiry addressed in quite differing terms what each of them considered to be the essence of reflective teaching and teacher education.

At minimum, there are three ways to interpret the intensified interest in reflective teacher education, accompanied by the continuing failure to achieve clarity and consensus about the nature of reflective teaching. Some observers of the current scene believe that we are merely experiencing another teacher education fad analogous to the competency-based teacher education movement of the 1960s and 1970s. According to this view, teacher educators are superficially attracted to reflective teacher education due either to its current popularity or to some external pressure such as the new requirement of the National Council for Accreditation of Teacher Education (1990) that all programs be grounded in a "model" for professional preparation.

Other observers believe that our definitional difficulties reside in the failure of "teacher educators to identify clearly the educational and political commitments that stand behind their own and others' proposals regarding reflective teaching" (Zeichner & Tabachnick, 1991, p. 2). In this case, external forces are not so much the source of the problem as is the reluctance of teacher educators to specify and make public their educational beliefs.

While I see merit in both of these interpretations, I also think that a third set of educational and cultural developments is important for understanding the fluidity—even the disarray—of the current scene in reflective teacher education. We teacher educators are, I believe, in the midst of a revolution of how we view the nature of teaching and, therefore, of teacher education. Gone are the days in which we presumed that the results from research on teaching would unlock the secrets of effective teaching and eventually yield prescribed skills or teaching behaviors for the professional curriculum, even though researchers on teaching continue to talk as if their work does provide a "knowledge base" for the professional curriculum (e.g., Good, 1990). The contribution of systematic research on teaching to the teacher education curriculum will likely be much more indirect and context-specific than researchers have envisioned.

In addition to this loss of faith in the efficacy of teaching effectiveness research, Linda Valli outlines in her introductory chapter several other factors that help account for the spectacular rise of reflective teaching and teacher education. These factors include the ascendancy of cognitive over behavioral psychology, an intensified interest in the moral basis of education, a growing movement for teacher empowerment, and in increased acceptance of ethnographic inquiry and action research. Though dramatic and wide ranging, these changes are relatively recent and do not necessarily complement one another.

In this context of ferment and possible realignment of the intellectual traditions within teacher education, we should not be surprised that debate and discord surround the topic of reflective teaching and teacher education. On the contrary, the absence of confusion and contention would be cause for alarm, as such a development would suggest a lack of insight on our part of the massive changes which seem to be occurring in how we view the nature of teaching and teacher education.

But what courses of action are most likely to move us toward a view of reflective teaching that is coherent yet comprehensive, and sophisticated yet practical? One obvious answer is that we need additional attempts to understand, conceptually, how various approaches to reflective teaching and teacher education compare to one another and how reflective teaching relates to broader intellectual developments within our society. Critics in this book address these and related conceptual issues.

At the same time, we can also profitably approach the issue from the viewpoint of what happens when a teacher education faculty decides to make reflective teaching the core—or a strong supporting element—of its program. Developing a teacher education program is a social process in which individuals need to develop shared perspectives and to articulate their teaching efforts with colleagues, all within the context of educational institutions. These social and organizational processes are much more complicated than having a single faculty member write a paper about the nature of reflective teaching. The case studies in this book begin the process of analyzing the intricate institutional processes involved in developing reflective teacher education programs.

Thus, the interplay between conceptual analysis and case studies in this book may help us develop a coherent conception of reflective teaching that is comprehensive enough to take into account the social and institutional realities that impinge upon program development. At the same time, this interplay between conceptual analysis and case studies should help us as teacher educators to balance our need to be practical enough to cope with the pragmatic demands of program development against our need to be more sophisticated than the platitudes that sometimes pass for teacher education rationales and goals.

I believe that the plan of this book does move us forward, both in conceptual and programmatic terms, toward answering two questions: How ought we define and practice reflective teaching? What issues are central to designing programs of reflective teacher education. The reader, then, will be left with the ultimate question: Is reflective teacher education worthy of being pursued? I believe that *Reflective Teacher Education: Cases and Critiques* will help the reader consider this paramount question.

LINDA VALLI

Introduction

What does being a good teacher mean? And how does teacher education contribute to the development of good teachers? Surprisingly, these questions are not always central to the design of programs to prepare teachers. All too often images of good teachers and knowledge about good teaching are left unarticulated, presumed to be part of a shared, but tacit, understanding. As a result, one of the most fundamental aspects of teacher preparation is left unexamined. In place of a coherent conception of good teaching, tradition, institutional forces, and external constraints often shape the teacher education curriculum, a curriculum which has become so standardized (almost reified) in its basic course requirements that conflicting purposes and unformulated assumptions have been obscured.

This standardized approach to teacher preparation is, of course, not without its critics. In their review of research on teacher education, Lanier and Little (1986) use the terms technical, fragmented, and shallow to characterize a curriculum they perceive as having been relatively static over the past few decades. Goodlad's recent *Study of the Education of Educators* faults teacher education for not clearly linking the curriculum "to a conception of what teachers do and should do" (Goodlad, 1990, p. 186). Barnes (1987) argues that programs lacking powerful, thematic, or conceptual orientations fail to dislodge prospective teachers' naive notions of teaching. And Tom is concerned that "without a concept of good teaching, a teacher education curriculum becomes nothing more than a means for preparing teachers to replicate current school practice" (1986, p. 11).

Departing from this fragmented approach to teacher education, the programs described in the first part of this book are characterized by a commitment to curricular reform around a conception of good teaching. They are further united by agreeing that this concept must embody a reflective orientation to practice, an orientation which emphasizes the knowledge, disposition, and analytic skills needed to make good decisions about complex classroom phenomena.

The authors of the seven cases have all worked to infuse reflection throughout the entire professional education component of their preservice programs. As implied by the preceding paragraphs, this work stands in marked contrast to the easier and more dominant practice of altering individual courses or instructional strategies (Zeichner, 1987; Ross, 1990). While numerous books (Schön, 1987; Grimmett and Erickson, 1988; Clift, Houston, and Pugach, 1990; Tabachnick and Zeichner, 1991) have discussed the possibilities and ambiguities of fostering reflective practice, none has provided an in-depth and comparative look at attempts to implement reflection at a programmatic level. The purpose of this volume is to provide such a perspective. As an introduction to the case study and critique chapters, I first explore the questions of why reflective teaching has attracted so much interest and whether or not it is a distinct approach to teacher preparation. This latter issue is revisited in the concluding chapter.

THE SOCIAL CONTEXT OF REFLECTION

The reader might well ask why an interest in reflective teacher education has emerged at this time and how this emphasis can benefit teachers, schools, and students? As with most trends, a combination of factors converge, including the perceived limitations of process/product research, the impact of cognitive psychology, renewed attention to the moral basis of education, interest in teacher empowerment, and the legitimation of ethnographic research.[1]

Recent years have witnessed what Doyle (1990) calls the breakdown on consensus about "technical rationality" being an appropriate model for the preparation of teachers. Process/product research has failed to generate a substantial and significant set of findings to guide the preparation of teachers. Even more damaging, the research paradigm itself has been seriously challenged as an inadequate way to explain and guide teaching (Shulman, 1987; Richardson, 1990; Tom and Valli, 1990). The fragmentation of knowledge into small, discrete elements and the treatment of knowledge as independent of goals and context hamper process/product researchers from even roughly approximating the real work of teachers. This failure explains much of the renewed interest in Dewey's notion of reflective practice and the appeal of Schön's concept of the reflective practitioner with its emphasis on uncertainty, artistry, and context-specificity as more helpful, relevant images of good teaching.

A related factor in explaining renewed interest in reflection is the increased dominance of cognitive over behavioral psychology. Focusing on thinking rather than observable behavior, cognitive psychologists seek to describe and explain the mental processes which underlie complex activities. When they study teaching, these researchers ask questions like: How do expert teachers plan? What are differences in the ways expert and novice teachers think about teaching? What is involved in teacher decision-making? This shift in psychology has provided fertile ground for explorations into teachers' thinking, problem solving, and reflectivity. In 1986, Clark and Peterson reviewed the wide array of studies on teachers' thought processes. This tradition has also produced highly personalized accounts of teaching (Elbaz, 1983; Grossman, 1990) as well as cognitively grounded, theoretical models of pedagogical reasoning and action (Shulman, 1987; LaBoskey, 1991).

Attention given the moral and political foundation of teaching by increasingly vocal and influential groups of feminists, multiculturalists, critical theorists, and mainline researchers has further eroded the orientation to teacher education as the prescription of pedagogical and managerial skills. These groups have been successful in arguing that the rightful agenda for teacher education is much broader than teaching technique and must include consideration of the goals and purposes of schooling, whose interests schools serve, and whose knowledge they legitimate (Valli, 1990). They have argued that in a pluralistic society, the goals of education cannot be taken-for-granted but must be debated and negotiated; that answers to complex, value-laden problems of schooling are not ready-made; and that the preparation of teachers able to function in such a society requires critical reflection on the normative issues of teaching and schooling.

Renewed concern about teacher empowerment and professionalization has also stimulated interest in reflective teacher education. Autonomous, self-renewing, and self-directed professionals must be capable of more than executing the curriculum designs conceived by others. They must be dispositionally and cognitively prepared to engage in dialogue about the proper goals of schooling and the educational needs of an increasingly diverse population of school aged children. Within the context of this social responsibility, teachers must be prepared to solve complex educational problems, make wise decisions, reflect in and on action, and collaborate with colleagues. Prospective teachers will not be prepared for this type of practice if they have merely learned to transfer findings from effective teaching research to their practice.

Although not directly accounting for the emergence of reflective teacher education, the increased interest in and legitimation of ethnographic and action research has also contributed to its development. More and more teacher educators are becoming trained in naturalistic and ethnographic methodologies. Because these research orientations emphasize the context dependence of research findings and the importance of attending to the meanings actors give to and take from their milieu, they tend to support the type of goals associated with reflective teacher education programs. Teacher educators who themselves use these methodologies are apt to promote reflection by encouraging teacher candidates to use ethnographic and action research to examine and improve classroom life.[2] The fact that feminists and critical theorists are among those most strongly proposing the use of action research is no small coincidence. Regarded as a form of authoritative knowledge, action research can empower the typically female and relatively powerless classroom teacher. It can liberate teachers from being regarded as lesser partners in school reform—as the subordinate element in the thinker/doer, scholar/practitioner dichotomies.

The convergence of interest in teacher thinking and reflectivity by scholars ranging from cognitive psychologists to critical theorists suggests a broad based and long-term commitment to understanding and fostering reflective practice. In contrast to mechanistic, behavioral models of teacher preparation, reflective models are more in keeping with the holistic way in which teachers actually think and act in classrooms; they have more intuitive credibility (Richardson, 1990; Shulman, 1987). Moreover, reflective approaches to teacher preparation hold out the promise of a new cadre of teachers ready to be active partners in school renewal—teachers who can make wise classroom decisions and who can help define the direction of schooling as we approach the start of a new century.

REFLECTION AS A CONCEPTUAL ORIENTATION

Several attempts have been made to distinguish conceptual orientations or paradigms of teacher preparation. These typologies are generally developed for the purpose of illuminating implicitly conflicting conceptions of good teaching. They are useful guides for action and can serve as "heuristic device(s) for organizing discussion about desirable teacher education practices" (Zeichner, 1983, p. 3). Some typologists are primarily descriptive, some advocate a particular vision of teaching and teacher education, while still others examine strengths and weaknesses across paradigms. Most often, reflective or inquiry-oriented teacher education is described as one of these paradigms.

While most typologists distinguish four or five conceptions of good teaching and teacher education, Kennedy (1989) offers just two: the reflective practitioner model and the professional standards model. In her schema, reflective practitioners have a thoughtful, contextualized sense of teaching and must ultimately make their own choices about preferred goals and practices. They construct working knowledge out of various frames of reference and alternative viewpoints. This ambiguous working knowledge, which favors personal experience but also includes theory, research, values, and beliefs, is used to critically analyze and continually improve teaching.

In contrast, the vision of good teaching found in the professional standards model is more clear-cut and prescriptive. Good teachers apply special knowledge and engage in practices widely agreed upon. Using prescribed knowledge, not personal judgment, is the key to successful teaching. This model is commonly referred to as technical rationality, the goal of which is to ensure that teachers conform to acceptable patterns of behavior (Doyle, 1990).

Unlike Kennedy, Zeichner (1983) offers four alternative paradigms of teacher education which are "held together by a set of common assumptions that distinguishes the basic goals of one general approach from another" (p. 3). In the behavioristic paradigm, good teachers are those who carry out the prespecified competencies and principles of effective teaching. The personalistic paradigm equates good teaching with psychological maturity and personal growth; professional beliefs and perceptions are reconstructed around students' perceived needs. Good teaching in the traditional-craft paradigm results from assimilating the often tacit, cultural knowledge of expert teachers. In Zeichner's preferred inquiry-oriented paradigm, good teachers skillfully and reflectively act upon ethical, political, as well as pedagogical issues involved in their everyday practice. A fifth paradigm, the academic, is briefly mentioned. Equating it with a sound liberal education, Zeichner assumes this paradigm is a basis for the others.

Drawing upon Zeichner's paradigms and Joyce's earlier conception of economic, progressive, academic, personalistic, and competency orientations to teacher education, Doyle (1990) identifies five themes which determine the direction and substance of teacher education: the good employee, the junior professor, the fully functioning person, the innovator, and the reflective professional. These themes roughly correspond to Zeichner's craft, academic, personalistic, behavioristic, and inquiry-oriented categories and seem to be partially determined by the different interest groups who advocate the various themes. School administrators, for example, would tend to promote preparation of good employees while phenomenologically-oriented education professors would advocate the reflective professional. For Doyle:

> the knowledge base for the preparation of reflective professionals includes personal knowledge, the craft knowledge of skilled practitioners, and propositional knowledge from classroom research and from the social and behavioral sciences. (p. 6)

Though he emphasizes critical analysis and deliberation, Doyle gives less weight to consideration of normative questions of "what ought to be" than Zeichner does in his inquiry-oriented paradigm.

Despite some variation in the number and types of categories and in the specific ways they define each category, Kennedy, Zeichner, and Doyle each view reflection or inquiry as a distinct model of teacher education. Feiman-Nemser (1990), on the other hand, has recently challenged that perspective by omitting reflection from her list of conceptual orientations, which includes the academic, the practical, the technical, the personal, and the critical. Rather than a conceptual orientation, she calls reflection a generic professional disposition. To explain this conclusion, Feiman-Nemser states that many of the programs she reviewed "explicitly endorse the goal of reflection, even though they embody different conceptual orientations" (p. 221). Since models of reflective teaching and teacher education differ on substantive goals, she concludes, these models cannot be grouped into a distinct category or conceptual orientation.

The implicit definition of "substantive goals" offers a key to Feiman-Nemser's conclusion. Referring to van Manen's (1977) ways of knowing, she defines substantive goals as different levels or foci for reflection. Van Manen offers three levels of reflection: the technical, the interpretive, and the critical. (These levels, as the reader will see, are used in many of the teacher education programs described in this volume.) The examples offered by Feiman-Nemser (1990) equate different levels or foci for reflection with content of reflection. Thus, "a technological orientation might focus reflection on the most effective or efficient means to achieve particular instructional objectives" (p. 221). In that same vein, the academic orientation would focus reflection on the explicit school curriculum or subject matter; the practical orientation on the messy problems of teaching; the personal orientation on the (re)construction of self as teacher; and the critical orientation on the school's role in creating a more just and democratic society. These differences in substantive focus, Feiman-Nemser concludes, mean that reflection is not so much an orientation as a disposition underlying other legitimate orientations.

Like Feiman-Nemser, many who have compared approaches to inquiry-oriented or reflective teacher education have also noted that variation exists among them. Their claim, however, is that, as in all paradigms, variation is bound to occur. The task they set for themselves is to systematically explicate differences within the paradigm rather than to fuse it with other approaches. Some authors identify differing dimensions of reflection; others develop classification schemas within the reflective paradigm.

Tom (1985), for example, found three dimensions upon which inquiry-oriented teacher education could be distinguished: the arena of the problematic, or that aspect of teaching which is the object of problematic thinking; the model of inquiry, or mode of reflection brought to bear on a particular problem; and the ontological status of education phenomena, or how real, observable, and law-like one views the components of schooling. In an analysis of instructional strategies used to prepare reflective teachers, Zeichner (1987) adds to these dimensions. Among important differences he finds are the degree to which program goals are linked to broader changes in schools and society, and the degree to which the approach is justified by reference to theory.

Grimmett, MacKinnon, Erickson, and Riecken (1990), Valli (1990), and Tabachnick and Zeichner (1991) have each developed different classification systems for reflective programs. Focusing on the role of knowledge in reflective teacher education, Grimmett, MacKinnon, Erickson, and Riecken find three distinct perspectives on reflection: as instrumental mediation of action, as deliberating among competing views of teaching, and as reconstructing experience. Valli, on the other hand, limited her scope of inquiry to examples which had an explicit commitment to examining teaching as a moral enterprise. Even within this more narrow scope she found three approaches: the deliberative, the relational, and the critical. And based on an historical analysis of educational philosophies and traditions, Tabachnick and Zeichner offer four conceptions of reflective teaching practice: academic, social efficiency, developmentalist, and social reconstructionist.

How one determines an orientation depends on how it is defined, what its elements are, its level of generality, and on what basis distinctions are made. At the highest level of generality is Kennedy's distinction between a model of good teaching based on the image of a reflective practitioner and one based on professional standards or technical rationality. The basis for Feiman-Nemser's categories seems to be sources of knowledge or content for reflection. Doyle arrives at his classification scheme by looking at the perspectives of various advocates for teacher education reform. Kennedy's are derived from contrasting views of good teaching, while Grimmett, MacKinnon, Erickson, and Riecken emphasize epistemological criteria. Categorizes can also be a function of what are perceived as dominant and supporting goals: is reflective practice the dominant goal for a number of aspects of teaching (e.g., content delivery, personal growth) or is it the primary goal for a particular aspect of teaching which reflection refines and supports?

While the authors of the cases presented in this volume view reflection as either the organizing principle or an essential organizing theme of their programs, the reader is encouraged to ponder the question of whether or not reflection is a distinct conceptual orientation in teacher education. Do the programs present such differing approaches to the preparation of teachers as to be separate paradigms? Or are they varying approaches within one basic paradigm? Is it possible to have diversity about the purposes and goals of reflection, what is reflected upon, sources of reflection, how reflection occurs, what happens as a result of reflection, and still have a conceptual orientation? Do the programs presented here vary so widely on these dimensions that any sense of conceptual coherence is lost, or are there commonalities which provide an underlying unity?

OVERVIEW OF CASES AND CRITIQUES

The seven case studies in the first part of this volume represent public and private institutions, four and five year programs, undergraduate and graduate programs, alternative programs, as well as efforts to transform all teacher education programs at particular institutions. Some programs have a generic (K-12) learning to teach emphasis; others maintain the traditional divisions between elementary and secondary preparation. The authors describe the history and assumptions of their program, their understanding of reflection, implementation strategies, evaluation procedures, and difficulties they encountered. The chapters also reveal authors' struggles to answer core questions. How do prospective teachers reflect? Upon what content should they reflect? How can reflective qualities be fostered? Are some teacher candidates disposed to reflection while others are not? What do we mean by reflection, anyway?

The second part of the volume comprises chapters which critique reflection as a conceptual orientation and assess the implementation of reflection in these specific programs. Authors approach this work from varying perspectives: developmental, narrative, social reconstructionist, feminist, and postmodern. All active teacher educators, the critics use their backgrounds in cognitive psychology, curriculum studies, sociology, and philosophy to analyze what is present in and what is missing from the programs. They propose new possibilities and reconsiderations.

The Case Studies

The first two chapters represent five year programs at public, research universities. The first program, at the University of New Hampshire, dates back to 1974 when faculty began to formulate a program to prepare reflective decision makers and autonomous teacher leaders. In the intervening years this image of a good teacher has shifted to teachers as co-explorers whose personal teaching styles and philosophies develop through participation in communities of inquiry and support. The New Hampshire program rejects traditional notions of preservice teachers being either practice teachers, who merely apply professional knowledge in their field sites, or apprentices, who merely imitate the wise practice of their mentors. Instead, preservice teachers are co-explorers who, as part of communities of inquiry and support, commit themselves to hearing the varied perspectives of group members, to empathic understanding, and to voicing their own emerging decisions and philosophies. Small group meetings also support and challenge supervisory teams as they identify common goals, expand their knowledge, and explore mutual concerns.

While both the University of New Hampshire and the University of Florida (chapter 2) stress the importance of the personal development, reflective judgment, and autonomy of new teachers, Florida's PROTEACH program puts additional emphasis on the knowledge base for teaching. At Florida, PROfessional TEACHers "master the expanding knowledge base about teaching" (p. 4). But unlike many uses of the term knowledge base, which are restricted to propositional knowledge about generic, effective teaching behaviors, Florida's definition is broadly inclusive of pedagogical and ethical knowledge, subject matter knowledge, "knowledge of ways to increase self-knowledge," and so on (p. 5). Moving from a more dominant concern with the process of reflective judgment, the program now balances that concern with simultaneous attention on the content of reflection. Faculty now communicate to students that reflection is "a way of thinking about educational matters that involves the ability to make rational *and ethical* choices and to assume responsibility for those choices" (p. 7). In keeping with their constructivist beliefs about the teaching/learning process, faculty have been developing ways to deal with students' tacit perspectives on teaching. That collaborative work, which includes reflective modeling and think aloud procedures, typifies the evolving nature of the program.

Developed as a selective, fifth year alternative route for prospective elementary and secondary teachers, the University of Maryland's Masters Certification program (chapter 3) emphasizes three Rs: reflection, research, and repertoire. Like New Hampshire, Maryland views the small cohort group as a powerful source of learning to teach. Like Florida, it considers the knowledge base for teaching a primary source for reflection. Students' grasp of this knowledge base (research on teaching, learning, teacher education, and school effectiveness) is essential to the program's goal: the development of reflective scholar-teachers committed to improving teaching. This model of good teaching orients candidates to Dewey's notion of problem solving: having "the ability to look back critically and imaginatively, to do cause-effect thinking, to derive explanatory principles, to do task analysis, also to look forward, and to do anticipatory planning (p. 13). Prospective scholar-teachers are given numerous opportunities to examine the uniqueness of various teaching situations, to explore the fit between theory and practice, and to avoid unthinking adoption of research findings.

Although a four year undergraduate program, the Academically Talented Teacher Education Program (ATTEP) at Kent State University (chapter 4) is also an alternative for scholastically strong and conceptually flexible students. Four seminars distinguish this program. Besides the student teaching seminar, the program is structured around learning, teaching, and schooling seminars in which students are urged to question teaching practice, use different modes of inquiry (psychological, sociological, and critical), and engage in complex problem solving. In the ATTEP model, a good teacher is an inquiry-oriented teacher researcher who makes reasoned choices by analyzing knowledge generated from research in light of their own values and ideas and the ambiguous nature of teachers' work. A culminating "Learning to Teach Autobiography" indicates that ATTEP students engage in three types of reflection: about themselves as teachers, about the practice of teaching, and about critical issues involved in the process of schooling.

The last three case chapters describe four year programs designed for the general undergraduate population. In Michigan State University's Multiple Perspectives program (chapter 5), students learn that reflective decision making is dependent upon interrelationships among principles from the various academic disciplines and that teacher decisions must balance competing demands and expectations placed on the school: demands that it simultaneously promote academic learning, personal responsibility, social responsibility, and social justice. These four functions (or multiple perspectives) of schooling can cause conflict within a teacher's role and demand wise professional judgment. Thus, a good teacher is one who is capable of making sensible and sensitive decisions in the face of competing expectations. These decisions require an interactive ability to think and act on a number of levels: technical, clinical, personal, and critical. Multiple perspective teachers must learn to situate technical concerns within a broad set of social and value-oriented considerations.

A similar orientation to framing technical issues within normative ones governs the teacher education program at the Catholic University of America (chapter 6). Competing "dilemmas" of schooling are analogous to the Multiple Perspectives' four functions and both programs draw on notions of levels of reflection and commonplaces of schooling. This is not, however, where the problem-solving program at Catholic University began. Rather, this conceptual framework of dilemmas, commonplaces, and reflective levels, was introduced after faculty realized that problem solving was an insufficient guide for reflection—that students needed an explicit framework to expand the scope of their reflection and improve its quality. To become good teachers, graduates of this program are expected to critically examine their own teaching behaviors as well as the school context in order to bring about desirable change. They are taught to view classroom situations from multiple perspectives, to envision alternatives to and ethical implications of their actions, and to resolve teaching problems by assessing experiential and theoretical knowledge. By using this conceptual framework as an overarching instructional strategy, faculty hope to reconstruct the way students view the act of teaching: to move them beyond short-term, efficiency oriented decisions to decisions based on long-term, ethically oriented criteria.

TABLE 1
Features of the Seven Reflective Programs

Site	Type of Program	Guiding Image of a Good, Reflective Teacher
University of New Hampshire	5 year, leading to master's degree	A supportive, inquiry-oriented co-explorer
University of Florida (PROTEACH)	5 year, leading to master's degree	Personally defines good teaching using personal definitions and professional knowledge; makes rational and ethical choices about teaching
University of Maryland (Master's cert.)	5th year, alternative master's degree program	A scholar-teacher committed to improving teaching
Kent State University (ATTEP)	4 year program for academically talented undergraduates	A teacher-researcher who uses psychological, sociological, and critical modes of inquiry
Michigan State University (Multiple Perspectives)	4 year, alternative undergraduate program	Considers the competing demands of schools in decision making
Catholic University of America	4 year undergraduate program	Analyzes teaching in its normative context; considers ethical implications
University of Houston (RITE)	4 year undergraduate program	Inquires into teaching practice in ways which foster continuous professional growth

The last of the seven cases is the Reflective Inquiry Teacher Education (RITE) program at the University of Houston (chapter 7) where reflection is officially defined as "the disposition and ability to consider education as the result of many social, political, and individual factors accompanied by an understanding of the need to base subsequent action on careful analysis of the results of such inquiry" (p. 14). This orientation toward deliberative action (called a strategic conception of reflection) is similar to the orientation guiding many of the programs described in preceding chapters. Also like a number of the other programs, RITE engages students in different types or levels of reflection. But despite this deliberate range of reflection built into the program, the Houston faculty realized that their diverse assumptions about good teaching and learning to teach did not consistently support this definition. These diverse perceptions, coupled with student input, state legislation, and other external regulations ultimately undermined the RITE program. One way out of this increasingly common problem, the authors suggest, is to treat curriculum as a negotiated process requiring reflective conversations.

The Critiques

A number of the themes alluded to in this introduction are played out more systematically in the critiques which follow the case studies. Taking a developmental perspective, James Calderhead (chapter 8) compares the models of professional learning in these seven programs to what we know from the literature on learning to teach. In so doing, Calderhead analyzes the extent to which these programs conceptualize a developmental process of learning to teach; how they allow for individual differences in student teachers' learning; and ways in which they deal with the diverse conceptions of teaching, learning, and curriculum that student teachers bring to their professional preparation. By discussing institutional and developmental impediments to reflective preparation, he raises questions about the feasibility of reflective goals, recommends a research agenda, and suggests strategies to support ongoing reflective practice.

The next two chapters analyze the seven cases according to what the authors see as different conceptions of reflective practice. Georgea Sparks-Langer (chapter 9) proposes that three approaches to reflective practice (the cognitive, critical, and narrative) are found to varying degrees within the seven programs. The cognitive approach emphasizes "the knowledge and processes involved in teacher decision making" (p. 1). The critical approach presumes that schools are not value-neutral, that they work for those with power and influence and against those without it. Prospective teachers, therefore, are asked to examine and change teaching practices and contexts to effect a more just society. The narrative approach includes the voices of teachers. It proposes that the source and context of reflection should primarily be the practical experience of complex and uncertain teaching situations. Though trained in the cognitive approach, Sparks-Langer argues for more consideration of the other two approaches.

Seeing four rather than three orientations which have informed reflective teacher education, Kenneth Zeichner (chapter 10) analyzes the seven programs by situating them in relation to the traditions of reform mentioned earlier: academic, social efficiency, developmentalist, and social reconstructionist. Through this analysis, Zeichner illustrates how contemporary teacher education reforms emerge out of traditions of practice that have been developing throughout the twentieth century. Like Sparks-Langer, he argues for a particular tradition, the social reconstructionist, and cautions against a vague, generic orientation to reflective teaching.

Two critics view the programs from feminist perspectives. Jesse Goodman (chapter 11), like the two previous authors, supports a notion of reflection which includes a critical perspective. But for Goodman, the critical perspective best suited to inform reflective teaching is derived from feminist pedagogy. The chapter describes three aspects of this pedagogy—teaching as an occupation, classroom dynamics, and fostering reflection—and argues that reflective programs would be enriched if teacher educators incorporated these areas of concern into the curriculum.

Taking a more constructivist (or in Sparks-Langer's terminology—narrative) approach in her feminist critique, Anna Richert (chapter 12) centers her analysis on the concept of "teacher's voice." She sets forth a two-pronged argument. The first is that in order to learn to teach, prospective teachers must be encouraged to examine their beliefs, become self-conscious, and, hence, speak their own truth. The second is that for any sort of empowerment to occur, the voices of these prospective teachers must be heard. Though this might seem commonsensical, the author reminds us that a teacher's audience is usually herself alone, and that norms for listening to co-workers are often absent in schools. Teachers are often the silent (or silenced) ones. To break this pattern, Richert encourages the development of voice such as she found in these seven reflective programs.

The final critic, Lynda Stone (chapter 13), casts a philosopher's eye on the case studies. Two claims begin the chapter. One is that the philosophical question of the nineties concerns the debate between modernism and postmodernism. It is a question best understood as the problem of essentialism. The other claim is that reform conceptions of teaching and teacher education ought to take account of this debate. Further they ought (perhaps) to be moving toward postmodernism. Stone sets out the components of the debate as viewpoints about "the quest for certainty" and examines the exemplary programs with regard to the modernist/postmodernist tensions within them. Though the author does not use terms like technical rationality and reflective practice in her chapter, the reader will no doubt connect them with essentialism and non-essentialism. Closing the chapter is a postmodern reflection which emphasizes multiplicity, remaking, identity, and contextuality.

CONCLUSION

The institutions exemplified in the first seven chapters have not found ideal ways to prepare teachers. As the reader will soon discover, conflicts arose over definitions of reflection, implementation strategies, the time involved in delivering such a program, and faculty autonomy and responsibility. In some cases, due to either internal or external forces, programs are already in the process of being radically reconceptualized. Moreover, program implementation has been restricted to the professional education component of teacher education. As in most institutions, little progress has been made in integrating reflection into the general studies or specialty area components. Nonetheless, the cases selected for this volume are among the few examples in the United States where sustained, scholarly inquiry has been brought to bear on a program-wide approach to reflective teacher education. They represent current thinking in the field: programs which treat reflection as an important and complex construct.[3]

PART I.   CASE STUDIES OF REFLECTIVE
TEACHER EDUCATION

SHARON NODIE OJA
ANN DILLER
ELLEN CORCORAN
MICHAEL D. ANDREW

1

Communities of Inquiry, Communities of Support: The Five Year Teacher Education Program at the University of New Hampshire

Since 1974 the University of New Hampshire (UNH) has had a five year program designed to educate teachers who make thoughtful, effective classroom decisions. We have identified three program components to illustrate how we move toward our goal of the teacher as reflective decision maker. These are: (1) course work in Philosophical Inquiry; (2) the Internship Experience, and (3) the Collaborative Supervisory Team at the intern site.

In analyzing these three program components, the use of small groups emerges as critically important. We refer to these groups as "communities of inquiry" and "communities of support." Communities of inquiry and support are not confined to the three program components we describe here, but have been structured from the outset into all phases of the program.

Taken as communities of support these groups provide a "safe space" where members come together as persons who care about each other as people, "without masks, pretenses, [or] badges of office" (Greene 1988, 16-17). All members assume some responsibility (not necessarily equal responsibility) for mutual well-being and group outcomes.

Our concept of communities of inquiry follows from William James' premise that "the truth is too great for any one actual mind . . . to know the whole of it. The facts and worths of life need many cognizers to take them in" (James, 1899, 19). Every participant acts as a "cognizer" who brings their own partial perspective to bear on the common inquiries of the group.

Ideally all members of the communities of inquiry and support take part as 'co-explorers' (Diller 1990). Each co-explorer tries to satisfy what Maria Lugones calls "the need for reciprocity of understanding" (Lugones and Spelman, 1983, 30). This means that each person makes a methodological commitment not only to listen to others but to endeavor to understand them on their own terms, and, in turn, expects to have an equivalent effort directed toward understanding their experiences.

Our communities treat both inquiry and support as intrinsic values. Both functions of community are founded on the premise that something of value—social, personal, intellectual, and ethical—can be achieved from the ongoing exchanges among members. We have observed that any given group tends to alternate between giving the support function and the inquiry function primacy. This alternation helps the two functions to mutually reinforce each other.

Our focus on communities does not deny the importance of leaders. Appropriate forms of leadership serve to structure and to sustain the communities. We have noticed that those who are recognized as leaders generally set the tone; they model the forms of participation that become the norm. Leadership style often determines whether or not both support and inquiry become jointly established community practices.

PROGRAM STRUCTURE, HISTORY, AND VISION

To better understand how Philosophical Inquiry, Internship Experience, and the Collaborative Supervisory Team conjoin to produce the teachers we seek, we will first describe the program structure, program history, and vision. We then discuss each of the three featured components. Examples drawn from case studies of student interns are used as illustrations in all three discussions.

Structure

The five year program is an integrated, undergraduate-graduate program for elementary and secondary teachers. Students complete a baccalaureate degree in four years with a major in a subject area, not education. The program begins with a freshman or sophomore clinical experience as a teacher assistant, then moves through required foundations courses which may be taken at either the undergraduate or graduate level. Most students complete these foundations courses at the undergraduate level. At the graduate level, the program includes a full year internship, a twelve-credit graduate concentration in content or pedagogy, elective courses and a final project or thesis. Twelve months of post-baccalaureate study are typically required to complete the Master's degree.[1]

Much of the success in meeting our goals and approaching our vision is determined by the students we recruit and select for the teacher education program.[2] Students are screened formally twice in the program. The first screening is based on performance in the initial clinical experience. Approximately 40 percent do not go on after this experience.

Informal self-selection continues as students do their undergraduate course work in education and participate in affiliated practicum experiences prior to making a decision about applying to the graduate school. Students who continue after the first screening and who wish to complete the program must apply to the Graduate School in their senior year and take the Graduate Record Examination. A teacher education committee then examines transcripts, grade point average, GRE scores, recommendations, and evidence from education and academic department instructors plus a folder of papers and recommendations from the semester of clinical experience.[3]

Program History

The five year program had its first interns in 1974, following four years of discussion and planning involving the entire education faculty, representatives of all colleges and schools within the University and a consortium of teachers, students, school administrators, and State Department of Education officials. The vision for the program was described in an Association of Teacher Educators monograph (Andrew, 1974). Early documents describe a central program goal as "a teacher-leader: a competent educator with special skills in analyzing teaching, working with students, implementing change, and developing curriculum" (Andrew, 1974, p. i). Autonomy and individual choice were central themes in the program rationale. Small classes, discussion groups, and seminars were also an integrating thread through the program. Original descriptions of small groups describe "integrative seminars" as "recurring discussion groups of 10-15 students in the same clinically oriented experiences." Major group functions were "facilitating honest communication, developing effective group process, discussing students' personally relevant experiences and dealing with emerging professional identity" (Andrew, 1974, p. 48).

The vision of preparing teachers as decision makers and leaders in improvement of curriculum and instruction has persisted but the concept of autonomy in the teacher-leadership role has been balanced by increasing emphasis on the group as a collective force for change and a powerful vehicle for inquiry and support. In the past six years these group functions have expanded to communities of inquiry and support for faculty and school people as well as students. This has come about as several faculty members have focused their energies on discovering and nurturing new levels of collaboration and new networks for support and inquiry that now pervade our program.

This direction of growth is encouraged as schools are urged to become the unit of educational change and school based management models emerge in which the empowered teacher is part of a collaborative group. The teachers we prepare should serve as catalysts for this change. They should settle for no less than reciprocity of understanding, caring, and reflective decision making in the context of co-equal groups. In this way the preparation of teachers can conjoin and support the restructuring of schools.

Program Vision

Central to our vision is the teacher as reflective decision maker. Teacher decisions are called for across the range of classroom activity. Teacher decisions usually have value components. They are often moral decisions. When teachers own the decision making process, they work from their own philosophical constructs. They move beyond blind implementation of packages and prescriptions. They make informed choices that direct practice.

Our vision of teacher as decision maker challenges the orthodoxy of a single knowledge base where ends are undisputed and means are empirically revealed. We assume, as James T. Sanders (1972) has observed, that 'good teaching' is a "disjunctive concept," that there are many different ways to be a good teacher. These ways are not mutually exclusive, and over time a good teacher may accumulate a large repertoire that includes most of them; but they are nonetheless different and not necessarily cumulative.

Areas of Inquiry

In order for students to develop effective personal teaching styles and to become reflective decision makers in the classroom, as well as able leaders in the educational community, they need professional knowledge. We require all our prospective teachers to study issues in several areas of professional knowledge. Students in our programs encounter a range of alternative perspectives and choices as they investigate issues in each of these areas of inquiry:

- Theories of development and learning and teaching.
- Teaching models leading to the development of an educational philosophy and effective personal style of teaching.
- Structure of public education and procedures for effecting change in that structure.
- Significant assumptions and philosophical points of view that underlie teaching and schooling and that help define a personal philosophy of education.

All four of these areas of inquiry constitute major required components of our program; but for the purposes of this chapter we shall skip over the first three and leap directly into a discussion of the fourth area—philosophical inquiry.

PHILOSOPHICAL INQUIRY IN THE FIVE YEAR PROGRAM

In order to constitute a class in philosophical foundations as a community of both support and inquiry we call upon a number of procedures. Although the substantive course work in philosophy focuses on theoretical inquiry, the actual practices, structures, and professorial mode during the first month or so of classes is weighted toward creating a community of support. Students meet regularly in small groups where they discuss assigned readings, read and comment on each others papers, and also construct their own agendas for co-exploration. The students' own beliefs and ideas are treated with respect, and occasionally clarified, but they are not yet subjected to critique, or given conventional academic grades. Early written assignments receive only 'credit' or an 'incomplete', with no letter or numerical grades assigned.

Even though considerable care is given to the support function, inquiry is neither neglected nor postponed. As communities of inquiry, we construe philosophy classes as "Laboratories for Ideas"—as opportunities to do "Thought Experiments" (for example, what if I held this philosophy—what would it be like?) under laboratory conditions. It is a place where we can examine new untried ideas, as well as old comfortable ones, without having to worry immediately about political expediency or economic feasibility. It is a place where we can engage in acts of the imagination and in the practice of dialectic, wherein we work to uncover hidden presuppositions, to scrutinize habitual conventions, and to examine unquestioned assumptions, whether they belong to revered traditions, current thinkers, or our own belief systems. It is a place to take "time out" from the immediate demands for lesson plans and teaching strategies.

The explicit framework for courses in philosophical inquiry is a cycle with four phases: Acquaintance, Analysis, Appraisal, and Synthesis. We will now discuss each of these in turn.

Acquaintance

The first major step of inquiry is for students to become acquainted with a representative range of educational theories, using both classical and contemporary primary sources. The term 'acquaintance' is important here because we are more concerned with introducing students to a wide range of major traditions, and positions, than in having them master all of these theories at this initial stage.

During Acquaintance, students are invited to enjoy a "mountain view" of changing vistas, to explore alternate educational paths and trails, and to journey into separate, diverse villages each with their own teaching and learning cultures. Students are encouraged, and prodded, to experiment with, to "try on," strange and novel ways of understanding education, to consider alternative perspectives, unusual approaches, unconventional aims and values as possibilities for their own educational thought.

We are concerned with wide-ranging acquaintance and understanding rather than mastery, because we believe that each person's own evolving philosophy will rely on selected sources and traditions at different points—the sequence and the depth of reliance on any particular tradition will vary according to personal development, individual style, and the practical contingencies of specific educational settings.

But the acquaintance needs to be sufficient for usefulness and for future reference, neither so superficial, nor so imposing or alien that one is cut off from the possibility of ever appropriating its insights.

The task of Acquaintance is not limited, however, to established theories and philosophies. Students also start to become better acquainted with their own, often unarticulated, perhaps inconsistent and muddled, but nonetheless powerful, beliefs and assumptions about education. Students begin to notice their own responses, their spontaneous "gut reactions" to what's being read, studied, and said—and they keep track of (i.e., write down) these responses as important "clues" to their own embryonic position.

Furthermore, because we have constituted the class as a Community of Co-Explorers, students also work at understanding each others' views. Thus, more or less simultaneously, students become acquainted with standard texts and positions in educational theory, with early round clues to their own assumptions about education, as well as with the beliefs of their classmates. We then take all of these findings to be interesting, appropriate foci for exploration through individual study and writing, class and group discussion, and written small group reports, or "group logs," which are copied and distributed to all class members as part of our ongoing community records.

Analysis

In contrast to the effort during the process of Acquaintance, to immerse oneself in a whole series of new authors and educational perspectives, the tasks of Analysis are more akin to efforts to "sit back"; here we have students provide a bit of distance between themselves and the content they are studying. During Analysis, we put ideas out in front of us, stand back and take a look at all of them, whether they belong to a new and unfamiliar position or constitute our own cherished beliefs.

Thus our own principles of action, our standard, habitual ways of proceeding, along with their underlying assumptions become, temporarily, just one more alternative to be analyzed. Students come to realize that what they take for granted can also be treated as an hypothesis to be examined, tested, held up for scrutiny. Furthermore, standard assessments (worthwhile knowledge is . . .), value judgments (schools ought to . . .), and favored choices (my course, my method) also become merely more sets of data, to be observed, explored, and analyzed.

During both the Acquaintance and the Analysis phases we recognize that appraisals keep occurring, inevitably "happen" to us. Just as we make instantaneous subjective judgments when we encounter unfamiliar situations or meet new people, we also react when we meet a new idea; we may experience disbelief, distaste, perplexity, interest, or instantaneous agreement. When this happens for students, it is helpful not only to notice and acknowledge such responses, but also to have students keep a personal written record of these "primitive" forms of assessment, a record that they can refer to when they construct their own syntheses. But during both the Acquaintance and Analysis phases our "official" explicit framework endeavors to stay "open" to each perspective we encounter, to study it with the aim of understanding rather than of judging, and to withhold, or suspend, definitive evaluative judgments.

Appraisal

It is not until after a sense of supportive community has been established, after students have worked together as co-explorers on Acquaintance and Analysis, that we move on to enter the Appraisal phase where rigorous methods of evaluation and systematic criteria get formally introduced, and we begin to evaluate positions. Also at this point, students' work receives conventional grades, critiques are made, and challenging questions are raised.

When students of teaching are encouraged to choose and construct their own foundational philosophies of education, to have them start with what they themselves find meaningful is an energizing and connected way to begin philosophical study. But two specters arise here: (1) a relativism that would fail to provide any grounds to choose among theories; and (2) a subjectivism that might meet internal, personally coherent criteria but be unresponsive to the realities of classrooms and the community.

Thus while person-specific considerations continue to be a touchstone that is acknowledged and occupies a legitimate seat in deliberations, other criteria take central stage during Appraisal. As an antidote to relativism we call upon standard criteria for theory assessment such as clarity, comprehensiveness, and consistency. Once we apply a full range of systematic criteria, the grounds for choosing among theories becomes clearer, and the range of compelling possibilities gets narrowed. One can still envision a plurality of viable positions, but there is no longer a relativistic "anything goes" atmosphere.

But what about subjectivism? Might students of teaching satisfy theoretical criteria and yet still be unresponsive to persons in schools?

One quick answer to this question says that when students learn, as co-explorers, to practice "reciprocal understanding" subjectivism becomes less likely. The long answer tells us that questions of truth and morals must receive detailed examination. For example, we now introduce students to a range of standard ethical criteria to judge the morality of practices connected with any given educational theory. And we start to subject empirical claims and assumptions to epistemological scrutiny, to ask for evidence, to consider research findings, and to check truth claims against our own and others' experiences. It is here that participation in a public Community of Inquiry, such as the Internship Seminar, adds an important reality check.

For example, Sally, working with her small group, presented a problem from her internship which challenged the group's belief that schools can and should always work collaboratively with parents. Her problem centered around a parent who was disgruntled because his child was not placed with the teacher whom he had requested. After many meetings involving the teacher, the principal and the parent, it became clear that each side believed it was in the right and that neither side was willing to change.

This standoff between school and home continued for several months. The child's behavior deteriorated and he became the leader of a small group of children who were so disruptive that it became difficult to teach the rest of the class. Due to the fact that the child's parent refused to support the teacher or to discipline his child, the child assumed more and more power in the classroom.

The underlying philosophical question of how we should constitute school/home relationships often reflects tensions among at least three competing positions: (1) a collaborative, or relational approach; (2) a utilitarian approach that is concerned with what is best for the whole school and believes everyone's learning is better served when the educators make such decisions as classroom placement, based on their professional understanding of what is best for all the students and teachers; and (3) an individual rights approach. Each of these abstract positions took determinate form in Sally's case.

Initially, the members of Sally's small group held the first position; they believed that school and home should work collaboratively. The school principal and staff apparently held the second position, namely that the child's individual rights claim should not be allowed to override what they perceived as the best policy for the whole class or for the entire school. The parent who claimed that his child had the right to the placement he had requested held the third position, giving precedence to his individual rights.

Because this was a real problem for her, Sally would not let her group off the hook. Each time a solution was suggested, Sally pushed the group to play out the possible consequences. She wanted to make sure she got it right for herself. The easy answers weren't good enough for her. Eventually she decided that the path she wanted to pursue was to see if the child could be placed in the class his father had originally requested. Members of her group felt somewhat threatened by this position—her position seemed too much like giving in—the group had moved to the second position and maintained: "This kid and his parent do not have the right to mess up learning for the whole class." The small group thus became entrenched in the view that no parent has the right to tell the school what to do. But Sally now argued that nothing was being gained by sticking with the original placement.

As Sally came to see it, the teacher that the parent had originally requested could sit down with both the parent and the child to work out a set of conditions under which the child would be able to move to this new classroom. One of the conditions would be that the parent agree to support and reinforce the teacher. Complaints sent home would have to be taken seriously. If the child were disruptive or uncooperative, he would lose the right to stay in his new classroom. For Sally, her small group provided an ongoing context for her to work out a realistic set of conditions.

Educational goals and philosophical assumptions have indeterminate meaning at the abstract level. It is only when considered and applied in specific contexts such as Sally's that they take on determinate meaning. In this instance, Sally's group members were compelled to give determinate meaning to their initial presumptions about 'collaboration'. In doing so, their own tacit personal commitments were revealed—commitments that often ran counter to their avowed position on collaboration. Working with Sally's problem in their group gave them a public context and a concrete case to help them measure the adequacy of their philosophical presumptions.

Synthesis—Theory Construction and Reconstruction

If our efforts during the Acquaintance, Analysis, and Appraisal phases have been successful, students should now be ready to appropriate the systematic methods of philosophical investigation as their own precision tools for building a personally valid, relevant, and even theoretically elegant, philosophy of education.

Because we envision teachers as reflective decision makers who work best from their own philosophical constructs, we endeavor, throughout the program, to provide the conditions, instructions, and communities that will enable students to develop their own coherent ways of being teachers—ways that fit and arise out of their own person—not simply subjective, or complacently stuck in a rut, but nevertheless still in tune with their own reasons for teaching, their own sources of energy, own personal values, strengths, abilities, and interests. This effort is focused and intensified in the philosophy classes where we encourage students to seek out the traditions that seem closest to their interests and proclivities. In the Synthesis phase students articulate, and systematize, their own versions of the theories they find themselves drawn to.

During this phase the professor continues to reiterate the point that good teaching is a 'disjunctive concept' and that a number of traditions, both classical and modern, can provide viable philosophies of education given the right circumstances, and appropriate conditions. Another professorial concern at this juncture is to help students maintain a balance between achieving some workable closure, with definitive, defensible statements of their own beliefs, while at the same time remaining open and fluid enough in their thinking to allow for an evolving, expanding philosophy. Thus the synthesis paper at the end of the philosophy course is viewed as "work in progress" a statement that represents one's current, and inevitably "dated," reflections on a growing, changing philosophy.

This ongoing construction and reconstruction effort is played out pedagogically in a mini-series of steps during the course itself—students construct preliminary outlines or "proposals," which are often revised. Students then present key aspects of their position orally to the entire class, all of whom write written responses to the oral presentation. Follow-up conferences with the professor add further material which is then fed back into the writing of a synthesis paper at the end of the course.

During students' oral presentations it often happens that as one student expresses and embodies their own version of a tradition we have been studying, it will suddenly come alive for another student who had not hitherto been able to envision this as a possibility. For example, after one high school science teacher defended his own adaptation of Plato's theory of truth, other seminar members began not only to understand it better but also started to take Plato's position seriously in a new way.

When the course work in philosophy is successful, students take some large strides toward one of our ultimate aims—our aim that every teacher will develop their own philosophy of education—person-specific, contingently practical, theoretically sound, connected with one or more viable live traditions of educational thought, consistent and coherent, yet also open, fluid, and evolving.

THE INTERNSHIP EXPERIENCE

When students move from course work to internship, new communities of support and inquiry are formed: the internship seminar, the intern/cooperating teacher/university supervisor triad and the collaborative supervisory team. We will discuss each of these in the pages that follow. The year-long internship is the centerpiece of the five year program. The internship provides the principal instruction in teaching methods. A full year of closely supervised internship offers the opportunity to integrate methods instruction with actual classroom experiences.

Classroom experience as a learning vehicle is widely accepted among teacher educators. Nonetheless, there are still important differences in assumptions about the use of school experience. The traditional concept of "practice teaching" persists in many programs in which it is assumed that students learn the necessary knowledge and skills of teaching in college courses, and that field experience serves as the place to practice these skills and reinforce the knowledge. A second traditional concept of "apprentice teaching" is also attached to clinical experience. The teacher-to-be learns the trade from the master. The teacher is the model, the student is the apprentice. In contrast to these two traditional approaches, the internship concept in the UNH five year program places emphasis on other assumptions.

A key assumption for our present discussion is that to produce a teacher as an autonomous decision maker, we must move away from the notions of practice teacher and apprentice toward the notion of "co-explorer." The teacher-to-be must be the evaluator and decision maker in improving his or her own teaching. The cooperating teacher and supervisor must move toward roles as co-equals. To illustrate, Anne reflects early on in her internship year about how her cooperating teacher and university supervisor assist her in becoming a co-explorer.

> When Mark [cooperating teacher] or Ellen [university supervisor] observe, they write what they see, not what they think or feel. They let *me* do the thinking and feeling from what they see. I like that. I am able to make inferences about my lesson. If they just told me how they felt I did, I wouldn't have to think, I'd just listen.

From this excerpt it is clear that Anne's cooperating teacher and university supervisor are working together toward a shared goal of helping Anne to become her own evaluator and decision maker.

Site Selection

The success of the internship experience is closely tied to site selection. Placement is the result of a personalized process that begins in semester one of the senior year (i.e., the year prior to internship). The director of field experiences meets with each prospective intern and discusses placement possibilities, taking into account the intern's strengths, weaknesses, needs, and preferences. Several students will usually visit a particular intern site and placement decisions are much like hiring decisions. A successful placement requires mutual acceptance and concludes with a meeting of intern and cooperating teacher.

Throughout the placement process, it is extremely important that each school makes its norms and expectations explicit so that interns will have a basis on which to make an informed choice. Anne, for example, saw things in Mark's room which told her a lot about the norms of his classroom. She saw it as a creative and challenging environment, where she, as well as the children, would have ample opportunity to "develop a desire and a purpose for learning." When students choose placements with norms that are congruent with their own, they are able to join the school as members of its community and to derive support from that community which allows them to meet the challenges of the teaching internship.

Supervisory Load

Second in importance to an appropriate intern site is the intense nature of university support and instruction provided to interns. Supervision of five or six interns is the equivalent of a one-course teaching assignment in each semester. A supervisor's interns are often placed in a single school or district and the supervisor becomes a regular part of a school community. Supervisors are required to visit each intern a minimum of twelve times. The norm is a biweekly visit. With five or six interns in the same school, supervisors are in that school at least one day a week.

Inquiry and Support Group for Supervisors

All supervisors meet biweekly as a faculty subgroup. During these meetings, the supervisors function as a community of support and inquiry for one another. Because they are working in separate schools, the supervisors do not see much of each other except at these biweekly meetings. They have come to use these meetings as a place to discuss problems, explore issues, experience different situations and points of view, to share resources, and recommend policy changes.

As an example of the community of support function that members of the supervisors group provide, let us take the case of Amy, an experienced and highly regarded supervisor. She presented the group with a question about how to deal with an intern who was constantly negative in the intern seminar. The group asked Amy a great many questions, slowly forming a clearer picture of the situation—of what Amy had already tried, of what the seminar sessions felt like, of how the other interns were responding. During the course of the discussion, Amy felt supported by the concern and interest of the group. She learned about what other supervisors had tried in similar situations. She obtained a range of ideas to think about. At subsequent meetings, the group made it a point to check in with Amy to find out how things were going. When the situation was eventually resolved, Amy reiterated how important the group's support had been to her throughout a difficult process.

As an example of the community of inquiry function that members of the supervisors group provide, let us take the case of Helene, a relatively new supervisor with recent secondary school teaching experience. She presented the group with a general question about the extended use of videotape by interns in their teaching. She was concerned about an intern who had shown "Ghandi" to his class for several days in a row. She described how she had handled the situation with the intern, but she wanted to know how the other supervisors worked with similar situations. Helene's question prompted an extended discussion of the uses of media in teaching and ways of helping interns research and present alternative perspectives for interpreting an historical event or piece of literature. The discussion was lively and provided the supervisors with new information and a broader understanding of the issues.

The assistance and stimulation that the supervisors receive from their biweekly meetings helps to sustain the high level of commitment and energy that they put into their work. New supervisors are welcomed into the group and experience the effects of joining a community of support and inquiry. Experienced supervisors act as mentors, enjoying the opportunity to rethink and revise stale ways of doing things. Together, newcomers and oldtimers appreciate the opportunity to work together.

Internship Seminar

In many ways, the seminar is at the heart of our communities of support and inquiry. It is here that the supervisor, as seminar leader, has the opportunity to pull together the many components that make up the total internship experience. The supervisors lead the intern seminars. The six interns whom each supervisor observes form a seminar group. Each seminar group meets after school for a two-hour session once a week. A weekly writing assignment is used to connect the intern's individual classroom experiences with the weekly seminar meetings. Letters, journals, and observation notes are examples of the kinds of writing which interns are asked to prepare for seminars. These arrangements enable us to integrate our supervision and our seminars into a curriculum which meets the evolving needs of the interns as they progress through their full year internship (Corcoran and Andrew, 1987).

Information gained from observations of the individual interns at work in their individual classrooms permits the seminar leader to identify problems (with planning, management or grading, for example) which some or all of the interns have in common. Additional information gained from the interns' weekly writing assignments enables the seminar leader to introduce topics (such as mainstreaming or working with parents) with which some or all of the interns are trying to cope on their own. The seminar has enormous potential as a forum for using the group to help the individual, and the individual intern is frequently able to help a peer or the entire group.

For example, Joan, an intern, has been working on combining the processes of observation, assessment, and curriculum development as she works with children in her first grade classroom. For much of the year she has been experimenting with various methods of note taking which will permit her to monitor the progress of each child, to keep track of general problems that children are encountering with specific activities, and to oversee the work and interactions of the group as a whole.

From time to time she has reported her progress to her seminar group, sharing what has and has not worked for her. She has used the group to get suggestions and ideas when she has been stuck. And the group has profited enormously from seeing how she has revised and modified her system. By early April she was able to show the group a system that had been working for her for over a month. She indicated that she felt that she had finally succeeded in developing something that worked in her classroom. Others in her group were extremely interested in what Joan had developed and began to think about their own methods of assessment and curriculum development in new and challenging ways.

The Supervisory Triad in the Internship

The field experience component of the internship is where the intern, the cooperating teacher, and the university supervisor come together in the supervisory triad as co-explorers. The intern works with the cooperating teacher throughout each school day—teaching, observing, asking questions. Sometimes the cooperating teacher provides the support function by listening, encouraging, helping. At other times the cooperating teacher provides the inquiry function by questioning, observing and providing feedback, pushing the intern to take on something new.

The university supervisor works with both the intern and the cooperating teacher, sometimes together and at other times separately. Just as the cooperating teacher provides both the support and the inquiry function, so does the university supervisor. When either the intern or the cooperating teacher is discouraged or confused, the university supervisor is committed to providing the support necessary in order to sustain the triad and its members. When either the intern or the cooperating teacher is stuck and looking for alternative perspectives, the university supervisor shares the responsibility for contributing new ideas.

The interplay among the three members of the supervisory triad is complex. Together they try to construct their own understandings of a particular community of learners, "figuring out each kid, what makes her tick and how she shows it."

The purpose of co-exploration is often initiated in the supervisory triad and fuels the discussion in both intern seminars and supervisory group meetings. The process extends even further back to University classrooms where the realities of school life bring forth both inquiry and support.

COLLABORATIVE SUPERVISORY TEAM

Another area of the teacher education program where we have developed multiple communities of support and inquiry is within the supervisory team at the internship sites. Since the early days of the five year program, we have been working on ways to develop and refine the concept of collaborative supervision. For example, in 1985 members of the teacher education faculty and the local schools initiated the Collaborative Approach to Leadership in Supervision project (Oja, 1988).

This project focused on schools where "clusters" of three or more interns were placed. The objectives of the project were to increase collaboration among the cooperating teachers who were supervising interns, to increase collaboration between the university supervisor and the school personnel, and to expand the cooperating teachers' knowledge of supervisory models. Just as the teacher education program is committed to the belief that there are many ways to be a good teacher, it is also committed to the belief that there are many ways to be a good supervisor.

Within the cluster school communities, cooperating teachers, the principal, and the university supervisor met regularly to identify common goals and to use collaborative inquiry strategies such as Collaborative Action Research (Oja and Smulyan, 1989) to generate topics of investigation in supervision. They also supported and challenged one another in problem solving sessions. In one cluster, for example, teachers divided into subgroups of trios and pairs to work together on reviewing relevant literature such as adult development theory and alternative models of supervision. They reported their findings back to the whole group, with all members functioning as co-explorers in their study of supervisory models and practices.[4] They relied on their practical knowledge as well as theoretical knowledge as they worked together to analyze, understand, and evaluate their work with interns. They developed ways to vary their supervisory practices according to the capabilities, variety, and flexibility observed in the interns with whom they were working. They applied their knowledge of adult development to support the interns in new learning experiences and to challenge the interns to teach to new levels.

Many of the practices which were originated and formalized as part of the Collaborative Approach to Leadership in Supervision project have been expanded to other internship sites. For example, cluster site placement has become an increasingly valued aspect of the teacher education program. It is now common practice to place three to six interns at a single internship site. At each of these clusters, the cooperating teachers, principal, and university supervisor meet together on a monthly, biweekly, or weekly basis to (1) share and reflect on their experiences, (2) investigate issues in supervision, and (3) solve problems and coordinate expectations throughout the internship site.

Outcomes from Collaborative Supervisory Teams

Participants in collaborative supervisory teams report the discovery of new ways of looking at people. In particular, they note interns have different capacities and limitations at different developmental stages in the internship year. This accentuates the need for considering alternative supervisory strategies. As one teacher said:

> I learned about different styles and that each person . . . may have different strengths and weaknesses and that different styles of supervision are appropriate. It was a real eye opener.

Participants in collaborative supervisory teams in the cluster sites perceive benefits in terms of the opportunities for sharing and support. They appreciate the sense of common purpose and common challenges. They report that the mutual support and open sharing leads to feelings of less isolation. They believe that their collective learning needs to continue and the communities of support and inquiry in the collaborative supervisory teams provide the setting.

We have observed an increased sense of professionalism among the participants of collaborative supervisory teams; their roles have expanded and they have taken risks. (As one teacher said, "We are more willing to stick our necks out.") There is an increased sense of efficacy in working with interns.

The collaborative supervisory team discussions often focus on larger issues beyond the here and now supervision of interns but which affect the climate of the schools. A principal reports:

> Though I fully support the idea that we should improve what happens with interns, I think that the real payoff for me and the school is what teachers can do with each other . . . sharing their increase in skills, ability to supervise, to get to the point where they can challenge each other in meaningful ways, within a secure framework.

Another principal reports that "the collaborative supervision models are making the university supervisor's role more exciting and more valuable in different ways." For instance, collaborative research may be encouraged by the university supervisor's interest and expertise as a resource to ideas for inquiry.

One outcome of our research on collaborative supervisory teams in cluster sites is that no single best structure or site agenda exists. Flexibility and local decision making remain of primary importance in each cluster site's choices of form and focus for their collaborative supervisory team. As additional cluster sites are formed and collaborative supervisory teams develop, we are seeing a variety of issues chosen for investigation and a variety of structures for collaborative supervisory teams.

Integrating Collaborative Supervision Team in Cluster Sites

To get a sense of how one collaborative supervisory community works together in solving a problem, let us take the case of Joan, an intern at a cluster school with three other interns. About three to four weeks into the internship, it became clear that Joan's placement was not working as well as those of her fellow interns, yet both Joan and the cooperating teacher wanted time to see if they could work things out.

Both Joan and her cooperating teacher consulted with their communities (e.g., intern seminars and supervisory team) as they worked toward making a decision. By mid-semester both felt that it was necessary to change Joan's placement. Because each of them was a member of an ongoing community, each felt supported as she reached her decision. And because of the collaborative supervisory team context, it was possible to work together using the inquiry function to resolve the problem without setting up a win/lose situation. Interns, cooperating teachers, other teachers in the building, the principal, and the university supervisor collaborated to make sure that the change in placement went as smoothly and respectfully as possible for both Joan and her cooperating teacher. Joan was given time and support to work out how she wanted to say goodbye to her students. She was also given time to observe and interview in many other classrooms before reaching a decision on who would be her next cooperating teacher.

There are several points in this case that merit highlighting. One point is that both the cooperating teachers and the interns, in their respective communities, accepted the possibility that Joan and her cooperating teacher might not be able to work together. A second point is that both communities accepted the right of the individuals to reach their own conclusions in their own good time. A third point is that all members of both communities accepted responsibility for helping to resolve the problem. No one individual, including the principal or the university supervisor, was expected to take on the full burden of finding Joan a new placement or figuring out how to manage her transition out of her original placement. In the past, when similar situations have arisen between interns and cooperating teachers in other schools, it has been necessary to move the intern to a new school. In Joan's case there was never any question of that. The collaborative supervisory team had made a commitment to Joan and they were willing to take the time to follow through. Another important factor is the high degree of congruence between the leadership styles of the principal and the university supervisor. There was no playing off the school against the university. The intern seminar group worked through the problem in a way that was very similar to the way the collaborative supervisory team worked through the problem. Throughout the process there was a high degree of professionalism, concern, support, and inquiry.

Because both the principal and the university supervisor were equally involved in working through the problem, the support function provided for both Joan and her cooperating teacher was seen as legitimate. It is often difficult to find time in schools for the support function. It happens on a catch-as-catch-can basis. In this case, however, because there were norms established whereby cooperating teachers were expected to meet together on a regular basis, there was an established community already in place to handle the difficulty. It is interesting to note that the support function shifted to the inquiry function once Joan's decision was made. The collaborative supervisory group then began to question how such a difficulty might have been avoided and to explore ways of fine-tuning the placement process for the next year to decrease the chances of its happening again. Their inquiry also resulted in their better understanding the problem.

SUMMARY

Little attention has been paid in teacher education programs to the importance of support and inquiry groups. Popular reference to "cohort" groups in teacher education sometimes means no more than sharing a common date for program matriculation. We have stressed functional groupings for support and shared reflection. We have consciously structured a series of such groups to sustain and nurture the development of reflective practitioners. In these communities, the relationship between instructor and student progresses from instructor-student and mentor-mentee toward co-equals in systems of common exploration and support.

Throughout the program, from early courses structured around small groups to the internship seminar and supervisory triad, students move between both formal and informal communities of support and inquiry. So, too, do university supervisors and cooperating teachers move within such communities as the supervisors group and collaborative supervisory teams. School and university participants meet together for common goals. The net effect is an increasing sense of common understanding and shared responsibility in the preparation of teachers.

The concept of teacher-leader central to the initial vision of the five year program at the University of New Hampshire persists, but the emphasis on personal autonomy has been balanced by communities of inquiry and support. The reflective teacher with a personal philosophy of education and personal teaching style must function within the total school community to bring about meaningful change.

DORENE DOERRE ROSS
MARGARET JOHNSON
WILLIAM SMITH

2

Developing a PROfessional TEACHer at the University of Florida

Elementary PROTEACH is a five year teacher education program which, for most students[1] culminates in a Master's degree and/or teacher certification. After four years of program development activities, the first students were admitted in 1984.[2] At this point, the faculty had developed an organizational structure for the program and had identified the development of teacher judgment as our central goal. Over the next three years faculty worked to detail the content of new courses, revise existing courses, and develop and implement an evaluation plan. As a part of this process, faculty searched for ways to work with pre-service teachers which would support the development of professional judgment and autonomy.

Beginning with teacher socialization literature, faculty clarified their focus and identified reflection as their fundamental goal. Like other programs which have tackled this complex goal, faculty have been struggling to clarify the meaning of reflection, the nature of teacher education that supports its development, and appropriate means for documenting the development of teachers. This chapter provides a summary of the distinctive features of PROTEACH, a picture of the program in practice, and a summary of what faculty have learned about reflective teaching and about teacher education. Predictably, this chapter raises as many questions as it answers; however, the goal is not to provide answers to the many dilemmas facing teacher educators today but simply to contribute to the on-going dialogue.

WHAT IS DISTINCTIVE ABOUT PROTEACH?

Previous articles have described key features of elementary PRO-TEACH (Ross, 1989a; Ross and Krogh, 1988; Smith, Carroll, and Fry, 1984). These articles, which describe the basic structure and key components of the program, are useful in distinguishing PROTEACH from other teacher education programs. The focus for this chapter will be on those things that distinguish it from other programs stressing reflection. Features described will include program history, the evolving definition of reflection, and faculty commitment to preservice teacher education.

Program History

Barnes (1987) noted that learning to teach requires developing organized schemata which can serve as guides to action. To help students develop such schemata, Barnes stressed that a teacher education program must present a unified view of teaching that is grounded in research. Valli and Taylor (1987) noted that in most programs reflection is stressed within only a few components; that is, programmatic coherence is the exception, not the norm. While PROTEACH faculty have not solved the problems associated with developing coherence, there is a pervasive sense of common purpose. A common definition of reflection is used within courses and field experiences, and common core experiences are provided for all students. Two historical features seem important in achieving this coherence: (1) the nature of the program which preceded PROTEACH, and (2) the developmental processes which led to PROTEACH.

PROTEACH was built upon the foundation of the previous teacher education program at Florida, the Childhood Education Program (CEP). CEP was a nationally recognized program based upon principles of humanistic education (Combs, Blume, Newman, and Wass, 1974). The current emphasis on reflection was a logical outgrowth of the previous humanistic focus on the importance of the development of an autonomous individual. Additionally, CEP provides evidence of Florida's history of coherence and focus within teacher education. The idea that teacher educators should work together to accomplish articulated goals did not begin with PROTEACH. Rather the specific focus of PROTEACH arose from a history of ongoing dialogue about purposes of teacher education and a process of continual revision designed to improve the ability to achieve those purposes.

The second historical force was the process of developing PROTEACH. Ross and Krogh (1988) noted that the developmental years of PROTEACH were characterized by a great deal of conflict about purposes of teacher education and about the development of a "college-wide" program. Collaborative action with colleagues dispelled much but not all of that concern. However, the conflict itself helped to create coherence among faculty. Ross and Krogh (1988) noted:

> Our concern forced us to clarify what was important to us . . . and perhaps, in the process, we strengthened our commitments. . . . It was the value commitments we made during the developmental process that guided us as we developed the content within our courses and as we began to consider next steps in implementation. (p. 28-29)

Evolving Definition of Reflection

The impetus for PROTEACH was to design a program that helped preservice teachers master the expanding knowledge base about teaching and supported the development of professional judgment and autonomy. Once faculty determined the basic structure of the program, they turned to research on teacher socialization to help them make decisions about how to achieve their goals. Research about reflective teaching (e.g., Goodman, 1984; van Manen, 1977; Zeichner and Liston, 1987), reflective practitioners (Schön, 1983; 1987) and reflective thinking and judgment (Dewey, 1933; Kitchener and King, 1981) was reviewed resulting in a comprehensive definition of reflection (Ross, 1987).

Briefly, faculty initially defined reflection as a way of thinking about educational matters that involves the ability to make rational choices and to assume responsibility for those choices (Ross, 1987). This definition of reflection included a description of the component processes, attitudes, and content. Important processes included the ability to view teaching as problematic, the ability to analyze problems in terms of ethical and educational issues, the ability to make rational and intuitive judgments, the ability to monitor the effects of one's actions, and the ability to modify and extend one's educational appreciation system (i.e., theoretical and experiential knowledge base). Important attitudes included open-mindedness, willingness to assume responsibility for one's actions, and whole-heartedness (i.e., confidence and capacity for self-evaluation). Essential content was defined as pedagogical and ethical knowledge (i.e., knowledge of various educational practices and philosophies and of the purposes and consequences of educational practices), knowledge of students and human development, knowledge of material and ideological constraints on educational practice, knowledge of subject matter, and knowledge of ways to increase self knowledge. This definitional work led to the development of a set of criteria for evaluating reflective judgment in students. (See Chart 2.1)

CHART 2.1
Criteria Used to Evaluate Level Reflective Judgment in
Elementary PROTEACH Students (taken from student handbook)

— ability to recognize educational dilemmas
— willingness to assume responsibility for educational decisions
— ability to view situations from multiple perspectives (e.g., the perspective of the student, the teacher, the administrator, the research community). This includes the ability to evaluate real or potential consequences of a decision
— ability to search for alternative explanations for events occurring in the classroom
— use of adequate evidence to support a position or decision
— willingness to consider new evidence
— ability to judge the adequacy of a decision or position based on the context of application (i.e., a decision that may be "right" for one child or one classroom situation may be "wrong" in a different situation

---

In this definition faculty placed heavy emphasis on the development of both reflective judgment (processes and attitudes) and a knowledge base framework (content or appreciation system) as keys in creating reflective teachers. Initially, faculty saw these as developing together.

These components do not describe a discrete set of skills which teacher educators believe must or can be taught to teachers. Instead the components should be viewed as parts of an integrated scheme, a state of mind or an attitude. (Ross, 1987, p. 3)

While faculty believed reflection to be an integrated construct and assessed both the content and process of reflection in their research efforts, the criteria communicated to students tended to stress the process rather than the content of reflection. That is, their early work in describing reflection to students was heavily influenced by the work of Kitchener and King (1981) which documents abilities involved in the progressive development of reflective judgment with no focus on the content of reflection. Faculty believed that teaching the process involved in competent reflection as students worked to master the knowledge base framework within courses would help students construct both the content and process of reflection.

However, faculty research efforts have demonstrated that mastery of reflective judgment processes does not necessarily result in mastery of the knowledge base framework (or vice versa). For example, Ross, Ashton, and Mentonelli (1989) found that a student may demonstrate a high level of reflective judgment but not apply ethical criteria in making judgments (which would be necessary if one had also mastered the knowledge base framework). Conversely, they found evidence of a student with low reflective judgment who consistently dealt with ethical issues. Faculty now realize they must help students develop both simultaneously and see the connection between them. To stress this, faculty have revised the definition of reflection to place more emphasis on the application of ethical criteria in making decisions. Reflection is now defined to students as a way of thinking about educational matters that involves the ability to make rational *and ethical* choices and to assume responsibility for those choices.

Additionally, like many who stress reflection, our view has been heavily cognitive and verbal. Although faculty have talked about an intuitive or affective component to reflection, it has not been an integral component of our definition. An analysis of the teaching practice of one of our students is leading us to rethink the role of intuitive and affective judgments.

Another issue related to our evolving definition of reflection is recognition of a need to provide more emphasis on a theory of learning as a part of reflective teaching. Development of a theory of learning has been included as part of the knowledge base framework. Because a constructivist view of learning has been an organizing principle of the elementary teacher education program for many years, most faculty work to help students view learning as socially constructed by teachers and students. However, this view is not unanimous throughout the profession (or college), and faculty have hesitated to indicate that any one view of learning is required of reflective teachers. Although faculty have not resolved this issue, we have achieved enough consensus that we now communicate that a reflective practitioner views learning as constructed by rather than transmitted to students. It should be noted that this view in itself is problematic because not all faculty within the college share this theory of learning. Thus, elementary faculty work to help students develop a coherent theory of teaching and learning that enables them to make sense of conflicting theories of learning within the profession.

Faculty Commitment

Lanier and Little (1986) note that faculty in colleges of education often identify more strongly with their academic disciplines than with teacher education. Faculty at Florida are committed to various academic disciplines, however, Zeichner (1988) noted a clear commitment to teacher education in the PROTEACH program. He stated:

> I doubt that we could find a program in which as much thinking has gone on about the structure and substance of teacher education programs. Even acknowledging the gaps which appear to exist between the programs as described in the written materials and what appears to exist in reality . . . there has been, and continues to be, an unusual amount of effort put into the initial and continuing development of these programs (pp. 10-13).

One example of this commitment is that core courses (e.g., Research in Elementary Education, Practices in Childhood Education, Action Research, Pre-internship, Internship) were developed and are continually revised by a set of faculty who work collaboratively. Many of the experiences within the core courses have evolved over time based on formative evaluation studies. Additionally, substantive changes in these core courses are discussed by the collective faculty.

The reality of PROTEACH is that it consumes the attention of elementary faculty. Most elementary faculty do all their teaching within the program, and all teach heavy loads. Thus, much of the program is taught by faculty, and all full-time interns are supervised by faculty. (Part-time interns are supervised by graduate assistants.) While this is a strength, it also is a problem. The success of PROTEACH has increased enrollment which has meant heavier class loads, larger classes, heavier supervision and advisement loads, and a reduction in time devoted to evaluation studies. Because faculty believe in PROTEACH, it is difficult to identify areas of the program to cut. Yet, failure to reduce faculty loads may, over time, reduce faculty effectiveness and commitment, and may disrupt the evolutionary cycle of evaluation and revision that has been central within PROTEACH. Additionally, the quality of other programs may be affected.

THE PROTEACH PROGRAM IN PRACTICE

In previous writings the structure of the program has been described (Ross, 1989a; Ross and Krogh, 1988; Smith et al., 1984). The structural components which focus on the development of reflection include: (1) core courses (listed above); (2) key instructional strategies (reflective writing, curriculum development and analysis, inquiry oriented supervision, faculty modeling, development of action research projects, focus on teaching micro-political realities of schooling); and (3) ongoing commitment to graduates (Beginning Teacher Conference, evaluation efforts, establishing a PROTEACH graduate network).

The focus of this section of the chapter is a description of the evolutionary nature of instructional strategies within PROTEACH. Based upon formative studies, faculty identify problems in their work with students and make revisions within courses or the program. In this way, the faculty provide a continuous model of reflective practice. The example chosen demonstrates faculty modeling within a specific course as demonstrated through the implementation of a new program strategy, student clarification of personal theories of teaching.

Studies conducted by PROTEACH faculty led to concern about the difficulty of fostering and sustaining reflection within students (Ashton et al., 1989; Bondy, 1989; Kilgore, Ross, and Zbikowski, 1990; Krogh and Crews, 1989; Ross, 1989b; Ross et al., 1989; Weade, 1987). Studies by Bondy (1989) and Ross et al. (1989) suggested that a reason for this difficulty is that the entering perspectives of students exert a strong influence on their experiences within teacher education. This research (and similar research done by others) suggested a need to help students reveal and confront their perspectives about teaching.

Drawing on related work on collaborative autobiography (Butt and Raymond, 1989), teaching perspectives (Posner, 1985), teaching metaphors (Bullough and Gitlin, 1989) and images (Clandinin, 1986), faculty teaching the courses in Research in Elementary Education and Practices in Childhood Education decided to experiment with the development and analysis of personal theories of teaching. This assignment was added to both courses simultaneously. Students take the Research course at the beginning of the program, and the Practices course in their last year. Faculty believe that repeating the assignment will provide students with greater opportunity to reveal, test, and confront their perspectives about teaching.

Development of personal theories was approached differently within the two courses because of differences in the experience levels of students and the nature of the courses. The development of personal theories within the Practices course is described here. In the past, students in this course had written "beliefs papers." In preparation for the beliefs paper, students read articles describing various aims in education, reviewed notes from previous courses, and then described their beliefs about teaching and learning and set priorities for action within their internships. In contrast, personal theory papers were designed to help students clarify their "implicit" beliefs about teaching and learning and thus were based in autobiographical writings (e.g., significant learning experiences, descriptions of best and worst lessons they have taught, descriptions of excellent teachers). In describing the change, instructors shared with students a rationale based in analysis of the perspectives and practices of previous students. The following explanation is reconstructed from an instructor's notes:[3]

> We have found that students have "implicit" theories of teaching that seem more important in determining what they do than a statement of beliefs done in an academic paper. For example, we have studied one student (Ross et al., 1989) who articulated a view of teaching based in caring and an ethical commitment to reach all students, while calling on only the most vocal and insistent students. The student evaluates herself as successful because her lessons are fun and students "respond positively," ignoring the fact that some students do not participate in classroom discourse. . . . This inconsistency seems to exist because the student's implicit view is that teaching is performing. Good teaching means a good performance. If the audience responds, little else is required.

In discussing the revision in the assignment, the instructors noted that their study of the perspectives and practices of a few students helped them to determine where they fall short of reaching their goals and to identify practices which need revision. This type of modeling provides students with clear evidence that faculty not only urge them to be reflective but actually engage in the process. Additionally, sharing faculty reasoning provides students with a clear picture of the reflective process, a model of how one does it. Faculty stressed particularly the importance of active study of pupils' perspectives as part of the reflective process.

In addition to modeling the reflective process by sharing faculty thinking about instructional decisions, faculty used "think aloud" procedures as a way of teaching students to analyze their past experience, an important aspect of reflective practice. Helping students to "tease out" their implicit theories about teaching requires helping them to articulate and analyze past experiences as a teacher and learner. What made the assignment particularly problematic was that class size varied from thirty-two to forty students which meant that students were required to complete their analysis with little individual assistance from faculty. Yet, if the assignment was to be more than an academic exercise, thorough analysis of past experience was required.

Faculty approached the task in two ways. First, faculty completed all personal theory assignments with the students, including the writing of a personal theory of teaching. To model analysis based upon personal writing, faculty shared excerpts from personal writings and noted key words and passages that suggested implicit assumptions about teaching and learning. To demonstrate more specific analytical procedures, faculty used think aloud procedures to analyze students' writings.

Drawing from an assignment completed by students, the faculty selected several representative paragraphs and walked students through analysis procedures by sharing their thinking.

> As I look at this paragraph, I see the words "each child," "independently," and "understand" repeated multiple times. If I saw this same pattern across many writings I would conclude an image of teaching as "individual interaction between a teacher and each child in the classroom." The purpose of these interactions would seem to be to help each child understand the instructional content.

After the faculty member modeled the process of looking for key words and attempting to draw conclusions about the implicit assumptions that guide the selection of words, students practiced by analyzing other paragraphs working in groups. This practice on paragraphs written by others helped students see the importance of distancing themselves from the experience in order to look for implicit, yet perhaps unexamined, assumptions. After students articulated their views, they were asked to critique them drawing on professional knowledge developed within the program, and to examine the "goodness of fit" between their personal theory and the instructional context in which they would do their internship teaching. Following this students identified a set of personal teaching goals for their internship.

At this point, let us step back from our example. Our charge for this section of the chapter was to tell you about the program in practice, yet this section has described one assignment within one course. What does this tell you?

First, the example gives a sense of the evolutionary nature of instructional strategies within the PROTEACH program and a picture of faculty modeling and of student-teacher interactions. In fact, the personal theory assignment as described above was substantially revised for the 1990-91 academic year based upon our experiences with the assignment, feedback from students, and further reading.

Second, the example suggests an important shift in focus. Based upon their knowledge of research on teacher socialization and cognitive psychology faculty have long believed that learners construct new understandings on top of preexisting knowledge. Faculty now recognize that this belief requires confronting students' entering perspectives. While this is not done in every PROTEACH course, the issue of teachers' implicit perspectives has become increasingly important in core courses and in some methods courses. As Roland (1990) who teaches art methods courses notes:

> When students' preconceptions are at variance with the ideas presented by the teacher they actually interfere with intended learning outcomes and often persist despite instruction. . . . Finding out what preservice art teachers already know, feel, and believe about art and teaching is crucial to their learning about art and teaching. (p. 6)

Finally, although mentioned only briefly, the example illustrates another important focus within PROTEACH, the context of teaching. Requiring students to assess the fit between their theories and their teaching contexts is one of the strategies used to help students recognize the important role that context plays in their professional development. Although resources make ongoing support of graduates difficult, faculty realize that preservice teacher education is only one influence on the development of teachers. The context of their beginning years of teaching is another highly important influence. Studies by Hayes and Ross (1989) and Kilgore et al. (1990) suggest that context plays a critical role in sustaining or constraining a reflective approach to teaching. Unless faculty can find ways to support graduates, they recognize that their influence may, in reality, be minimal. At present our strategies for helping students sustain professional growth include: The Beginning Teacher Conference,[4] establishing a PROTEACH graduate network throughout the state, helping students recognize and find growth enhancing professional contexts, and teaching students micro-political strategies that will help them become teachers of influence within schools. These first three strategies have been discussed elsewhere (Ross, 1989a). For a discussion of micropolitical strategies see Ross and Bondy (1990).

DOES THE PROGRAM TRULY TEACH REFLECTION?

The previous section describes the evolutionary nature of instructional practice within PROTEACH. Changes made are most often based in the research efforts of the faculty as they have attempted to determine whether the program and/or particular strategies contribute to the development of reflective practitioners. What has been learned?

Two major issues are addressed in the fourteen completed studies and those that are continuing. The first relates to our struggle to define reflection. Faculty are still working to determine what reflection is, how to help students learn it and how to assess it. Without completely resolving the first issue, they have concurrently been studying students' perspectives and actions during the program and upon completion to try to determine program impact. Here faculty are trying to determine whether students are becoming more reflective, how various program experiences have influenced them and whether the program has an impact on their actions as teachers.

At this point, faculty have reached two major conclusions. First, learning to teach is influenced by a complex array of factors. These include: entering perspective, personal learning history, theoretical knowledge base, faculty mentors, peers, cooperating teachers, university supervisors, children within classrooms, student teaching experiences, image of self, perception of efficacy. Each of these things contributes to the development of the teacher's perspective. However, it is important to note that each also influences how other factors are experienced. That is, perspective is built through a complex array of factors. Perspective also acts as a screen that determines how new experiences are interpreted.

For example, Bondy (1989) describes a student who sees good teaching as organized activity. This image emerged from the student's out-of-classroom experiences (e.g., past experiences with organized versus disorganized teachers and her personal concerns about organization of time). This entering perspective then influenced how she perceived the PROTEACH program and the kinds of learnings she took from her courses and her internship. For example, when asked to describe problems in PROTEACH she focused on scheduling problems (as opposed to other students who have discussed problems in content or grading practices within courses or concerns about the practices, commitment, or ethics of fellow students). Similarly, in discussing what she learned during her internship, this student described practical tips related to classroom and lesson organization.

Because each student's entering perspective influences the nature and impact of the teacher education program, change in perspective (which faculty have come to see as the basis of the development of reflective practice) is very difficult. This difficulty can be exacerbated when the knowledge base discussed within the program conflicts with the practices encountered within elementary classrooms. For example, an issue raised in our program is whether Assertive Discipline can be considered a reflective approach to discipline. While many students can articulate the "party line" that Assertive Discipline is not reflective, the fact that few see an alternative approach within their field placements means that many come to accept the model, yet continue to describe themselves as reflective practitioners without confronting the underlying conflict.

As Weade (1989) noted, at times program participants engage in "procedural display" rather than true reflection. They may seem to have mastered the knowledge base, but perspectives remain unaltered. More importantly, unless faculty can help students move beyond procedural display, they have no access to underlying perspectives and minimal opportunity for significant impact on students.

Our second major conclusion is that reflective teaching is difficult to assess and difficult to teach. Helping students change their perspectives is slow, difficult, and time consuming work. Each study conducted refines our knowledge about what is involved in learning to teach and leads to program revisions designed to improve our ability to help students become reflective practitioners. Examples of changes which have already been discussed in this paper include increasing the emphasis on the ethical component of reflection, requiring students to clarify and analyze a personal theory of teaching at the beginning of their program and immediately before (or after) their internship, increasing the emphasis on theories of learning as a component of reflective teaching, and placing increased attention on the nature and importance of beginning teaching contexts and the development of micropolitical skills that will empower teachers.

Additional changes which have come out of the research efforts include the following. First, faculty throughout the program have increased the focus on issues related to teaching at risk students. Kilgore et al. (1990) found that graduates who are least likely to sustain a reflective approach to teaching were those who were teaching a large number of at risk students. Additionally, Hayes and Ross (1989) reported the difficulties experienced by a highly reflective teacher when teaching at risk students for the first time. Second, faculty have made changes in the structure of reflective writing assignments. Weade (1987) and Krogh and Crews (1989) conducted studies of student response and/or levels of reflection in reflective writing assignments using alternative structures. Their work suggests the difficulty of facilitating reflective thinking through written assignments within a non-graded course. Faculty are still working on this problem. And third, there have been changes in the nature of training experiences for graduate students who supervise part time internships for preservice teachers. Hoover and O'Shea (1987) found that field advisors who are trained using an instrument (Florida Performance Measurement System—FPMS) which stresses effective teaching behaviors tend to focus on those behaviors even when not using the instrument. Because faculty see this as an overly narrow focus, they have limited the focus on the FPMS in our training of supervisors.

Because the program is continually revised, our research lags behind. That is, each study evaluates the impact of a program that no longer exists. Additionally, almost all of research has been done with students within the program. Only one completed study focuses on graduates of the program, however, several studies of graduates are in process. Nevertheless, we do have some evidence of program impact. Every study conducted demonstrates that some students and graduates are moderately or highly reflective and at least some maintain their reflective abilities within their first year of teaching (e.g., Kilgore et al., 1990; Krogh and Crews, 1989; Ross, 1989b; Ross et al. 1989). Students perceive the program as positively influencing the development of their perspectives and abilities as teachers, and principals perceive our graduates as competent professionals. However, as already noted, reflective teaching is influenced by a complex array of factors, one of the most significant of which is the entering perspective of the student. Although our studies indicate the program has an impact on those who enter with a propensity to be reflective, the nature of our impact on those who enter with a more technical orientation is unclear.

In their study of the socialization of preservice teachers, Tabachnick and Zeichner (1984) conclude that teacher education enables students to clarify and elaborate their perspectives. It does not change them. The extent of our impact upon students is difficult to assess for several reasons. First, the entering perspective of each student is a powerful force which means that each student experiences the program differently. Second, although PROTEACH is a thematic program in which faculty have a great deal of consensus about goals and have collaborated in developing strategies to achieve our goals, the "program" is different for different students. For example, differences exist in instructors taken, in the peers with whom students most strongly identify, in the contexts in which student teaching is done, in the model provided by cooperating teachers, and in the nature of guidance and feedback provided by university supervisors. The interaction between differences in the nature of the experienced program and differences in the entering perspectives of students magnifies the difficulty of assessing programmatic impact.

Third, our definition of reflection is still evolving. Until faculty clarify the nature of reflection and its components, it is difficult to develop criterion measures useful in evaluating program success. And fourth, the real impact of the program can only be determined by studies of graduates during their beginning years of teaching. Perhaps the impact of reflective teacher education programs is best represented by the nature of the professional development and practice of their graduates several years later. These studies have just begun. However, here again it will be difficult to assess impact because of the differential influence of context on teacher development.

Perhaps, the relevant conclusion here is that the study of teaching and teacher development is messy. To isolate individual variables in controlled studies would violate our knowledge about the complexity of teaching. Consequently, in our view the most significant criterion for evaluating research in teacher education is whether the research is contributing to our understanding of what is involved in learning to teach and the nature of teacher education that is likely to improve teaching.

LESSONS FROM PROTEACH

Our research efforts thus far have contributed to knowledge about the complex array of factors involved in helping students learn to teach. At this point faculty do not have a total picture. Within PROTEACH, and within the field in general, teacher educators are still discovering the multiple pieces of this complex puzzle. Each study contributes but teacher educators do not yet have all the pieces, nor is there only one acceptable way to assemble the puzzle to create a good teacher. Understanding the process and components of learning to teach is important to all teacher educators, however they describe their particular goals.

Additionally, our efforts contribute to an understanding of how teacher educators learn to teach and the factors that contribute to their development and to the development of good programs. As faculty attempt to improve programs, they must consider curricular issues such as what content and experiences to include, and how content and experiences should be sequenced. This is where faculty began in PRO-TEACH. But for teacher education to have any significant impact on teaching and learning in schools, much more must happen. Faculty must examine their perspectives to determine their personal theories of teaching. These must be shared, critiqued, and revised to develop a sense of shared goals. Faculty also must assess and continually revise their goals and their instructional strategies in order to improve their ability to accomplish their goals.

It seems critical to recognize that a teacher education program is socially constructed. The effectiveness of the program is dependent on the development of common visions, goals, and definitions. This requires conflict, collaboration, and consensus building. If the PRO-TEACH faculty were to begin again, they would draw on literature in the areas of shared decision-making and group process skills to help us develop a better process for the social construction of a program.

Additionally, teacher education requires a commitment to continuous evaluation of programs and program components. Faculty believe PROTEACH is a strong program. They have clearly articulated goals, a logical programmatic structure grounded in the theoretical and research knowledge base, a strong student population and competent faculty. However, the program itself is only part of PROTEACH. The other, and perhaps more important part, is the ongoing process of evaluation that increases faculty knowledge about the impact of the program on students, the nature of students' perspectives about teaching and the experiences of graduates as they begin to teach. This knowledge leads to faculty growth, to clarification of their goals, and to changes in instructional strategies. It is this recursive, reflective process that is the core of PROTEACH.

While many give lip service to evaluation, high quality teacher education programs should be characterized by commitment of resources, including faculty time, to evaluation. Formative evaluation has been a strength within PROTEACH, but this has been possible because of external funding. It remains to be seen whether the college and university have sufficient commitment to teacher education to institutionalize the allocation of resources to evaluation efforts. It is time teacher educators recognized that evaluation is not a frill; it is an essential part of the process of teacher education that leads to faculty development and to the continual improvement of teacher education programs.

JOSEPH McCALEB
HILDA BORKO
RICHARD ARENDS

3

Reflection, Research, and Repertoire in the Masters Certification Program at the University of Maryland

The Masters Certification Program (MCP) at the University of Maryland is an alternative teacher education program designed for highly educated and capable persons who have completed baccalaureate degrees in academic fields. As the name suggests, completion of the program yields a masters degree and eligibility for certification to teach in either secondary or elementary schools. This chapter describes the distinctive qualities of the program and especially details the ways reflection is enhanced and evaluated.

The Masters Certification Program was designed and implemented in 1985 out of two different but complementary motivations. First, the chair of the Department of Curriculum and Instruction wanted to combine his interests in innovative, graduate-level teacher education with similar interests of several faculty members. The envisioned program was to focus on generic teacher education rather than on the emphases of grade-level and subject-area specializations that existed in the department. Generic teacher education was understood to concern basic principles of learning and pedagogy as represented by the research on teaching effectiveness and school effectiveness (e.g., handbooks of research on teaching). The program planners acknowledged the importance of sufficient preparation in the arts and sciences but did not focus directly on the specifics of the preparation. Another aspect of this motivation was the interest expressed by several faculty members who wanted to connect their research agendas with program development. An innovative, experimental program seemed an appropriate vehicle for this.

A more pragmatic motivation occurred as faculty recognized a need to respond to the large number of highly qualified college graduates who were inquiring about an alternative means of certification. These persons were often seeking a career change into teaching after five to twenty years in a first career. They already had a good liberal arts education, often with impressive majors in the arts and sciences; in addition, many had completed graduate programs and had worked in such careers as basic research in science, law, technical editing, or union organizing. Although they were willing to embark on additional preparation, they did not want to piece together a set of undergraduate classes spread over two to four years in order to fit into the existing accredited programs. The Masters Certification Program was designed as a creative alternative *within* teacher education to the other alternatives that were gaining popularity: credentialing through the apprentice model and "credit-count" certification by the state.

DISTINCTIVE FEATURES OF THE MASTERS CERTIFICATION PROGRAM

These two motivations led to the formation of a program with at least four distinctive features: selectivity concerning participants, an emphasis on developing a cohort group, a change in field placements so they could actually be experienced as laboratories or studios, and the identification of a specific knowledge base.

Selectivity

Given the faculty's desire for a small innovative program combined with the interest from a large number of well qualified applicants, the opportunity was available to be unusually selective about the "scholar-teachers," the term used for "students" admitted into the program.

Criteria for admission to the program include the College of Education's graduate school requirements: a bachelor's degree from an accredited institution with a grade point average of 3.0 or better, and a score at or above the 50th percentile on the Millers Analogy Test or the Graduate Record Examination. Applicants are also required to write a statement of purpose which is screened for writing and thinking ability and for commitment to teaching. The faculty decided that before admitting an applicant an interview should be held; this requirement exceeds those set by the graduate school. The interview enables program faculty to evaluate appropriateness of this program in relation to the applicant's interests and goals. The transcripts of persons interested in teaching at the secondary level are also evaluated to determine sufficiency of preparation in the subject specialization.

Although the quality of reflection was not an explicit criterion in the decision process, applicants were selected who displayed this quality. The written statement of goals and the interview with faculty were given an emphasis so that persons were selected who were thoughtful about their decision to enter the teaching force and who were knowledgeable and concerned about issues of education. Also, because high grade point averages and standardized test scores tend to represent a capacity for or orientation toward reflection, the use of these criteria also contributed to selecting reflective participants. Persons admitted to the program have averaged about a 3.25 GPA and have had test scores averaging at the 72nd percentile.

Cohort Group

A second distinctive feature of the program was the use of a cohort group. Existing programs within the university had little provision for students to experience more than one or two classes together. Very seldom did persons from different disciplines or teaching levels interact, and existing programs paid little attention to group formation. In contrast, the MCP consisted of a small group (fewer than twenty-six scholar-teachers in each cohort) and provided intensive experiences together over a twelve month period (a summer session, two semesters, and another summer session). An example of the degree of development of the cohort as a group was demonstrated the second year when the scholar-teachers began establishing rituals which have been continued by subsequent cycles. A continuing example was their initiation in designing and producing their own graduation ceremony.

The cohort structure reinforced reflection in several ways. Specific structures or "containers" were designed for the processing of group dynamics of the cohort. For example, the cohort met in a proseminar each semester and frequently addressed interpersonal and programmatic concerns. Journal writing which was responded to by the director of the proseminar also dealt with these matters.

In addition, because of the emphasis on generic issues in teacher education rather than on subject matter or grade level specializations, the cohort experienced more classes with persons of varied disciplinary orientations than occurred in the traditional programs where elementary majors seldom encounter secondary majors and math education majors rarely see English education majors. As suggested by attributions made by scholar-teachers and faculty, the cohort structure promoted reflection by providing a safe place for the scholar-teachers to reflect on the diverse perspectives they were experiencing.

Field Placement Schools as Laboratories or Studios

A third distinctive feature concerned the role of clinical and field experiences. Considerable energy was devoted to conceptualize field-placement schools as laboratories or studios rather than as "*the* real world." The intention was for participants to experience *both* the university and the school as a real world, both as parts of the same constructed world, a world characterized by continuing inquiry rather than by the transmission and incorporation of predetermined information.

University and clinical faculty have strived to inculcate in candidates the value that they are reflective scholar-teachers rather than apprentices. Schools and cooperating teachers were carefully selected and were given orientations and training related to the program's design and its mission as well as instruction about current research on learning and teaching. The schedules for field placements were continually rearranged to promote inquiry, diversity of experience, and opportunity for reflection. Intensive work in the field was interspersed with intensive work on campus where they could reflect upon and discuss the experience. Each year the time allocated to each setting was scrutinized and usually adjusted. The general design for the major field placements was for scholar-teachers to have an extended period (about ten weeks) in one school, then a week on campus, then a shorter placement in a second school (about five weeks), and finally spend the remaining time at university. Even during the long placement, most weeks for at least one-half day the scholar-teachers returned to campus to reflect on their experience. A primary intention of this design of the field placement was to counteract uncritical adoption of school practices as "the way it is."

An action research project conducted during the field experience also served to influence the conceptualization of that experience. The project, which produced the data for the second of two major scholarly papers required for the program, entailed identifying and studying an issue of interest in one's own teaching. (A more complete discussion of this project is provided later in the implementation section of this chapter.)

Conducting action research generated tension against the familiar routine associated with student teaching. This tension forced continued dialogue and negotiation around the differing perspectives on the real world, thereby meshing reflection with practice. Viewing the field experience as the setting for action research helped to change the perception, both in the university and in the public school, toward schooling as a laboratory/studio and away from the prevailing notion that becoming a teacher was a transition from the ivory tower to the real world.

Knowledge Base for Reflection

The fourth distinctive feature of the MCP concerned the "what" of reflection. Although many of the scholar-teachers came to the program as reflective individuals, their conceptions of teaching and schooling were often naive and limited. Therefore, the program planners recognized the importance of developing a knowledge base as substance for reflection simultaneously with promoting the practice of reflection. This knowledge base that became the core of the curriculum came mainly from five areas of inquiry: theory-based studies of classroom methods; research on effective teaching; studies of learners, learning, and learning strategies; school effects studies; and learning to teach studies. (These program components are described in the section on theoretical foundations.)

Together these bodies of research and theory represented the orientation and expertise of the faculty who worked most closely with the scholar-teachers during the first years of the program (the "program faculty"). Faculty with other perspectives (e.g., a subject matter specific focus) also interacted with the scholar-teachers; also some members of the program faculty broadened their orientations as the program evolved to incorporate increased attention to different paradigms (for example, more attention was given to radical social critique of schooling, Giroux, 1983; Shor and Freire, 1987).

Despite these variations, the faculty most involved in planning and implementing the program worked from a reasonably discrete knowledge base and expected the scholar-teachers to reference this base in their reflective activities (e.g., examinations, papers, and class discussions). While scholar-teachers were not restricted to this body of literature, they were expected to acquire the capacity to apply it to their classroom observations and teaching experiences. The distinctive characteristic is that the program not only emphasized the practice of reflection, but it emphasized being reflective with a particular paradigm and knowledge base, and this critical stance was consciously acknowledged.

THE ASSUMPTIONS AND THEORETICAL BASE FOR THE PROGRAM

Alternative teacher education programs are not needed unless existing programs are not adequately serving all prospective teachers and learners. A fundamental assumption underlying the Masters Certification Program is that the basic structures of existing programs are limited. Structures that have been criticized in reviews of teacher education include: the lecture format dominating college instruction (Carnegie Forum, 1986; Holmes Group, 1986), the conception and design of student teaching (Berliner, 1985; Evertson, Hawley, and Zlotnik, 1985), the isolation of participants and lack of integrating experiences (Joyce and Clift, 1984), and identification with content fields rather than with teaching and learning in general (McCaleb et al., 1987).

In responding to the perceived need for an alternative method of teacher preparation, the program faculty designed the Masters Certification Program around three conceptual goals. Scholar-teachers are expected to develop (1) a thorough command of the *research* and knowledge base on teaching, learning, teacher education, and school effectiveness; (2) skills and dispositions for *reflection*, problem solving, and decision making; and (3) a *repertoire* of teaching strategies and routines believed to be effective and essential for beginning teachers. After hearing repeated references to these goals, participants in the first cohort were overheard discussing them as the "3 Rs" of learning to teach. This label caught on, and the "3 Rs" has become a trademark of the program. Thus, a primary assumption undergirding the MCP is that research, reflection, and repertoire are the foundation of an effective teacher preparation program for persons already having acquired background in academic content through the completion of a baccalaureate degree.

A third major assumption of the MCP is that schooling as currently practiced is failing and that teachers must acquire knowledge and skills to bring about change. This means that teachers must become knowledgeable about the processes of educational change (Fullan, 1991) and, most important, they must develop a technical language and a shared memory (Lortie, 1975) for talking about teaching specifically and about education in general.

Unlike other professions where initiates acquire new vocabulary, persons preparing to teach already possess idiosyncratic language based on extensive experience in schools. This preexisting language, and the presumption accompanying it, may impede acquisition of more sophisticated language and in turn reflective, critical thought. The program faculty observed that, unless convinced there is a body of knowledge that they need to acquire, prospective teachers often act as if they already know enough about what happens in schools. This third assumption concerns the recognition of a specific body of knowledge that informs effective teaching.

A related assumption that has been prominent in developing the MCP is that a crucial characteristic of the professional teacher is the quality of being reflective and that being reflective as a professional involves referencing a special knowledge base. This knowledge base and associated technical language enables the professional teacher to observe instructional events and episodes, to explain them with principles from learning and from pedagogy, and to see how instructional events relate to numerous contextual variables. Teachers also use the knowledge base in considering moral and ethical aspects of what they and others are doing.

Prior to program implementation and in the first years of the program, the knowledge base was identified in self-study reports as emphasizing five areas of inquiry:

Theory-based studies of classroom methods. Over the past several centuries a variety of teaching models (as labeled by Joyce and Weil, 1986) were invented by teachers, philosophers, university researchers, and psychologists. Most of the models were designed based on the inventors' perceptions (theories) of good teaching and beliefs about what is important for children to learn. A knowledge base was built around each model as inventors and others used it and evaluated its effects. Cooperative learning, the advance organizer model, the inquiry model, the concept attainment model, direct instruction, and synectics receive considerable attention in the program beginning with the course titled Models of Teaching.

Studies of learners, learning, and learning strategies. This research came out of a variety of areas but mostly from cognitive sciences. It opened up new paradigms about the nature of learning and how students approach learning tasks and also the nature of teaching and how teachers teach (Berliner, 1986; Gagne, 1985; Garner, 1987; Leinhardt and Putnam, 1987). This knowledge base is introduced in and serves as the core of the course titled Cognitive Basis of Instruction.

Research on effective teaching. Over the preceding thirty years, researchers observed teachers in classrooms as they taught. By comparing behaviors of more effective teachers with those of less effective teachers (as defined by the researcher) a set of pedagogical concepts was structured which informs some aspects of teachers' work: classroom management, use of time, questioning, the demands of various instructional tasks, etc. (e.g., Berliner, 1979; Emmer, Evertson, and Anderson, 1980; Evertson and Emmer, 1982; Evertson et al., 1983; Good and Grouws, 1977; Good, Grouws, and Ebmeier, 1983; Stallings, 1976). More recently, research has emphasized cognitive processes of effective teachers such as planning, interactive decision making, and problem solving (e.g., Borko and Livingston, 1989; Borko and Shavelson, 1990; Leinhardt and Greeno, 1986; McCaleb, 1985; Yinger, 1981). This knowledge base became the focus of the course titled Research on Effective Teaching.

School effects studies. During the preceding twenty years, research from such fields as organizational psychology, anthropology, and education provided ideas about the positive effects which follow certain processes in schools. These processes especially involved teachers and others coming together and reaching common agreements about school goals and processes (Brookover et al., 1979; Good and Brophy, 1986; Goodlad, 1984; Rutter et al.,1979). This knowledge base is addressed in the course which came to be labeled Teaching as a Profession.

Learning to teach studies. The final component of the knowledge base includes the recent literature which identifies the unique features in the process of learning to teach. This literature focuses primarily on the special experiences and needs of beginning teachers (Applegate, 1987; Arends, 1988; Borko, 1988; Feiman-Nemser, 1983).

STRUCTURAL CHARACTERISTICS OF THE MASTERS CERTIFICATION PROGRAM

The Masters Certification Program was designed to be completed in one calendar year. Classes begin in the first week in July with a six-week summer session, continue through the fall and spring sessions (each with about fifteen weeks), and conclude in late June with another summer session. Upon successful completion of forty-three to forty-nine semester hours of work, two scholarly papers, and comprehensive examinations (written and oral), candidates receive a Master's degree in education and certification to teach in Maryland and states with which the state education agency has reciprocal agreements.

A series of carefully planned and integrated field experiences was designed to occur throughout the program. During the first summer, participants typically visit a staff development center in a public school system, a special education center, educational agencies in the federal and state governments, and a professional teachers' association. During the fall session, special arrangements are made to enable scholar-teachers to observe the beginning of school. Additional experiences in public and private schools continue throughout that semester and are coordinated with assignments given in the university courses. The internship occurs in the spring session with placements in two sites especially selected for multicultural diversity. Scholar-teachers are encouraged to visit each other and to negotiate with the program director for their special interests concerning what and where they want to teach.

The specific courses in the program have evolved and changed over the six years. Some changes were made based on feedback from scholar-teachers who identified weaknesses in the program; other changes resulted from "turf battles" as the new courses were submitted to departmental and college-wide program review. Courses and field experiences currently required are illustrated below.

First Session (six-week summer school)
  1. Models of Teaching: Theories and Applications (three credits). Theory and research on teaching as applied to models of instruction. Practice in developing an initial repertoire of teaching models and in providing thoughtful critique of teaching based on these models. This course has evolved to include more social criticism with attention to different views on literacy and education.
  2. Cognitive Basis of Instruction (three credits). Psychological and educational research literature on human cognition, especially as applied to learning and teaching in classroom settings.
  3. Teaching as a Profession (three credits). The profession of teaching and the knowledge base that defines teaching and schooling. Current and social issues that affect teaching and learning; role of research and experience in learning to teach.

Second Session (fifteen-week regular session)
  4. Research on Effective Teaching (three credits). Survey of the research

literature on effective teaching and effective schools. Observation and analysis of teaching in a variety of school and classroom settings.

5. Teaching Reading and Writing (three credits). The study of principles of reading and writing instruction. Reviews specific research studies and develops instructional strategies. Practice in conducting research and in providing effective instruction.

6. Quantitative Research Methods I (three credits). Introduction to research design principles and the scientific method as applied to behavioral phenomena. Instrumentation procedures including the planning and construction of simple data collection instruments, and assessment of the reliability and validity of such instruments. Statistical procedures appropriate to the analysis of data from simple research designs.

7. Specific methods courses (three to six credits). Objectives, selection and organization of subject matter, appropriate methods, lesson plans, textbooks and other instructional materials, measurement, and topics pertinent to specific subject matters.

8. Content specific courses (three to six credits). Dependent on analysis of prior course work, scholar teachers take a variety of class options.

Third Session (fifteen-week regular session)

9. Conducting Research on Teaching (three credits). Application of the knowledge base on effective teaching to the analysis and improvement of educational practice. Research methods used in the study of classroom teaching. Design and conduct of an action research project.

10. Proseminar on Teaching (one credit).

11. Internship (eight credits).

Fourth Session (six-week summer session)

12. Trends in Curriculum (three credits). The study of the complexities of design and evaluation in curriculum specialities, grades K-12. Examination of curriculum materials and reflection on teaching experiences. Review of values, assumptions, and knowledge which influence decisions about curricula design and evaluation. Includes attention to social and ethical concerns broader than the classroom and school level.

13. Independent study to complete action research report and for the written and oral comprehensive examinations (three credits).

All courses except numbers six through eight are restricted to participants in the MCP.

One significant evolution of courses occurred with regard to the two classes which are now named Research on Effective Teaching and Conducting Research on Teaching. These were initially conceived as a two-course series to develop the knowledge base on effective teaching and to guide the scholar-teachers in their action research projects. Some topics from the knowledge base were considered each semester. The idea of action research was introduced in the first course in the fall along with a discussion of methods of data collection. In the second class (Spring Semester), scholar-teachers selected topics for their action research, received guidance in designing their studies, and discussed methods of data analysis.

The division of content in the two courses was revised over the first few years of the program, primarily as a result of feedback from scholar-teachers. Members of the initial cohort groups reported difficulty in concentrating on theoretically-oriented substantive issues when faced with the immediacy of classroom problems during their internships in the Spring semester. Further, they were not yet receptive to ideas about data collection in the first class, before having sufficient classroom experience to decide upon topics for their action research projects. As a result, the current version of the Research on Effective Teaching course (taught first in the series) introduces the knowledge base of effective teaching and focuses on substantive discussions of that knowledge base. The second course (Conducting Research on Teaching) introduces the idea of action research, discusses methods of data collection and data analysis, and provides guidance for individual projects. The knowledge base of effective teaching is considered as it relates to scholar-teachers' action research projects. This revised division of course content is preferred both by course instructors and scholar-teachers.

THE PERSPECTIVE ON REFLECTION

The curriculum of the MCP was built on the premise that knowledge should guide practice but research cannot be translated into a set of recipes and formulas for teachers to follow blindly (Fenstermacher, 1980). Similarly, having a theoretically-based repertoire of methods to employ was considered essential but not sufficient. The third R of the three goals, reflection, provides the individualizing necessary to appropriate both repertoire and research into the contextually complex environments of the classroom and the school. Reflection also offers a primary means for the continued growth beyond initiation as a beginning teacher and beyond the teachings of the program (Feiman-Nemser and Buchmann, 1983), which of necessity cannot match the specific instructional demands of each individual's teaching placement.

As these comments indicate, reflection was conceptually understood as a problem-solving process, not too much different than that described by Dewey at the beginning of the century. Operationalized it means: (1) taking action (sometimes routine); (2) reflecting (thinking back, analyzing) upon that action (what happened, why, what it meant); (3) if resolution is not reached, moving on to a higher level of reflective or critical thought (multiple causes, conflicting goals, larger moral or ethical conflicts); and (4) coming up with alternative actions and thus continuing the cycle. Having surpassed the criteria for admission to the program, most scholar-teachers already had habits of reflection; therefore, a major task of the program was to instill a common knowledge base as the formulation of plans and as a primary consideration in the analysis and evaluation of action.

The program faculty held a retreat to reflect upon the success of the program midway through its first cycle. Focused attention was given to the conceptual understandings of the goals of the program. Notes from that retreat reveal a shared understanding of reflection as: "the ability to look back critically and imaginatively, to do cause-effect thinking, to derive explanatory principles, to do task analysis, also to look forward, and to do anticipatory planning (that is, to plan for options, to use an 'if-then' approach)." The connections of reflection with research and repertoire were affirmed at that retreat; additionally, reflection was extended beyond technical classroom analysis as some faculty stressed the development of professionalism in the scholar-teachers. Professionalism included involvement in teachers' organizations and broader issues than the individual classroom.

Operational Definition of Reflection as Shown in Implementation

From the outset, the program faculty were acutely aware that discussions about the meaning of reflection, even with scholar-teachers, would not contribute sufficiently to establishing effective practice of reflection. The program faculty therefore designed program features for demonstrating and practicing reflection, and they monitored the implementation of these features and their impact on reflection at regular intervals. These features include the following.

Faculty modeling. The faculty determined to "think-aloud" for the scholar-teachers in order to give more access to their processes of reflection. Sometimes this occurs as an in-flight decision in which the faculty member externalizes the considerations that lead to a change in plans, the alternatives being considered, and the criteria for deciding. On other occasions, an end-of-class reflection is offered. For example, in the Models of Teaching course, scholar-teachers requested a demonstration of the synectics model. The teacher had never used that model, but designed a lesson, taught it while being videotaped, offered his self-evaluation, and invited the scholar-teachers to critique both the lesson and the self-evaluation. The intent was to model the kind of reflection scholar-teachers might do at the conclusion of the microteaching lessons they were doing for the class.

The cohort and the help lab. The cohort has already been discussed as a container or safe place to risk self-criticism. The "help lab," one vehicle for doing self-criticism, is a weekly event (usually in the proseminar) when scholar-teachers present issues or problems for consideration of their peers, without faculty supervision unless it is specifically requested. Although an activity like the help lab may not be an unusual feature, when the participants are a cohort rather than just classmates, the level of risk-taking, insight, and growth seems significantly improved.

Journaling. As one of the faculty remarked to the scholar teachers, "Experience is not the best teacher; reflection and analysis is." The weekly journaling, required throughout the year, encourages reflection upon experience. It is viewed as a means of promoting disciplined reflection on a regular basis. The faculty often respond to the journals thereby turning them into a dialogue.

Microteaching. In their first semester, scholar-teachers are required to complete several microteaching cycles (teach, critique/reflect, reteach, reflect) under the supervision of the instructor of the Models of Teaching course.

Action research projects. Scholar-teachers conduct action research projects simultaneously with their internship. Guidance and support for these projects is provided in the course titled Conducting Research on Teaching and in the proseminar during the final two semesters of the program. The projects are completed as seminar papers in partial fulfillment of the requirements for a master's degree. They are also presented orally to faculty and other scholar-teachers as the oral component of the comprehensive examination.

The definition of action research that guides this assignment is that it should be research conducted in a "field setting," by participants in that setting, to help them improve their teaching. The focus is on a "problem of practice" identified by the teacher/researcher (the scholar-teacher) and the goal is to discover possible solutions to that problem. Implicit in this notion of action research is the premise that teachers are autonomous, thinking professionals who can and should take an active role in making their own histories and directing and improving their own teaching (Hopkins, 1982, 1985).

Early in their internship, scholar-teachers select an aspect of their own teaching which they want to understand better (a problem of practice). Through the action research project, they engage in systematic inquiry about the problem, with the goals of self-reflection and improvement. Consistent with the program's focus on research, they are asked to draw on previous research, as well as their own concerns as a teacher, in deciding upon the specifics of what to study and how to study it. They are encouraged to consult textbooks used in the program (e.g., Arends [1988] *Learning to Teach*; Good and Brophy [1987] *Looking in Classrooms*), as well as original research reports, for examples of observation and interview instruments that might be modified for use in their projects. They are also encouraged to continue research on the same topic which they investigated in their first seminar paper, a review of research on an educational issue of interest.

Several scholar-teachers in the most recent cohort designed their action research projects around teacher cognition and reflection. One planned a study comparing the effects of wait time and scripted wait time. The intention was to look at thought processes of students and of the teacher during wait time where students are given written direction on how to think. Another planned to study her thinking during discussion periods, specifically how call outs were thought about and handled. She intended to record her own thought processes through scripting and daily journaling. Scholar-teachers from earlier cycles submitted reports with titles such as: Improving the Quality of Clarity in the Classroom, Impact of Different Questioning Levels and Wait-Time on Student Interest and Participation, A Study of Two Self-Evaluation Methods in the Art Classroom, Teaching Writing through Response, and Planning and Interactive Decision Making.

Theory-practice wheels. In order to facilitate the transfer of principles from pedagogy to instructional practice, scholar-teachers received instruction in the use of charts or graphic organizers for representing the principles and their connections. Like journaling, these theory-practice wheels were viewed as a tool to promote disciplined reflection and principled pedagogical thinking. When focusing on classroom problems in their journal writing, the scholar-teachers often use the wheels as a source for the concepts to frame the reflections.

Class assignments. Several classes use assignments that were designed specifically to promote reflection. For example, Research on Effective Teaching has a primary goal that scholar-teachers learn to reflect on classroom teaching, using theories and research findings related to effective teaching as a source of issues to address in their reflections. The course is designed to encourage scholar-teachers to ask the following questions about their own teaching and the teaching of others:

> (a) To what extent does this classroom teaching exemplify principles of effective teaching, as identified in the body of research on teaching? What elements of effective teaching are evident in this teacher's classroom? What elements are not evident? (b) In what ways do findings from research on effective teaching seem to be appropriate standards against which to judge this classroom teaching? In what ways do they seem to be inappropriate?

Two written projects, based on observations at practicum sites, address these goals: an Academic Learning Time exercise and a Teacher Questioning and Feedback Techniques project.

The Academic Learning Time exercise requires the collection of data on allocated time, engaged time, and success rate by observing a classroom teacher in the practicum or by being observed. Observations include at least two classes (secondary) or two content areas (elementary) on two or more occasions. Based on these data, scholar-teachers compute Academic Learning Time (Berliner, 1979) and analyze patterns of time use. The assignment states:

> Discuss results of this exercise. For secondary classrooms, compare the two classes observed; for elementary, compare the two content areas. When analyzing time use, be sure to look for patterns in all of the information collected in the class. For example, when examining engagement rates, look for patterns of attention over time . . . and across students . . . If data were collected about your teaching, consider the following questions: In what area(s) are you strongest? In what area(s) are you weakest? How might you improve your time management skills? If data were collected about the teacher in your placement, consider a parallel set of questions.

The Teacher Questioning and Feedback Techniques exercise encourages self-initiative and responsibility and therefore is less structured than the Academic Learning Time exercise. Scholar-teachers are expected to identify a small number of research questions and to develop or modify an observation instrument for use in data collection. The assignment states:

> Based on existing research on questioning and feedback, select a small number of aspects of teaching on which you would like to focus . . . Then collect data (observations of your own teaching or the teacher in whose class you are participating). Analyze the data, paying particular attention to patterns in the data and comparisons to previous research. Present and discuss your results. Be sure to address the issue of what this observation activity has taught you that will be useful to understanding and/or improving your own teaching.

Course and program examinations. Course examinations are also designed to encourage reflection. In the course just described, an examination question used in Fall 1989 was:

> Ms. Maxwell, a beginning teacher, comes into your office one morning and says, 'I just read an article on the self-fulfilling prophecy and realize that it's wrong to hold expectations for students' performance. How can I stop myself from having expectations about my students?' How would you respond to Ms. Maxwell's question? Cite evidence from the research on teacher expectations to support your response.

In the Models and Processes of Teaching class, some of the final examination questions were:

> (a) You have been graded on the first three microteaching lessons with two different approaches. Identify the two methods of criticism that are associated with the grading. (For example, 'For the practice model, the _____ method of criticism was used . . .') Name 1-2 relative merits of each of these methods of criticism. (b) In 500 words or less critique your final presentation. In another 500 words critique your critique. What kind of critique did you do? What other kinds of critique were discussed in class? Why were they not used? What is the most important theory and/or research related to the best critique you could have done?

A written comprehensive examination is one of the College's requirements for a Master's Degree. Faculty in the MCP decided to use the examination as an opportunity to have students examine their personal development as professionals, using the three cornerstones of the program—reflection, research, repertoire—as focal points for their reflections. The questions for the examination have been modified only slightly over the years. The Comprehensive Examination for the 1988-1989 cohort asked:

> 1. As you know, the three goals or themes of the MCP are repertoire, research, and reflection. Discuss your development as a professional over the year, focusing on each of these three themes. We encourage you to use any assignments you have completed during the year (e.g., journals, essays, literature reviews, action research projects) as stimuli for your response. We expect you to incorporate ideas from courses and readings you experienced in the program. 2. Look ahead toward your career in education (or in another field if you have decided not to pursue a career in education). What do you hope to accomplish as a professional educator (or in another career)? Support your response with reference to your experiences in the MCP (e.g., courses, readings, projects); the three themes of repertoire, research, and reflection; and your understanding of the structures of schooling and the meaning of education.

Case studies. Some courses provide case studies to provoke thoughtful critique of the larger social and political issues of schooling and teaching. These issues include grouping practices, working with at-risk youth, the cellular school, outmoded curricula, and dynamics related to differing philosophical orientations of teaching (liberationist, executive, and therapist; e.g., Fenstermacher and Soltis, 1986).

Research conference. Near the end of the third cycle, a spring conference was established at the initiative of and with extensive collaboration by graduates of the program. The conference has as its theme the "3 Rs" of learning to teach. Each year current cohort group members present recent research, and program graduates present ideas from their expanding teaching repertoires and give reactions to their teaching experience and the preparation they received. Prominent educators in the area are featured as keynote speakers on one or more of the program themes. This conference has provided an additional means to extend the processes of reflection into the beginning years of the candidate's teaching career.

Field supervisor training. Each year, faculty provide a full-day workshop for teachers who work with the scholar-teachers in their internships. These cooperating teachers are provided with information about the "reflection" component of the program and are given opportunities to practice strategies they can use to help candidates reflect on internship experiences. Cooperating teachers are also given demonstrations of teaching models that the scholar-teachers have been adding to their repertoire and are coached in conferencing with the teacher who used the model. Purposes of this workshop include gaining increased support from the field supervisors for the innovative program and the continued development of a common language. Prospective teachers have often worked under the disadvantage of having university and field personnel who use different dialects for similar pedagogical concepts.

EVALUATION PROCEDURES AND RESULTS

Although there have been some discrete evaluative activities in the life of the Masters Certification Program, the emphasis in evaluation, in keeping with the process approach to reflection, has tended to occur more in a continuous manner. The discrete evaluations included a survey of graduates, two self-study reports accompanied by external reviews (conducted by the Maryland State Department of Education), and two major research studies.

The ongoing evaluation occurs within frequent meetings, both formal and informal, of program faculty; within a continuing dialogue with scholar-teachers in the context of their classes, especially the proseminar; and through the annual research conference. During recent cycles, scholar-teachers have selected representatives to attend formal meetings of the program faculty. These conversations have served as the basis for many changes in the program since its inception. For example, courses have been changed as noted earlier and modifications have been made to field experiences.

Evaluating Reflection

The perspective on evaluation was reflected in a statement one of the program faculty prepared for a task force on essentials of teaching (under the auspices of the Maryland State Department of Education):

A reflective teacher who has command of the knowledge base on teaching can: (1) Explain the core ideas emanating from the knowledge base and cite appropriate best practices associated with them; (2) Cite key pieces of research associated with the knowledge base and provide thoughtful critique of this research; (3) Execute effectively (at a novice level) selected best practices which grow out of the research in simulated and laboratory settings and in real classrooms; and (4) Engage in critical reflection and intellectual dialogue about the knowledge base and understand how the various ideas are connected and how they interact to inform (situationally) a particular teaching/school event or episode. Evaluative activity related to each of these four categories has occurred.

Understanding and application of the knowledge base. Evaluation of this component of reflection occurs through examinations (as described earlier), and it is monitored in journal entries. One scholar-teacher stated in a journal entry:

> I feel the pod system I observed does a lot to alleviate some of the problems arising from isolation that were pointed out both by Lieberman and by Goodlad. The issue of isolation aside, teachers do have their own personal styles and create their own unique atmosphere for their students. Goodlad pointed out that teaching techniques did not vary much between good and bad teachers. What did vary was the quality of the relationship and caring between and respect between students and teachers.

Critique of research. The most obvious place where this has happened is in the two seminar papers (one on a review of research and the other on the action research project). A sample from one of those papers shows the analysis of research studies:

> A case may be made for some cooperative learning with intergroup competition in a science classroom as well. Cotton and Cook (1982) argued many of the points made in the D. W. Johnson meta-analysis . . . For example, pure cooperation is not necessarily better than cooperation with competition, not enough studies were analyzed to draw such a conclusion. More data is necessary to support such a theory. A number of science classroom studies, (Okebukola, 1985, 1986a, 1986b) showed that cooperation with intergroup competition contributed to significantly higher student achievement than pure cooperation, competition, or individualization; particularly in high level problem-solving individual process skill tasks.

Moving understanding into teaching. As described earlier in the section on examinations, the scholar-teachers are asked to critique their microteaching during Models of Teaching. One self-critique shows the application of conceptual language from the course and the beginning of a constructive critical appraisal. Scholar-teachers were not demonstrating these characteristics in their initial self-evaluations.

> Despite my difficulty with the concept attainment model, I like the model and want to try it again. I think the model lends itself very well to scientific concepts, and is well suited for a science class. However, it was a lot more scary to use than some of the models we have practiced because I had very little control. I had to trust the students to really focus on my examples and think about the concept I was getting at. I am sure my control could have been improved with more concise examples of the attributes, but I still have to depend on the students to develop the ideas I am looking for. I think that when I do this model again I would like to allow more time and give more examples to see if students can really attain the concept.
>
> I wasn't overly pleased with my lesson when I had completed, and I began thinking back to a few class sessions ago when we discussed the importance of developing a philosophy and finding our center . . . I *felt* today the importance of developing a philosophy and becoming centered. I am sure that some of my ideas for the classroom will fall flat, especially on the first try, and if I allow that disappointment to govern how I teach, it won't be long before I am a teacher who drones on in front of the class day after day. I think I gained a little insight on why some teachers do become dry . . . I don't think my philosophy is close to being developed yet, but I am working on it and I realize that reflection allows me to see how I can improve and accomplish my goals with another try, rather than a criticism of everything I do wrong on my first try.

One of the research studies also investigated the teaching practices and reflection of scholar-teachers. Eight participants in the MCP were compared to a matched sample of student teachers in the traditional teacher preparation program at the university by observing their teaching on two consecutive days and interviewing them about their planning for, and evaluation of, observed lessons (Borko et al., 1988). Across both programs, three factors were related to student teachers' planning and post-lesson reflections: subject matter and pedagogical knowledge, content area influence, and teaching multiple sections of the same course.

The one clear difference between students in the two teacher preparation programs was that the MCP participants were less likely to attribute classroom successes and failures to external factors. They seemed to have a greater sense of control over classroom events than did student teachers in the traditional program. In turn, student teachers who perceived themselves as responsible for, and in control of classroom events (some in the traditional program also fit this category) more frequently took active steps to correct problem situations and improve their teaching.

MCP participants' greater sense of control over classroom events may be related to the experimental nature of the program. This study was conducted during the first year of the program's existence. The program underwent many revisions in the course of that year, and the scholar-teachers participated actively in the change process. Through their role in program revisions, they may have come to perceive that they did have control over, and responsibility for, their professional preparation experiences. Also, the program's focus on reflection may have helped scholar-teachers become better able to identify strategies for improving their teaching.

Critical reflection and intellectual dialogue. The development of critical reflection was evaluated in a more informal way through the research conference and in a formal manner in the second research study. A feature of the research conference each year is panel presentations by graduates just finishing their first year of teaching, those completing more than one year, and those just finishing the program. Members of each panel reflect on their teaching experiences in light of the research they have studied and their perceptions of the goals of schooling. Program faculty observed the scholar-teachers' retention of and facility in using the research literature, and they were generally impressed with what they saw. The second research study investigated the nature of pedagogical expertise by comparing the planning, teaching, and post-lesson reflections of three scholar-teachers in the MCP (two secondary and one elementary) with those of the cooperating teachers with whom they were placed (Borko and Livingston, 1989). The researchers observed the participants teaching mathematics for one week of instruction and interviewed them prior to and following each lesson. Differences in the thinking and actions of these experts (cooperating teachers) and novices (scholar-teachers) were analyzed by perceiving teaching both as a complex skill and as improvisational performance.

The novice teachers showed more time-consuming, less efficient planning, and they encountered problems when attempts to be responsive to students caused them to deviate from scripted lesson plans. They reported more varied, less selective post-lesson reflections than experts. The researchers accounted for these differences by the assumptions that novice teachers' cognitive schemata are less elaborate, interconnected, and accessible than experts' and that their pedagogical reasoning skills are less well-developed.

Additional Program Evaluation

The preceding sections on evaluation concerned items most related to reflection. Other evaluations of the program have occurred. Particular questions have been asked about the program: Has it been innovative (has it changed the curriculum significantly, for example)? Has it influenced other teacher preparation programs and the local public schools? Has it been of value to the faculty (both participants and nonparticipants)? Has it helped bring critical leaders and leadership to schooling? As might be expected with questions of this scope, unambiguous conclusions have not emerged. In general, the program faculty, the scholar-teachers, and school personnel who have supervised or employed scholar teachers have considered the program an impressive success. Further, several similar programs have been implemented in other universities throughout the state and region. As indicated in the next section, faculty not working with the program sometimes have expressed differing views and evaluations.

DIFFICULTIES, PROBLEMS, AND CONSTRAINTS

A report written in the first years of the program (McCaleb et al., 1987) identified four problem areas facing innovation in teacher education: curricular change, passivity, identity, and control. The program has continued to encounter problems in these areas.

Curriculum

Faculty with commitment to subject-matter specializations modified initial ideas for the design of the program. Attempts to infuse more attention to group dynamics and leadership were eventually dropped. Classes with one or two credits have disappeared; sometimes they have been incorporated into the three-credit format which more easily fits with structures regarding faculty load and other institutional conveniences. In some cases, the topics have received reduced emphasis. After an extended battle over the contents of the measurement and evaluation required course, the program faculty finally gave in to the uniform course taken by all persons in the college. Most of the program faculty still thought a special course could be tailored which would meet the statistics requirements and would better serve measurement needs of the scholar-teachers.

Passivity

The innovative quality of the MCP went against the characteristic passive grain of teacher education. As the program faculty and some scholar-teachers assumed a more assertive stance regarding the need for changes in education, objections began to appear from some faculty and staff who seemed to resent change, perhaps assuming the MCP was critical of their particular programs. Gaining formal approval for the new courses required extensive time and energy as certain faculty on the procedural committees persisted in asking for editorial changes in documents. One course continued to be offered under a temporary provision while its approval was held up. Another example concerns the resistance to changes in the field experiences. Attempts to reconceptualize duration and locations of experiences has required continued negotiation. The successes have related to having or getting "friends" as director of placements within both the university and the school systems.

Identity

Because the program has both elementary and secondary preparation and has persons from various academic fields, it crossed many of the existing units within the governance structure of the department. The program did not fit well within the established structure. It resided for five years within the department without being placed within a specific unit. This led to some loss of representation in governance decisions, and some difficulty in scheduling courses. Another problem related to identity concerns having a "special" program without offending persons who were not invited to participate intimately in it.

Control

Questions about control issues continue to exist. One critical problem concerns admission of persons wishing to teach at the secondary level. Transcripts must be evaluated for content sufficiency. Non-program faculty with specialization in the content area have been asked to do the evaluation. Persons who conceptualized the MCP had not intended an exact correspondence between the transcript and the content courses required in the traditional program. However, some non-program faculty continue to operate under the "exact" assumption, making it difficult to admit many otherwise well-qualified applicants unless the admissions decision disregards the content-specialist's recommendation. Disregarding the recommendation obviously leads to discontent and thus to conflict related to control.

Beyond these four areas of curriculum, passivity, identity, and control, a general difficulty concerns the area of evaluation. Reflection is not easily evaluated, and the ways it can be evaluated may not provide the most useful information toward program improvement. For example, scholar-teachers can be measured on the use of conceptual language from models of teaching or on their references to research literature; however, it is much more difficult to evaluate the blending of personal knowledge with critical perspectives in order to break open significant problems in their classrooms or in the broader educational enterprise. So it appears problematic to continue or expand evaluation of the technical reflection and by so doing to potentially restrict growth in critical reflection.

FUTURE PLANS AND RECOMMENDATIONS

The future of the Masters Certification Program seems quite uncertain. The department and college have been in extended debate over adoption of the Holmes Group proposals. The MCP has often been a referent for proposals related to new or revised programs. One direction would be for the MCP to dissolve into new/revised programs. It also seems possible that the program continue for some time in a form similar to what it is now. The program faculty remain open to new forms but continue to assert the importance of the critical distinctive features of the MCP and that they remain in existence in some form within the university's options for teacher certification. These features include the development of reflection in teachers through the activities described above, the development of a repertoire of pedagogical methods, a focus on particular knowledge bases and supporting research related to teaching, learning, and learning to teach, special attention to the cohort structure, and reconceptualizing the field placements as a laboratory/studio.

The program should not be xeroxed onto other programs. Instead, the reflective impulse that gave the program its inception should continue to yield explorations into alternative methods of effective teacher preparation. In the Masters Certification Program that impulse is reaching toward expansion beyond the technical concerns which dominated its early years and toward more ethical or social criticism. The very conception of reflection itself should be open to growth and transformation.

JANE APPLEGATE
BEVERLY SHAKLEE

4

Stimulating Reflection While Learning to Teach: The ATTEP at Kent State University

The Academically Talented Teacher Education Program (ATTEP) was developed at Kent State University in response to the need for the preparation and retention of high quality teachers for our nation's schools. Stimulated by OERI's call for proposals, "Using Research Knowledge to Improve Teacher Education," (1984) we began a search for knowledge from the practice of teacher education which could stimulate our thinking about different ways a program for bright students could evolve. Schlechty and Vance (1983) noted in their study of the teaching force, teacher education does not attract recruits from among the academically able. "That teaching is unattractive to the more academically able and disproportionately attractive to the less able creates a significant public relations problem for the teaching occupation and probably serves to discourage potentially competent teachers from pursuing careers in teaching" (p. 6). Policy makers and practitioners taking Schlechty and Vance's work to heart have begun to look at the working conditions of teachers and the rewards of teaching with an eye toward making teaching more attractive as a profession. Recruitment programs with monetary incentives have blossomed on college campuses. However, getting the interest of academically talented students is only part of the problem. Keeping and stimulating those students' interest in teacher preparation is yet another concern.

The problems and concerns related to traditional teacher preparation are well documented. Issues of relevance, redundancy of coursework, lack of focus, lack of challenge, lack of critical thinking, poor role models in both college faculty members and classroom teachers are but a few of the criticisms levied at teacher preparation. Cruickshank (1984) iterated six categories of variables to be considered when contemplating change in the teacher education enterprise: (1) characteristics of the teacher education faculty, (2) characteristics of teacher education students, (3) the context of teacher education, (4) the content of the teacher preparation curriculum, (5) the instructional experiences in teacher education, and (6) the learning outcomes of beginning teachers. We believed that if academically talented students are to pursue careers in teaching, the teacher preparation curriculum must be sufficiently demanding intellectually; the instruction by teacher education faculty must be sufficiently stimulating; and the experiences students have during their college preparation must be sufficiently challenging for students to sustain interest in a program of preparation for teaching.

The alternative program we developed addressed four of Cruickshank's categories: the individual characteristics of teacher candidates, the teacher preparation curriculum, the instructional experiences of teacher candidates, and the external or school-based context in which teacher preparation occurs. Utilization of knowledge generated from research provided a foundation for both the decision-making process and the content for changes in the development of this experimental teacher education program.

—The program was conceived based upon the following assumptions: There are attributes, particularly cognitive attributes, of teacher education candidates which could be encouraged and developed to reflect upon classroom activities.
—There are attributes of curriculum in teacher education which, if shaped, could stimulate the development of cognitive schema.
—There are instructional strategies in activities of learning and teaching which could stimulate a reflective attitude or disposition.
—Practical experiences, if structured appropriately, could provide the opportunity for knowledge integration and reflection to occur.

It was agreed that the program would be open to prospective teacher candidates across all teaching fields and would be for undergraduate students. A two-year time frame was established as was an initial cohort size of twenty-five. Because the nature of the program was experimental it was not designed to replace other traditional teacher education efforts.

We believed that there are certain preconditions, particularly related to the characteristics of persons entering teacher preparation that are necessary for reflection to emerge, that learning to teach is a developmental process, that there are particular kinds of activity structures that can stimulate reflective thought and that if the integration of thought and action are to occur during the process of learning to teach, we would have indices of growth through assessing students' reflective thinking and changes in cognitive complexity.

DISTINCTIVE PROGRAM FEATURES

What sets this experimental effort apart from traditional teacher preparation at our institution are the following attributes:

—The program has a specified focus. Students experience a variety of approaches to inquiry as they acquire knowledge about teaching, learning, and schooling.
—A specific identification, recruitment, and selection strategy which was developed with the hope that attributes of an inquiry orientation could be identified and cultivated.
—Identification of a cohort group whose identity rests not with a subject matter specialty or a certification preference but with an understanding of one another's talents and growing professional commitment.
—Individualization of program requirements with a recognition that learners can acquire knowledge about teaching from different sources and under a variety of circumstances.
—Identification of mentor teachers to work with undergraduates for an extended period of time.
—A recognition of teacher expertise in the learning to teach process.
—Incorporation of action research into the culminating internship as a strategy for verifying the acquisition of an inquiry approach to teaching.
—An approach to teacher preparation which encourages faculty team members teaching courses to exchange perceptions of content and students.

—Development of a support system for students that extends beyond the academic challenges faced in a given course. Students know one another and faculty know students.

—A comprehensive program documentation effort which allows for data collection and data analysis on an entire program and its students.

THEORETICAL UNDERPINNINGS FOR THE PROGRAM

In developing a theoretical base for this program we attempted to integrate together two schools of thought relating the way teachers think about their work with what is known about academically talented students. First, we accepted the assumption that teachers' work is often ambiguous and uncertain. Because teaching is a dynamic set of social and intellectual actions which requires an integration of knowledge, a simplistic view of reflective inquiry was not accepted. Perhaps the most useful view of reflective inquiry for us initially was described by Tom (1985) as "the arena of the problematic" (p. 37). Throughout the ATTEP seminars, students are encouraged to question their own practice, that of their professors and that of their school-based mentors. Assumptions about teachers, teaching, students, learning, schools, curriculum, and community are consistently challenged by professors and the students themselves. We want our students to examine the fabric of teaching and be able to make reasoned choices about their own practice.

We also recognized that for students to develop a reflective style they must be conceptually flexible. Drawing upon the work of conceptual developmentalists like Harvey, Hunt, and Schroeder (1961) as well as the work of Stuck (1983) and Taylor (1983), we have learned that as conceptual levels of individuals increase, the person becomes more capable of generating his or her own concepts, better able to consider alternatives and more self responsible. Other attributes studied included independence, creativity, stress tolerance, and responsiveness. As noted by Hunt and Joyce (1967), the more abstract a teacher candidate's conceptual level, the more likely the candidate is to prefer a reflective style in which generation of optional approaches to a variety of teaching problems is encouraged.

Our challenge in this program was to bring together our desire to stimulate reflection in teacher candidates by stimulating conceptual development through providing different kinds of information about teaching, learning, and schooling with complex problem solving tasks derived from conceptually different views of knowledge (sociological, psychological, and critical theory). We hoped, at the onset, that the complexity of our program design would, in fact, stimulate reflection while students are learning to teach.

When examining the literature base about academically talented students we selected the following definition: students who demonstrate superior performance in specific academic areas when compared to their agemates. For the purposes of this program, academically talented students are identified by grade point average, standardized test scores, evidence of critical thinking, and complexity in written and oral expression. Additional characteristics and abilities considered were: the ability to plan and do independent work; ability to understand, analyze, and synthesize concepts; interpersonal communication skills; leadership potential; commitment to teaching; and breadth of life experiences. The literature pertaining to academically gifted students characterizes this population as demonstrating significantly different patterns of learning (Feldhusen, Van Tassel Baska, and Seeley, 1989) than their chronological peers. Through extensive research, differences among this population have been identified which related to the rate of learning, ease of learning, levels of abstract thinking, critical thinking, ability to process information, and the need for intellectual peer groups (Gowan and Demos, 1964; Van Tassel Baska, 1985; Kulik and Kulik, 1982).

In order to recruit and, more importantly, retain talented students in teacher preparation the program must be designed to complement and enhance the unique learning skills and abilities of this population of learners. For example, the ease with which academically talented students process information indicated that the time frame for delivery of instruction could be modified to include more in-depth information on a particular topic. One of the most common complaints from bright students considering teacher education is the quality of instruction and the repetition of previously mastered material. Students often expressed the desire to delve more deeply into a topic, not to master "more facts."

Another characteristic of academically talented students is their ability to ask complex questions. Able students are more apt to challenge the existing models in teacher education as well as the professor's values and beliefs (Hutchinson, 1989). In addition to specific learning abilities demonstrated by this group of students, one must also consider the necessity for continued intellectual stimulation. Bright students require the opportunity to interact with other bright students in order to develop an accurate assessment of their own skills and abilities. This interaction enables the bright students to see a continuum of learning abilities which is often a more accurate reflection of the real world (Tannenbaum, 1983; Van Tassel Baska, 1983). Cohort grouping can also provide the opportunity to express thoughts and ideas in a psychologically safe environment. While this configuration may be appropriate for all students, bright students frequently express divergent ideas which often do not find acceptance in more traditional settings (Benbow and Stanley, 1983).

Therefore, the basis for differentiating the curriculum of a teacher preparation program resides, in part, on the unique learning skills and abilities of the population recruited for the program. ATTEP provides a differentiated curriculum which recognizes the demonstrated characteristics of able learners. This includes attention to the use of cohort grouping, the rate and pace of instruction, the variety and depth of material offered for study, and focus on reflective inquiry.

PROGRAM IN PRACTICE

Currently in its fifth year, ATTEP is a time-intensive program which begins with recruitment during the spring semester. Each new cohort begins in the fall term by enrolling in a seminar, Inquiry Into Teaching. As the semester unfolds the Coordinator of ATTEP begins the process of locating potential mentors for the new cohort. Former and current mentor-teachers, administrators, university field supervisors, and university faculty are contacted to make recommendations for potential mentors. Potential mentors are recommended for participation based on skill in teaching, professional demeanor, flexibility and creativity in teaching. Each nominee is cleared through the required school district procedures and invited to attend an informational meeting. At this meeting potential mentors have an opportunity to hear current mentors describe their roles, ask questions, and meet ATTEP students. Nominees who accept the invitation to participate are interviewed by ATTEP students for a potential match. Both the potential mentor and the ATTEP student must agree to the match; either person may decline without penalty. After a match is made the ATTEP student begins working with the mentor-teacher one-half day per week in the second semester, one full day per week in the third semester and completes a sixteen week internship during the final semester.

Complementing the practical on-site experience for each of the semesters are three additional inquiry oriented seminars: Inquiry Into Learning; Inquiry Into Schooling; and, Research in Teaching. Each seminar is designed by an outstanding faculty member within the area;

e.g., Inquiry Into Learning is taught by a professor in Educational Psychology. Additionally, each seminar is discursive and represents a particular inquiry-oriented focus for student instruction: sociological for the "teaching" seminar; psychological for the "learning" seminar; critical theory for the "schooling" seminar. Action research becomes a base for the fourth seminar.

During the first semester, ATTEP students are matched with faculty advisers from the College of Education. The education adviser is responsible for individualizing the planned program for teacher preparation. Based on professional educational knowledge and consultation with liberal arts faculty members, as well as consideration of the student's educational background and goals, the faculty adviser may waive, delete, or replace coursework in the traditional plan for teacher preparation. Each ATTEP student and faculty adviser creates an individualized prospectus which includes approximately sixty hours of study in the liberal arts, thirty hours in a professional content area, twenty-six hours of professional education coursework, and twenty hours of electives. ATTEP students are eligible for graduate level coursework or study abroad when recommended by their faculty adviser. Upon successful completion of an approved program prospectus, ATTEP students are certified by the State of Ohio as beginning teachers.

HOW THE PROGRAM HAS SOUGHT TO DEVELOP REFLECTIVE THINKING

Five different strategies to stimulate reflective thought have emerged as the ATTEP program has been implemented. Perhaps the central feature in stimulus for reflection is the four inquiry-oriented seminars. The seminar format, unlike traditional didactic interaction often provided for undergraduate students in teacher preparation, allows professors and students to engage in an orderly but informal manner in their examination of issues and dialogue about content materials. Frequently the students have their beliefs challenged by the professor and by one another. In these seminars, each with a different content focus and each with a different inquiry orientation, students and professors become jointly responsible for the learning which occurs. Students are encouraged to constantly measure and sort information and knowledge in relationship to their own values, ideas, and conceptions of teaching. Professors seek to create dissonance, a creative tension, and sometimes mild stress to encourage self-analysis. Because each professor enacts a different inquiry tradition as he or she teaches, students are exposed to conflicting views of knowledge about teaching and learning. These conflicting views seem to force introspection on both personal and professional levels.

A second strategy which, perhaps, is an outgrowth of the seminars is the modeling of these inquiry strategies by the seminar leaders. For example, the schooling seminar is taught by a professor who holds a critical theory view. Students are constantly challenged to support their beliefs and assumptions about the teaching-learning process in the context of studying schooling in America. The students, likewise, challenge the professor to be clear about the beliefs which undergird his own practice.

A third strategy is that of journaling. As students begin the program they are asked to keep a reflective journal and to focus upon their own learning process. The act of journaling has been well documented as a strategy for influencing reflective thinking (Holly, 1989). We are learning that in the mentoring process some of our classroom teachers are co-journaling with the students which further enhances the opportunity for reflection.

A fourth strategy which we have encouraged is active experimentation in actual classrooms with mentor teachers. We do not expect ATTEP students to be passive when they are in their mentors' classroom. We are asking them to actively engage themselves in the teaching process and to try new and innovative strategies for approaching classroom problems. Because the mentor teachers are carefully selected, they are willing and eager to support students' active engagement of their classroom.

A fifth and final strategy is the implementation of individual action research projects during their final semester in the program, another strategy well documented for this purpose (Noffke and Zeichner, 1987). In their seminar, Research on Teaching, students enact the action research cycle as they identify a problem which they can study during the course of the semester. During seminar time, students have the opportunity to discuss their research projects, to raise questions when they are having difficulties, and to seek advice from other students in the class. It is through these five strategies that these students are given both the opportunity and the encouragement, the "challenge and support" that is necessary for reflective thought to occur.

As we have observed the implementation of these strategies we noted that multiple meanings of the concept of reflection are apparent. Not only is reflection cognitively complex reasoning and wondering, but we have seen it become an attitude toward one's own practice. For some students, reflection is a way of thinking about, thinking back, standing apart from one's self and reviewing one's own action. For others it is an integration of knowledge and experience. For others still it is a sense of self renewal. As there appears to be, at least in Perry's mind, a variety of levels of cognitive complexity for college students, there also appears to be a variety of levels in meanings of reflective thought.

PROGRAM EVALUATION

ATTEP employs a complex design for evaluation which posed special challenges. To determine the relative effectiveness of the program components, a multifaceted documentation effort was developed at the beginning of the program. Our interest was in understanding the complex interactions and patterns of human behavior which occur in learning to teach (Applegate and Shaklee, 1990). We selected a naturalistic, inquiry-oriented approach to evaluation which was congruent with the goals and outcomes of the program. As Guba and Lincoln (1988) noted, "naturalistic inquiry is an inquiry model aimed at understanding actualities, social realities and human perceptions . . . Naturalistic inquiry attempts to present slice of life episodes documented through natural language." (p. 78).

To determine the relative effectiveness of the program as a whole as well as its component parts multiple procedures were used to provide continuous documentation (see Applegate and Shaklee, 1990, for a complete description).

For the purpose of this chapter we will focus on the question: "How effective were the research-based inquiry-oriented seminars in developing reflective teacher candidates?" Each semester ATTEP students, faculty members, and Planning Council members are asked to contribute their responses to this question. Documenting and validating their responses were anecdotal records, observations, structured questionnaires, and the "Learning to Teach Autobiography. "

In addition to the data collection at the end of each semester, ATTEP students were given the *Measure of Epistemological Reflection* (MER) (Taylor, 1983) prior to entering the program and again as they exited the program. The MER assesses the development of cognitive complexity in relation to critical incidents in young adult development. The MER was the only standardized instrument used in data collection. This instrument was developed to provide specific stimuli and a standard scoring procedure to reduce the degree of influence necessary to assess the scheme of intellectual development and cognitive structures as identified by Perry (1970). It was hypothesized that a structurally and conceptually different program of teacher preparation aimed at developing and enhancing a student's inquiry ability would influence the student's cognitive structures. According to Perry, individuals move from one structure to the next when they encounter experiences that are discrepant with their current structure. Cognitive conflict provides the stimulus to reorganize the structure to reduce the discrepancy. The MER assesses six domains of intellectual development: decision-making; role of the learner; role of the instructor; role of peers; evaluation; view of knowledge, truth, or reality. Each of these domains is represented on the instrument by open-ended questions. The content of each response is analyzed by Perry's five positions or "reasoning structures." The results of the MER indicated the continued development of cognitive complexity on the part of students enrolled in ATTEP. Obviously, the continued development of cognitive complexity cannot be attributed to ATTEP alone. Maturation, other life experiences, as well as other college endeavors are known to contribute to intellectual development.

Videotaped seminar sessions provided information about the types of conversation and interaction that contributed to the development of reflective teacher candidates (Hutchinson, 1989). The analyses of the videotaped seminars indicated that the teaching style of the professors encouraged student participation, decreased the role of professor as information giver, increased the number of open ended questions, and turned questions back to students to answer. For their part, students actively participated in structuring seminar sessions, provided experiential examples to extend discussions, asked substantive questions of each other and professors, and evaluated their peers and professors' statements. Descriptive evidence that these seminar conversations were reflective in nature was found in the uncertain and inquiring attitudes expressed by students in their questions, the way they examined themselves and their actions as well as the motives and actions of others, and the openness they exhibited when faced with new information or conflicting points of view. From our experimentation in ATTEP it appears that the seminar format, coupled with the role modeling of an inquiry-oriented professor contribute to the development of reflective thinking on the part of ATTEP students.

The culminating activity for all exiting interns is the completion of the "Learning to Teach Autobiography." All data (application packet, demographic questionnaires, end of semester evaluations, journals, and anecdotal records) are returned to each student. Along with their documents twelve questions relating to five general areas provide focal points for students as they begin writing. These areas include: past, present, and future career experiences, including commitment to teaching; changes in self, knowledge, and learning; problems and conflicts encountered in all aspects of the learning to teach process; specific examples of direct and indirect learning, and future directions (Applegate, Shaklee, and Hutchinson, 1989). The following section summarizes the results obtained thus far.

ATTEP students have demonstrated, to varying degrees, the ability to reflect upon the art and craft of teaching. The themes which appeared as part of this data analysis appear to revolve around three major areas: (1) self-reflection, (2) reflection on the practice of teaching, including the bridge between theory and practice, and (3) reflection about education, including the analysis of critical issues which impact the profession.

Self-reflective thoughts such as, "when I began teaching I worried about how I was going to get there. Now, I worry about how I am going to get my student there" show evidence of the level of reflection on self which was developed. ATTEP students consider the act of learning to teach as "forcing me to look at myself in a new light" or to "take a real deep look inside yourself, examine what you believe, and establish a personal plan for defending the position you have taken."

Reflection on the practice of teaching was clearly evidenced throughout the "Learning to Teach Autobiography." The combination of seminar and extensive field experience allowed students to "discover relevant points especially when it came to actual problems faced in the classroom" and to tie together their "intellectual strengths with their social conviction." Furthermore, ATTEP students viewed teaching as challenging stating, "teachers have many decisions to make that are not easy or clear cut" and that, "teaching would not prove to be nearly as easy as learning has been; and learning to teach has proved to be the most challenging of all."

ATTEP students have also been able to reflect about the institution of education. Comments such as, "I gained a much better understanding of all of the prevalent social issues that shape the structure and nature of our schools and influence the lives of students" or "the fact that a myriad of powerful social forces are beyond our individual control and have profound impacts on our students and our schools that we can often neither anticipate nor project" demonstrate their awareness of the forces which shape educational institutions.

The reflective nature of the bright student can be developed by providing a challenging interactive environment which integrates theory and practice. What is the future for these students and more specifically, what do they perceive their future to be? The sum perception of the ATTEP students could not be expressed more eloquently than by this quote entitled "Conscious Competence":

> I was able to join together the conceptual content of my liberal arts years with the professional orientation taught to me by my professors of education and do, I think, a firmly competent job in the real-life setting of a city public school. For the first time in my life I have found something that I do well, that is productive, that is connected to real people, that I feel truly good, in a Gestalt sense of feeling good, about doing. I am now educated. I am now ready to teach.

DIFFICULTIES ENCOUNTERED

Each of the individual elements of ATTEP as well as the program as a whole has not been without problems. Aside from the fundamental issues embedded in defining inquiry and reflection for ourselves and our students, three additional areas of difficulty were: student selection; mentor selection and participation; and individualization.

Though ATTEP has been successful in the recruitment of academically talented students to the teaching profession, we have consistently recruited more students than we have the capacity to educate. We cannot accept all of the students who apply to the program due to the nature of the program itself. We have wrestled with the issue of elitism. We have an exclusive program for specific students. Would other students also benefit from similar experiences? Should we employ a selective identification procedure for all teacher education candidates? The answers to these questions are still under review.

In addition to the inclusion of students, we also must deal with the exclusion of students. There is a very real possibility that through our screening procedure we have missed students who would not only benefit but excel in a program such as ATTEP. The inaccuracy of screening and the reliance on standardized testing and grade point average as the initial screening measures may preclude the admission of students who should be included in the program. The Screening Committee has attempted to mitigate these factors by including oral and written samples of student work as well as references from other professionals; however, we do realize the potential sources of error. We are not yet convinced that the criteria we have established are appropriate indices of "reflective potential. "

Another key element to the success of the program has been the establishment of a continuous field based experience under the guidance of a master professional. Without question this is one of the most highly regarded aspects of the program from all perspectives. Not only has the mentorship provided an environment for the preservice teacher to develop it has also provided substantial benefits to the mentor-teacher as well (Shaklee and Applegate, 1990). We are now concerned about two issues: the available resource pool and increasingly complex collaborative efforts with the local school systems. We have found little difficulty establishing effective mentorships at the elementary and middle school levels, but we have been less effective in secondary and special education. For example, in foreign languages the availability of teachers is very inadequate and the quality of nominees is based more on scarcity than reflective teaching. As we recruit more students from foreign languages and other content specific domains we must be able to provide suitable placements for them. While our resource base for potential mentors has grown from two school districts to eight, the actual availability of master teachers who are willing to participate in a two year program is still in question. The most effective means for recruiting mentors is still a recommendation from a current mentor.

Although original agreements on the recruitment of mentors had been established we still struggle with "administrativia" in the public school setting. Each of the eight schools has established a different procedure for the recruitment of potential mentors. Some school districts are more open to recruitment than others. The key factor appears to be related to who has the authority within the district to recognize a "master" teacher. In most districts this is vested within administrators as well as peers; in a few districts only an administrator may recognize a potential mentor. The result has been a decrease in nominees within some settings and reluctance on the part of the university personnel to continue to recruit from those districts; thus, limiting the potential pool of teachers from which to draw.

An unanticipated outcome of the cohort grouping for the two year sequence has been the development of the personality of the cohort. Each group has established a stake in the program and, seemingly, in one another. It appears that the formation of a cohort empowers the group sometime during the second semester. This "power" is often demonstrated by challenging the program itself.

Students bring issues such as the practical value of coursework, load assignments, unmet needs, instructional style, grading practices, and even the name of the program to the attention of the directors. This typically occurs in the second semester of the cohort. Each issue is examined and students are encouraged to utilize active problem solving strategies to develop possible solutions. While we do not "solve it for them" we have been open to alternative resolutions.

The individualized program prospectus has caused serious questioning of the traditional teacher preparation program in the College. As faculty members have been asked to examine the traditional teacher preparation program for ATTEP students they have been challenged to investigate the efficacy of planned series of coursework for all students. This has created a feeling of dissonance for some faculty members. In one program area, the faculty has begun to closely question the usefulness of some coursework and to examine alternative ways to structure preparation programs for undergraduates.

IMPLICATIONS FOR STIMULATING REFLECTION
IN TEACHER EDUCATION

Our experience with the implementation of ATTEP has taught us a number of lessons about reflective teacher preparation not only for bright students but for all students desiring to become teachers. The following implications were derived from the study of this program and suggest some direction for the reform of teacher education locally and nationally.

1. *Use a broad-based collaborative council in the design, implementation, and monitoring of teacher education.* The project's planning council with cross university representation as well as cross school district representation allowed for exchange and debate of fundamental principles in teacher education. Each of the constituents were helpful providing dramatically different views about reflection in teacher preparation from the selection of potential teacher candidates to advice on bridge-building with local school districts. The integrated planning process allowed for ownership of the project among all groups to emerge. Such ownership has built credibility for this project which assured its institutionalization. It was here that issues of "the problematic" first emerged.

2. *Provide a multifaceted assessment process as part of admission to teacher education programs.* The assessment process which specified multiple criteria and a team approach to selective admission allowed both prospective students and faculty "judges" the opportunity to examine criteria indicative of reflection and scrutinize the abilities and characteristics of prospective teacher candidates accordingly. Poten-

tial problems were identified early. Ownership was evident for students who were admitted. Faculty began to know the students early and thus were able to make program decisions based upon evidence provided through the admissions process.

3. *Develop a program with a clearly articulated conceptual focus.* When "inquiry" became the guiding focus for program development, faculty made content and instructional process decisions to support the conceptual focus of the program. Students became aware of a variety of inquiry orientations and were able to structure their learning outcomes accordingly. Thus, assessment of program goals was more clear than a traditional "shot gun" approach to teacher preparation.

4. *Continuously monitor student progress.* When data are collected about students at admission and at the conclusion of each phase of the program it is much easier to identify students' growth and development in the teaching process, and to examine attributes of reflective thinking. Students, although academically successful, may not be successful in the classroom. Continuous monitoring has enabled us to identify students with social, emotional, and interpersonal problems and to advise them accordingly.

5. *Recognize students' strengths and abilities in curricular program planning.* Just as we have studied and supported the recognition of differentiated learning experiences for children and youth especially with regard to language development and the learning of mathematics, so, through ATTEP, we have acknowledged individual differences in learning to teach. Some students are ready for different kinds of learning at different times. Some students bring to the teacher education process rich life histories which influence the rate at which they learn to teach. Through an individualized approach to learning to teach these distinctions can be acknowledged and extended, allowing for more effective preparation to occur.

6. *Recognize teacher expertise in the teacher education process.* Classroom teachers have much to offer prospective teacher candidates. Their context rich "wisdom of practice" and their experience working with other teacher candidates enabled us to identify a cadre of potential mentors who were eager for the challenge of having a reflective teacher candidate in their classrooms for an extended (two year) experience. These teachers did not need to be "trained." They only needed support as they developed the role and responsibilities associated with mentoring. Acknowledging their professional worth through the partnership with ATTEP was a strength.

7. *Build parity and ownership with school district personnel.* The identifi-

cation, recruitment, and selection of teachers to work as partners in teacher education cannot be done using a traditional chain of command through administrative offices with administrative criteria. Prospective teachers and practicing teachers must have the opportunity to interact directly for "goodness of fit" to be enhanced. This cannot occur unless school district personnel and university personnel development mutually conceive parity and ownership for the teacher development process.

8. *Develop a vehicle for program documentation and self-study for data-based, data rich program decision making.* Throughout this program development effort data have been gathered to document all aspects of the program from multiple perspectives. Through continuous data collection and analysis we were able to make program modifications on an ongoing basis. The data summaries also provided evidence of progress and program impact of the Planning Council and to College and University Policy makers. Such evidence was also useful when the program was institutionalized.

9. *Develop cohort groups of students for teacher education programs.* The cohort group proved to be a vehicle which enabled ongoing communication and support for the teacher education candidates. Their positions related to teaching, learning, and schooling were able to be articulated and challenged for and by one another.

10. *Provide opportunities for colleagueship among teachers, students, and university faculty members.* Each semester opportunities for students, mentor teachers, and university faculty members are provided to enable dialogue about the program. A notable impact was felt by university faculty members who were encouraged to share with one another course content, instructional processes and insights about the students. They were helpful to one another as they each prepared their course. Springing from this dialogue is a cross program research team that is working together to design a study of program options available in our College. Such exchanges build program support and power.

CONCLUSION

Although the Academically Talented Teacher Education Program developed for creating cohort groups of bright, reflective students for teacher education seems to have been very effective, several conflicting issues and questions still exist. Even though the professional preparation of bright people for teaching may be possible, will the profession itself be able to sustain their talents? Over time, will these students continue to view the activities of teaching in a challenging and complex fashion or will the routines of teaching become discouraging? Will campus colleagues continue to support our efforts, especially when the coursework and program design are put forth for consideration by curricular bodies? How will we deal with students who are admitted to the program but later are judged ineffective in the classroom? How tolerant might others be of the intellectual and social demands put forth by bright, reflective students?

The implications of our work in this arena suggest that it is indeed possible to use what is known about teacher education to improve the likelihood of attracting bright students into an experimental program of teacher preparation and keep them challenged. To make this happen, one needs a broad, supportive, representative (and politically astute) base of colleagues who have a commitment to the improvement of inquiry in an educational experience for bright students. Also needed is time for discussion and deliberation.

The Academically Talented Teacher Education Program which was developed as a result of the challenge to "experiment" and "take risks" in order to develop a reflective orientation in teacher preparation has been successful. We have taken risks and have learned that the risks are worth taking. We believe that what we have done and what we have learned from doing this may have meaning for others interested in the improvement of teacher education for all future teachers.

JOYCE PUTNAM
S. G. GRANT

5

Reflective Practice in the Multiple Perspectives Program at Michigan State University

Historically, public schools in the United States have been expected to serve society by helping America's youth become knowledgeable citizens and effective participants in a democratic society. As teacher education programs have developed, the intent has been to provide the course work and experiences which would best provide prospective teachers with the requisite knowledge, skills, and dispositions to effect this expectation.

HISTORY AND OVERVIEW OF THE PROGRAM

The Multiple Perspectives program at Michigan State University (MSU) was developed after a serious examination of traditional approaches to teacher education. From this examination, which began in 1977, MSU faculty and department heads concluded that existing programs were fragmented and bound to superficial knowledge. In subsequent discussions it was suggested that new efforts reflect current research on teaching and in teacher education, the College's earlier successes with alternative programs, and the notion of tying program emphases to major role demands on teachers and schools.

A four year planning and development period culminated in the creation of five alternative teacher education programs. Four of the programs, Academic Learning, Heterogeneous Classrooms, Learning Community, and Multiple Perspectives, were organized around conceptual themes; the traditional teacher education curriculum was represented in the fifth, or Standard, program. Creating alternative programs gave planners the opportunity to build coherent and sequential programs of study through which instructional experiences could be selected and organized. The intent was to break the prevailing one-size-fits-all view of teacher education and to promote programs both more realistic in scope and more focused in conception.

Multiple Perspectives, like the other alternative programs, reflects a particular view of teachers and schooling. Grounding all of the alternative programs are the functions of schooling as described by Schwab (1974): academic outcomes, personal responsibility, social responsibility, and social justice. While all four functions are present within each program, three of the programs—Academic Learning (academic outcomes), Learning Community (social and personal responsibility), and Heterogeneous Classrooms (social justice)—cast one or two of the functions as central. What distinguishes Multiple Perspectives from the other alternatives is the premise that all four functions are considered of equal rank. In fact, the strength of the functions as outcomes develops through their integration. Therefore they merit equal attention within the program framework. Reflection and decision making become necessary if teachers are to make use of these ideas appropriately.

Program goals

The functions of schooling outlined by Schwab (1974), while integral to educating students, often create complex and competing roles and responsibilities for teachers and institutions. To meet these multiple expectations, teachers must become reflective decision makers capable of distinguishing between conflicting alternatives. In part this means that graduates of the Multiple Perspectives program must adopt a professional rather than a technical orientation to teaching. In more specific terms, they are expected to develop the knowledge, skills, and dispositions to:

1. develop integrated units of instruction which are (a) based on assessment of individual student performances, (b) promote achievement of identified knowledge and skills used in everyday life, and (c) account for individual differences while promoting equal opportunity for all students,
2. provide systematic instruction for diverse students based on reflection and continuous data collection,
3. exhibit valid information processing and knowledge verification skills that are requisite to rational and informed decision making, and
4. function as life-long learners characterized by an ongoing intellectual and scholarly curiosity about the practice of teaching and learning.

Set within a context of the functions of schooling, these goals help establish a functional direction for the program. In effect, while the functions of schooling provide a philosophical orientation, the Multiple Perspectives program goals explicate the practical dimension.

From these goals come a number of assumptions. These assumptions operate as the underlying premises on which decisions regarding the implementation of the program are made. The assumptions which follow speak both to requisite knowledge and understanding, as well as to teaching behaviors. Both concerns contribute to a comprehensive portrait of the Multiple Perspectives program.

The foundational assumptions can be grouped into three nested categories. Issues related to schooling comprise the first category. Here assumptions include the notion that public education is rooted in a philosophical, political, and socioeconomic context. It is also assumed that based on the issues of equity and equality, efforts to construct helpful and humane environments for all students will be made. The second category of assumptions focuses on teachers and the teaching and learning experience. Principal assumptions in this category include the recognition that teachers work in an environment that allows for a substantial amount of individual judgment and autonomous decision making. Judgment and decision making, however, are not value-neutral; teachers must make decisions continuously which are normative and ethical, and at times, controversial. The final and overarching category of assumptions supports reflective thinking and practice. Effective and humane instruction requires that teachers have a functional array—a repertoire—of teaching behaviors and strategies at their disposal. These behaviors and strategies, however, are context specific. Thus teachers must be able to assess the context (e.g., learners, subject matter) and their own goals in a reflexive fashion.

These assumptions reflect the general orientation of the program which hopes to develop in beginning teachers the ability and inclination to work towards the multiple goals of schooling, and the ability to manage obstacles which interfere with the ready accomplishment of those goals. This expectation would be impossible without a program orientation toward reflective thinking and practice. Thoughtful decisions based on information, predictions, and experiences that are guided by long range expectations are the basis for the reflective work of the professional teacher. Thus the program attempts to prepare beginning teachers whose idealism is tempered by realistic expectations of themselves, students, curriculum, and the school context.

Organization and Structure of the Program

To implement this conception, Multiple Perspectives is organized to provide a systematic, coherent program of experiences which encourage teacher candidates[1] from diverse academic areas to come together to study and reflect on the problems of teaching and learning, and to share in their development as professionals. Working together as a cohort in both their courses and in their field experiences, teacher candidates have numerous opportunities to learn from one another, their cooperating teachers, the university faculty, and field instructors.[2]

In practical terms, students apply for admission to either an elementary or secondary cohort.[3] Elementary teacher candidates complete a six quarter[4] program comprised of twenty quarter credits of course work and field experience before student teaching. Secondary teacher candidates are in the program for four quarters and finish twelve quarter credits previous to their student teaching term. The program is structured so that during each term before student teaching, a teacher candidate engages in both formal course work and a participatory field experience.

Reflective thinking and practice are central to the Multiple Perspectives orientation to teacher education. Attention to teacher candidate reflectivity is evident in course work, field experiences, and in teacher candidate/field instructor conferences. To frame a discussion of reflection, however, it is necessary to begin with an understanding of the program structure.

Teaching and learning is defined as the interaction between a teacher, students, and the specified pupil outcomes in all four functions of schooling. These functions (academic outcomes, personal responsibility, social responsibility, social justice) serve as program parameters and are reflected in the program knowledge base which develops through course content and school-based experiences.

Foundational course work accounts for a significant portion of the knowledge base for teaching and learning. In the first term of the secondary program, for example, teacher candidates take a course in instructional design which emphasizes the functions of schooling with both in and out of school applications. As a practical matter, teacher candidates learn to write unit and lesson plans as a means of guiding their instruction. However, this exercise transcends a purely technical orientation as the teacher candidates are asked, based upon reflections on subject matter knowledge, developmental knowledge of learners, and specific learner assessment data, to translate the functions of schooling into appropriate student outcomes.[5] Unit plans also include, in a separate section, written rationales or justifications for the identified outcomes. Justifications are written responses generated through reflection on questions related to: learner knowledge and skills; the question, "what is worth knowing?"; and current conventions and research in a given discipline area. In practice, a teacher candidate might have a unit goal which examines twentieth-century American literature. In the goal statement, the teacher candidate attempts to establish a real-world context and application that suggests why American literature is important for students to spend time studying. To reinforce the importance of the functions of schooling, the teacher candidate must then show how the unit goal contributes to students' deeper understanding of subject matter, personal responsibility, social responsibility, and social justice.

Also in the first term, secondary teacher candidates take a classroom management course. The course sets technical concerns within the broader context of the functions of schooling (e.g., those dealing with personal and social responsibility and social justice) as related to the classroom group and society. Thus the organizing principle becomes that of creating a classroom learning community (Putnam and Burke, in press). Teacher candidates discover that reflection on the functions of schooling, their own experiences, and the specific context is necessary to create a learning community plan.

In the second term, the foundational courses consist of a generic instructional methods course and a human growth and development course. The generic methods course functions to continue the development of teacher candidates' thinking about instruction by linking it to larger theoretical constructs (e.g., the four functions of schooling). The course focuses on a variety of instructional methods and on the process of decision making a teacher might use to select appropriate strategies for specific outcomes. In this course, all four functions of schooling are developed. Realizing the tendency of novice teachers to slight all but the academic function in their teaching practice, instructors of this course hold teacher candidates responsible and accountable for examining how their instruction impacts the development of personal and social responsibility and social justice goals.

Teacher candidates also take a course in human growth and development during their second term. While attending to traditional topics such as physical, emotional, social, and intellectual growth, instructors highlight salient cultural issues such as the structures and functions of peer groups and families. This information becomes particularly valuable to teacher candidates as they continue to develop their awareness and understanding of the personal and social responsibility and social justice functions.

Course work in the third term centers on the social and philosophical foundations of education. With the functions of schooling still in the fore, this course examines those functions from a societal perspective. Class assignments and discussions enable teacher candidates to explore, for example, functionalist, Marxist, and interpretivist perspectives. As might be expected, this context provides a valuable opportunity to map the implications of each perspective against each of the four functions. The course proves quite challenging for teacher candidates as many of the assumptions implicit in their own schooling and in their emerging practice rise to the surface. Many students report that this course, while unsettling, helps them synthesize the theory and practice embedded in the four functions.

Another of the foundational courses, the Teacher Decision-Making Laboratory, extends over the three terms. Taken in conjunction with the field experience, the Decision-Making Lab attends to a number of needs. For example, teacher candidates learn about, and gain experience in, various decision-making processes (e.g., problem solving, conflict resolution), communication skills (e.g., self-disclosure, paraphrasing, praise), assessment, and evaluation. The Decision-Making Lab provides a vehicle for exploring issues of equity and diversity in school classrooms and materials. One of the projects that teacher candidates complete is an exploration of curriculum bias in school textbooks and other classroom resources.

Teacher candidates take a variety of formal courses throughout their program. They also participate in a field experience each term. They begin teaching, first to small groups of students, during their first term.[6] In that term, they work in pairs to develop units of instruction which they then individually teach and evaluate. In succeeding terms, teacher candidates teach both more frequently and to larger groups of students until, in their fourth term, they are placed in full-time student teaching assignments.[7]

In the student teaching term, teacher candidates teach four classes each day. During what would normally be the fifth teaching period, teacher candidates engage in a self-designed study of practice. The intent of this exercise is to encourage teacher candidates to look critically at the development of their thinking and practice as part of their role as a teacher. For example, a teacher candidate might choose to study how she uses learning community norms to develop a sense of community in her classroom. Or, a teacher candidate may study how his students respond to higher level thinking questions posed on homework assignments. In practice, the cohort of student teachers meet weekly with a program instructor to talk about their studies. At this meeting, the student teachers can share both their successes and frustrations as they develop and conduct their inquiries. The study of practice culminates in a dinner conference where the student teachers present their findings to program staff and cooperating teachers. Within the Multiple Perspectives program, the study of practice serves as a vital component in helping teacher candidates understand the value of reflection as part of their regular teaching practice.

REFLECTIVE THINKING AND PRACTICE

We strongly believe in the power of combining course work with field experiences in each term of a teacher candidate's program. The brief explication of the knowledge base of Multiple Perspectives presented above was not meant to be exhaustive or fully formed. Instead it serves as a footing on which to construct our conception of reflective thinking and practice.

Teacher candidates in Multiple Perspectives are taught and encouraged to become reflective thinkers and practitioners principally for the purpose of helping their students grow in each of the areas outlined in the functions of schooling. We contend that reflective thinking makes a critical difference in how teachers think and go about their work. Creating environments in which all students can flourish will occur most often, we believe, in the classrooms of reflective teachers. But this will only occur if teachers fully understand the concepts and the context in which they teach. In short, reflective teaching is much more than technical knowledge applied to classroom situations. Instead, it is the thoughtful and adaptive exercise of reflective thinking, planning, doing, and evaluating. Our rationale for this position follows. In the

Multiple Perspectives program, teacher candidates develop theoretical perspectives through courses at the same time they develop practical experience through their field work. This program orientation supports our sense that reflection lies at the intersection of theory and practice. We contend that neither theory nor practice provides both the necessary and sufficient conditions for dynamic teaching and learning. Schwab (1978), among others (cf. Kennedy, 1987), points to the inherent disparities between theory and practice and suggests that, "the incongruities of theory and practice cannot be corrected by a fundamental change in either one or the other" (p. 323). Both theory and practice have beneficial features, strengths that the other can not possess. Experience has shown, however, that the benefits of theory and practice are not simply additive; as with most things, the whole (in this case, reflective thinking and practice) is something larger than a sum of the component parts (i.e., theory and practice). In fact, the incongruities that can, and often do, arise between theoretical knowledge and practical experience may lead to disparate perspectives of the same situation. Inherently problematic, this remains a common situation. Schön (1987) calls such dilemmas the "indeterminate zone of practice" characterized by "uncertainty, uniqueness, and value conflict" (p. 6). Recognizing that different perspectives exist, and understanding that they are not always reconcilable can prove discomforting. Such realizations, however, remain critical to reflective thinking and practice.

In functional terms, reflective thinking and practice is characterized by the interactive ability to think, understand, and act on a number of levels. One means of grasping the complexity of these interactions comes from Zimpher and Howey's (1987) representation of technical, clinical, personal, and critical competencies. Though cast in terms of supervisory practice, Zimpher and Howey's framework provides a particularly rich conception in helping teacher candidates develop their thinking. Technical competence speaks to the primary, functional skills of planning, instruction, and evaluation which are part of the classroom routine. Clinical competence focuses on the teacher's ability to identify and think through classroom problems using practical reasoning and judgment. Personal competence results from a teacher candidate who has developed a sophisticated sense of self and can use that knowledge to create supportive and humane classroom environments. Critical competence demands attention to the social conditions (e.g., the extant norms and values within the school culture) of schools and the attendant influences on teachers and students.

In the Multiple Perspectives program, Zimpher and Howey's (1987) areas of competency are interpreted as levels of reflectivity which overlay with Schwab's (1978) notion of the four commonplaces: learners, teachers, subject matter, and milieu. The commonplaces provide a context within which teacher candidates can engage in reflective thinking at all levels. Teacher candidates learn to describe, explain, predict, and act in deliberate fashion while keeping the commonplaces in mind (though not necessarily in that order or always to the same outcome). Clearly this is no simple order. For example, the ability to manipulate a number of positions and perspectives while, at the same time, working with third graders on how to make sense of subtraction is problematic. Kennedy (1987) uses the term "deliberate action" to describe the "interactive relationship between analysis and action" (p. 15). Similar to Schön's (1983, 1987) conception of "reflection-in-action," Kennedy's sense of the interplay between analysis and action works only to the extent that "each influences the other."

Taken together, the aspects of reflection described become important for teacher candidates as they develop a deeper understanding of, and make more informed decisions about, their work in classrooms. In this sense, we view reflection as a transformative process rather than a reproductive process. Lortie (1975) describes the enormous effect a prospective teacher's experience as a student has on an attendant conception of teaching. As such, the impulse to reproduce the kind of teaching an individual has experienced is quite powerful and highly resistant to change. Recognizing this tendency, faculty and field instructors lead teacher candidates to think about what they know and how they came to know it. The aim is not to force the teacher candidates to reject all that they have experienced. Instead, the objective is to bring to the surface the teacher candidates' prior knowledge and experience so that it becomes another source of data to consider when making reflective decisions about current practice.

Implementing Reflective Thinking and Practice

With reflective thinking and practice as a central theme in the Multiple Perspectives program, each component of the program serves to support its development. Organized around the functions of schooling, course work helps teacher candidates become reflective through the construction of a conceptual knowledge base. The fieldwork component also supports reflective thinking and practice by contributing to a teacher candidate's experiential base. The third component of the program focuses on the field conference. Such conferences between teacher candidate and field instructor serve to assist teacher candidates as they begin to reflect on and make sense of this new knowledge and experience.

Most standard teacher education programs provide formal theoretical course work and some sort of field placement. The assumption prevails that teacher candidates will, on their own, be able to put their theoretical and practical knowledge together in constructive and reflective ways. The Multiple Perspectives program holds no such assumption. As teacher candidates progress through their program of course work and field experiences, they do so with the assistance of field instructors who help them bridge their course and fieldwork knowledge and develop their capabilities for reflective thinking and practice.[8]

The primary vehicle for such interactions is the field conference. Teacher candidates and field instructors meet each week of each term. Frequently the conversation occurs after the observation of a teaching episode. In the conference, a teacher candidate and field instructor use the long range unit plan, the specific lesson plan, the context of the lesson, and a set of program debriefing questions to engage in a conversation. While grounded in the four functions of schooling, these conversations focus on one or more of Zimpher and Howey's (1987) technical, clinical, personal, or critical levels. Teacher candidates talk specifically about their preactive, interactive, and postactive thinking and decision making. In doing so, both teacher candidates and field instructors explore the connections between the teacher candidates' emerging professional knowledge base, their observations while teaching and planning, and their teaching practices. For example, as a preactive question, a teacher candidate might be asked to talk about her thinking while planning a particular lesson. An interactive question could focus on what a teacher candidate was observing and thinking about while teaching a particular concept. Finally, a postactive question might ask the teacher candidate to reflect on how his observations of the students' thinking and actions and his professional and discipline knowledge will be used in planning the next lesson. In effect, teacher candidates are asked: What sense are you making of all this? How can you explain it? What do you infer? What do you predict? What do you wonder about? And what do you need to learn?

Evaluating Reflective Thinking and Practice

The reflective thinking and practice of teacher candidates in the Multiple Perspectives program is assessed in two ways. On one level, teacher candidates are evaluated on their individual growth. On another level, information about teacher candidates is used to assess current program practices.

The progress of an individual teacher candidate's levels of reflectivity is monitored each term throughout the program. Through their weekly conferences, field instructors assess how teacher candidates think about their work. Twice during the term, all of the field and course instructors for a cohort meet to discuss the teacher candidates' strengths and weaknesses. These mid and end-of-term meetings cover a wide expanse of the teacher candidates' knowledge and practice—for example, content and professional knowledge, unit and lesson planning, instruction, and evaluation. Special attention is given to an assessment of the nature and level of each prospective teacher's ability to engage in reflective thought and action.

Weekly field conferences and mid and end-of-term meetings are two means of evaluating an individual teacher candidate's professional knowledge, practice, and ability to reflect. To get an aggregate sense of these variables, a professional knowledge examination was created. Administered during the teacher candidate's final term, the examination is designed to represent the professional knowledge base taught in the program. The examination is structured around a series of vignettes posing classroom-based problems of practice relative to the four commonplaces—teacher, learner, curriculum, and milieu. Teacher candidates must interpret and respond to each situation drawing from their professional knowledge and field experience. In general, evaluators look at how a teacher candidate's analysis and reaction to the situation is posed. More specifically, they evaluate the candidate's exit ability to integrate information and apply it to a specific teaching and learning situation. In the past, results from this assessment have indicated strengths and weaknesses in: (1) initial courses, (2) field instruction ties to professional knowledge, (3) linkages with field practice, and (4) internal program coherence. Analysis of these data provide information that facilitates the determination of program effects.

Impediments to Reflective Thinking and Practice

While the Multiple Perspectives program has matured, issues that need to be addressed remain. Of these, three relate directly to the notion of reflective thinking and practice. One emergent concern lies in the teacher candidates' knowledge of subject matter. The rationale for the Multiple Perspectives program posits the integration of Schwab's (1974) functions of schooling, one of which concerns academic outcomes. Thus one's knowledge of subject matter, one of Schwab's (1978) commonplaces, stands as an essential consideration during the reflective thinking process. Despite this program emphasis, examination of field conference data shows that teacher candidates have two different, but related, problems regarding academics (LaForce, Putnam, and Johns, 1986).

The first problem centers on disciplinary knowledge. This problem relates to the requirements for majors and minors at the university. The MSU College of Education Task Force on Teacher Education report, produced to guide the current reform of teacher education, identifies the need for teacher candidates to possess a deeper knowledge of subject matter. Specifically, the Task Force Report calls for disciplined study that includes four aspects: (1) shared understanding of a field, (2) understanding the various perspectives scholars of a field take, (3) understanding how seminal knowledge in a field has come to be, and (4) understanding that ideas are nested in historical, socioeconomic, and political contexts (Department of Teacher Education, 1990). Recognizing the importance of disciplined study of one field does not, however, preclude the necessity of being able to see broadly. Thus, cross-disciplinary experiences, long considered to be an important aspect of teacher preparation, remain part of the current plans to revise programs.

The second concern relative to teacher candidates' knowledge of subject matter involves the linkages made between subject matter and the other functions of schooling. Teacher candidates must make connections among the various functions in the justification section of their unit plans. That they are generally able to do so reflects at least a partial success; they begin to understand that academic outcomes are one, but only one, measure of schooling. Teacher candidates, however, have been less able to demonstrate an ability to dig deeply into the nature of a discipline to unearth issues related to gender, diversity, and equity. Instead, their discussions of such topics belie a thoughtful and critical understanding of subject matter.

The full responsibility for these deficiencies does not rest solely on the shoulders of teacher candidates. The nature of the content and instruction in academic courses is problematic. For example, Sarason (1982) points to the pedantic and uncritical nature of most teaching of academic disciplines at the undergraduate level. Such experiences tend to reinforce the teacher candidates' prior conception that teaching is telling and that the transmission of subject matter is the principal goal of education (Cohen, 1988). That these are longstanding issues in no way diminishes the difficulties they pose for the preparation of teachers.

Some of the professional program experiences of teacher candidates may also contribute to the problem. For example, data from field conferences show that when questions about a teacher candidate's knowledge of subject matter surface, novice field instructors do not always pursue them. Instead, they tend to pursue questions about instruction, pupil outcomes, and planning. Thus questions about the teacher candidate's subject matter knowledge tend to get lost. An example of this might occur when a teacher candidate asks children to explain their thinking in relation to a subtraction problem. Rather than address the academic implications of this instance, the field instructor may focus on who gets a turn, the accuracy of a response, or wait time rather than on the substance of the teacher and pupils' talk.

Thus, we infer that one of the reasons that teacher candidates may have difficulty integrating subject matter into their thinking is that new field instructors place more emphasis on technical deliberations rather than critical competencies. In fact, evidence from field conferences with novice field instructors shows that the conversation tends to lean toward technical and personal levels of thinking rather than toward clinical and critical levels (Putnam et al., 1989). In part, this situation stems from the conference methods employed by novice field instructors. Attempting to gain consistency in their role as field instructor, novice program staff tend to gather data that is focused on observable behaviors that can be recorded on checklist-type forms. When these data are brought into the conversation by new field instructors during the field conference, the checklist data provides a concrete form of what they know about the candidate's teaching. In effect, these data act as a "security blanket" for the novice field instructor. The novice thus avoids the more difficult, but critical issues related to reflective thinking and practice.

One means of addressing this issue is through a set of standardized guidelines for conferences. These guidelines provide the novice field instructor and the teacher candidate with a structure for their conversation. The structure helps to focus the conversation on the teacher candidates' preactive, interactive, postactive thinking and decision making and their rationale for these decisions. Structured in this manner, the conference form encourages discussion of the clinical, personal, and critical levels as well as the technical.

The overemphasis on technical issues may also have another source. In the initial instructional design course, teacher candidates are taught to construct unit and lesson plans according to a prescribed pattern. The premise behind such practice suggests that teacher candidates will, once they have learned and worked with the prescribed structures, use this knowledge in flexible and reflective ways to design, implement, and evaluate lessons. Experience has shown, however, that some teacher candidates do not understand the unit and lesson plan forms as conceptual elements. Instead, they reify the form, viewing it as a separate and distinct end rather than as a means to help them think through and integrate the component parts of their units and lessons. Encouraging teacher candidates to become more sophisticated in their thinking and use of lesson and unit plans is a frequent theme of conversation between field instructors and teacher candidates. The Multiple Perspectives program standards call for candidates to demonstrate non-technical applications of lesson and unit planning by the end of the term prior to their student teaching.

A final area of concern regards the training and retention of experienced field instructors. As we suggest above, the field instructor plays an integral role in helping teacher candidates develop the capacity for reflective thought. In the field conference, an effective field instructor can assist a teacher candidate in making connections between professional knowledge and practice in thoughtful and reflective ways. The problem is that it takes up to three years for field instructors to acquire the professional knowledge taught in the program and to learn how to effectively carry out their role (Putnam et al., 1989). Predominately doctoral students, field instructors tend to be a transitory group rarely staying with the program more than three years. Thus, some field instructors do not develop a full understanding and practice of program goals. As a result, field conferences can exhibit an uneven quality.

One means of addressing this problem is through Clinical Studies, a program of weekly field instructor meetings. In these sessions, field instructors and program faculty discuss questions and issues related to field instruction. Though procedural matters occasionally infringe on the discussion time, in general these meetings center on topics directly related to the field instructors' work. In the past, discussions have focused on issues such as the professional knowledge taught in the program's courses, how teacher candidates perceive themselves in the role of teacher, how they talk about their practice and what issues are of the greatest concern to them, and how field instructors learned to teach. More recently, the focus of conversation has been on gaining a shared understanding of the functions of schooling.

The genesis of the Clinical Studies sessions came from the realization by program faculty that with the incidence of new field instructors, a shared understanding of the foundational elements of the program had been lost. Often operating exclusively from prior knowledge and experience, field instructors did not necessarily hold common understandings of constructs such as academic outcomes and social justice. As a result, field instructors were not helping teacher candidates consciously and consistently examine the relationships between their emerging knowledge and practice. This situation became particularly problematic when new teacher candidate/field instructor assignments were made.[9] Teacher candidates became understandably confused when their new field instructors, for example, used terminology in different, and sometimes conflicting, ways. To address this problem, Clinical Studies participants have focused their attention on developing shared understandings of the functions of schooling and how they might better talk with their teacher candidates about them.

EVALUATION OF THE PROGRAM

The Multiple Perspectives program has been periodically evaluated since its inception (Polin and Putnam, 1987; Putnam, 1987; Putnam, 1985a, 1985b; Putnam, 1984; Putnam and Johns, 1987a, 1987b; Putnam, Johns, and Oja, 1987). During the first three years of the program, evaluative measures were principally formative and yielded a number of significant changes in both structure and practice. In years since, research efforts have produced additional information related to the success of the program (Hoerr and Putnam, 1989, 1990; Putnam, 1988; Putnam and Johns, 1987c, 1987d). These research efforts have also had a direct influence on the decision to reexamine all of the teacher education programs at MSU. That reexamination, in combination with work done with the Holmes Group (Holmes Group, 1986), will result in the redesign of teacher education programs as the College of Education moves to a five year model for the preparation of teachers.

In the early years of the Multiple Perspectives program, formative evaluation measures were developed to collect data from teacher candidates, field instructors, and program faculty (Polin and Putnam, 1987). These data were used to make adjustments in faculty assignments, and in the sequence and substance of courses. The evaluation also played a role in the creation of staff development activities such as weekly field instructor meetings. By the end of 1985, the third year of operation, program staff felt that the program had structural and functional integrity. From that point on, an intensive research phase began.

The first major research endeavor began in 1985 when the Project Director undertook a study of graduates of the first three cohorts (Putnam, 1988). Attempting to understand the impact of former teacher candidates' experiences within the program, Putnam engaged in a series of case studies of the graduates in their first teaching positions. The three year study involved interviews with nine graduates, observations of their classrooms, and debriefing sessions. Interviews with each teacher's principal and selected colleagues yielded additional data.

Findings included consistent agreement among graduates, principals, and colleagues that the graduates, when compared with standard program first year teachers, were better prepared to teach, more confident, better able to attend to pupil outcomes, more interactive with experienced teachers, and more capable of providing leadership in curriculum development activities during their first year of teaching. All principals volunteered their impressions that these graduates were "thoughtful" decision makers.

Also, in 1985, research initiatives related to teacher candidate learnings from teacher educator demonstrations and teacher candidates' perceptions and performances related to classroom organization, management, and discipline were initiated (Putnam, 1985a, 1985b; Putnam and Barnes, 1984; Putnam and Johns, 1987a, 1987b). Findings from these studies indicated that (1) teacher candidates gained different understandings from different demonstration models, and (2) teacher candidates' perceptions related to classroom management changed over the time that they were program participants.

Research more directly related to the development of teacher candidates as reflective thinkers was initiated in 1983. In this work, a number of instruments were employed to gather baseline data on teacher candidates' entering characteristics and on the nature of field conferences. A series of studies concerned with teacher candidate and field instructor conferences began in the early 1980s. From 1983 to 1988, four hundred conferences were audio-taped and transcribed. The preliminary purpose of these studies was to identify the characteristics of conferences that support autonomous reflection. Analysis of these data has yielded multiple findings which have contributed both to changes in current program practices and to the college redesign plans. For example, the amount of time spent in the field instructor role is correlated with field instructor quality; field instructors receiving the highest ratings demonstrated an understanding and identification with program outcomes rather than with generic supervision models; staff development for field instructors is critical (without it field instructors operate from a personal orientation which may or may not coincide with program goals); teacher candidates with higher conceptual level scores on the Hunt Conceptual Level Survey rate higher in the quality of their conference talk than do candidates with lower scores; and, field instructors rated low in terms of their conferences roles, are rated low in conferences by both high and low-rated teacher candidates.

The net effect of the research cited, while helpful in understanding the impact of the program on teacher candidates, has also been instrumental in the efforts to phase out the five current alternative teacher education programs. Over the past ten years, significant changes have developed in the way we think about teaching and learning. Current thinking about teaching for understanding and for conceptual change have encouraged a serious review of the present program goals. Other issues relating to equity and diversity continue to be problematic and demand more focused attention. In short, the field of education has matured and study of the present programs has, in part, resulted in the decision that a major revision of the preparation of teachers is in order.

CONCLUSION

The effort of the College of Education at Michigan State University to prepare quality teachers has meant that teacher education programs have undergone serious and sustained study and development. The Multiple Perspectives program resulted from that effort.

Born from a concern that standard programs lacked conceptual and practical coherence, Multiple Perspectives and the other alternative programs at MSU have attempted to build coherent structures along thematic lines. The result, in the case of Multiple Perspectives, has been a program grounded in an integration of academic outcomes, personal responsibility, social responsibility, and social justice. The full integration of these functions is possible, however, only when teacher candidates engage in reflective thinking and practice. From this premise, the Multiple Perspectives program has taken shape.

Since the inception of the alternative programs in 1981, research on teacher education has expanded dramatically; we are now a lot smarter about the practice of teacher preparation. As a result, while certain features of the present programs, like reflective thinking and practice, will be retained, faculty in the College of Education are reconceptualizing teacher education efforts and will offer students redesigned programs in the Fall of 1992.[10]

MARIA J. CIRIELLO
LINDA VALLI
NANCY E. TAYLOR

6

Problem Solving Is Not Enough: Reflective Teacher Education at the Catholic University of America

Typically, the professional education component of teacher education programs consists of a series of foundations and methods courses, selected field experiences, and an extended period, usually a semester, of supervised student teaching. The assumption is that this model develops persons with specific technical skills who become effective teachers.

Until 1986 the teacher education program at The Catholic University of America (CUA) approximated this model. The program required a stringent set of liberal arts courses taken in conjunction with a prescribed set of education courses. These professional courses incorporated some field work and culminated in a student teaching semester. But there was no compelling image of what shaped or constituted "good teachers" guiding the professional requirements of the program. The program lacked focus and integration. Education faculty taught separate courses with no clearly articulated, shared "vision" or common language. Formal professional dialogue about the goals of the teacher education program seldom occurred. More importantly, a growing conviction developed among some faculty that a program which primarily promoted the development of teaching skills was inadequate. To be empowered as professionals (Wildman and Niles, 1987) teachers need to exercise deliberative decision making. They ought not be satisfied simply to use methods or techniques that "work." Rather, professionals examine their practice to uncover hidden problems. Such teachers consider the long-term ramifications their actions have on pupils, the school, and the broader community and alter their practice accordingly.

Supported for three years by an Office of Educational Research and Improvement (OERI) grant, the CUA's Department of Education embarked on an improvement project focusing on an undergraduate elementary education program which would promote a reflective orientation. The goal was to improve the process of teacher preparation by helping prospective teachers become more reflective about their work. The purpose of reflection was to foster the use of professional knowledge to inform teaching and to enable teachers to become more self-directed.

Presently, a teacher education program with a strong emphasis on reflection is institutionalized to serve all students seeking teacher certification. Yearly cohorts consist of twenty-five to thirty early childhood or elementary education majors, twelve to fifteen secondary majors, and five or six graduate students across both programs. The examples in this paper are confined to experiences relating to the elementary education program.

REFLECTION

Reflection, the keystone of the teacher education program at Catholic University, is a theme in many current teacher education programs. However, the term assumes different connotations depending upon the context of the institutions and the intent of the developers. The Catholic University program is influenced by the work of Berlak and Berlak (1981) who define reflection as the ability to stand apart from the self in order to examine critically one's actions and the context of those actions. The purpose of such a stance is to facilitate efforts to think and to act from conviction based on professional knowledge rather than simply functioning because of habit, tradition, or impulse. Such a reflective orientation includes: relating theory and experience-based knowledge to practice; analyzing one's own teaching and the school context for the purpose of effecting change; viewing a situation from multiple perspectives; seeing alternatives to and consequences of one's actions; and understanding the broad social and moral embed-dedness of teaching (Valli, 1990). In other words, thinking about, questioning, or evaluating the effectiveness of one's teaching from only a technical standpoint is insufficient. Teachers must deliberate about the ethical implications of their practice and be willing to modify actions according to these insights (Valli, 1989a).

IMPLEMENTATION APPROACHES AND PROGRAM EVOLUTION

Specifically, the objectives for the revision of the elementary education program were: to facilitate students' transfer-of-learning from the university to the classroom; to foster the types of school environments which encourage student teachers' professional growth; and to implement a conceptual framework wherein preservice teachers are urged to reflect actively about both technical and normative aspects of schooling (Blum and Valli, 1988). This third objective was added when initial program revisions failed to help students internalize a broad definition of reflection. The description of efforts to promote transfer of learning and to foster reflective school environments is presented separately for the sake of analysis but because the goals overlap some reference to these topics occur in other sections of the paper.

Transfer of Learning

The literature in cognitive psychology and teacher education notes that novice teachers have problems with transfer of learning (Feiman-Nemser and Buchmann, 1985). Frequently new teachers revert to childhood memories of teachers, uncritically imitate their cooperating teachers' practices, or become dependent on mandated curricula instead of using professional knowledge to guide their practice (Valli, 1989b). Two common errors beginning teachers make are failing to see relationships between theory and practice and overgeneralizing the applicability of knowledge.

Dewey's ideas about learning influenced the approach first taken to encourage preservice teachers to reflect about their experience. For Dewey, the learner must actively engage in discovering the meaning of experience through problem solving. Experience is truly educational only when a person reflects with informed awareness on a problem within a particular context (Hook, 1966). Grant and Zeichner (1984) build on Dewey's idea of reflection on experience by noting that there must be conscious, determined, and cautious "consideration of any belief or practice in light of the grounds that support it and the further consequences to which it leads" (p. 4). The purpose of teaching preservice teachers to use a reflective problem solving approach is to counteract their tendency to respond to events by simply imitating the actions of cooperating teachers or by indiscriminately applying knowledge without thorough analysis. Students are cautioned that knowledge is not always directly transferable but that it takes reflection on specific circumstances to discern whether and which experiences or principles apply.

Research cites at least four reasons why transfer fails to occur: lack of modeling, little connection to experience, conflicting expectations, and unrelated supervision. Koehler (1985) indicates that university professors seldom demonstrate the kind of teaching behavior they recommend to their students. In response, more of our department faculty began modeling their own thinking processes to demonstrate to students ways problems can be approached. Elliot (1980) suggests that theory tends not to make sense unless it is linked directly to experience. Therefore efforts were instituted to help students make connections between their past experience and course content. Griffin (1984) notes that school sites and universities frequently reinforce conflicting norms and expectations, putting the preservice student in an awkward position. Closer collaboration between the university and the field sites was initiated to mitigate inconsistencies. And last, Cohn (1981) observes that little supervisory feedback draws on issues discussed in teacher education courses. In fact, preservice teachers receive little supervision at all. Weekly supervision seminars are now conducted which revisit course content.

Helping students see the relevance of course content by modeling reflective approaches and linking experience to professional knowledge facilitates transfer of learning. One example of modeling takes place in the Teaching and Learning in the Elementary School course through a teacher demonstration of thinking out loud as she uses reflective questions to correct a sample assignment. Students then practice by first doing a silent critique of their own assignment using the same type of reflective questions. Then, by working in "thinking out loud" pairs students share with one another comments about the assignment and critique each other's progress.

Both modeling and encouraging students to relate new knowledge to their experience are accomplished in the Reading, Language and Literature class when the professor models how to approach reading assignments. Explaining that reading comprehension depends on active processing of ideas and concepts in the text and class discussions, she provides written directions and examples of the following assignment. The students are asked to be alert to statements in the readings that give them an "Aha!" feeling, that is, new insight that changes or enlightens their thinking. Then students are to give three statements which either link text information to their background information (personal or academic) or relate to other concepts within the chapter. Linking course content with personal experience is also a goal in the Foundations of Education course and will be discussed in the conceptual framework section of the chapter.

In this same Foundations course students are required to incorporate their personal experience within a series of papers addressing the contribution of particular disciplines to educational theory and practice. Each paper must include three parts: a response based on assigned readings related to a particular discipline, a personal experience related to the subject under consideration, and a third source (book or article) which supports or refutes the perspective of the reading or the personal experience. These papers encourage students to examine their views on educational issues by comparing the position taken in the reading to their own opinions and explicitly looking for other arguments which either support or refute their position. For instance, one student addressed the legal obligations of teachers when suspecting child abuse. She then recounted the stress she experienced in deciding how to proceed when as a camp swimming instructor she had to comply with these directives. In the third part of the paper she referred to an article that discussed the ramifications for both teacher and child victim in abuse cases.

Transfer of learning to field sites involves working with cooperating teachers and supervisors to explain the expectations of a reflection oriented program and to provide information which will enable them to support program goals. Steps were taken to develop collaborative problem-solving processes with field site schools. Our goal was to encourage environments which would model reflective problem solving and encourage preservice teachers to draw on professional knowledge to examine their practice. In addition, university supervisors and cooperating teachers are encouraged to guide the preservice teachers by asking questions which call for problem solving and by prompting students to articulate and justify the reasons for their practice. The comprehensive examination and journal writing required in the junior practicum are two major revisions of the program that specifically address transfer of learning.

Comprehensive examination. The comprehensive examination was revised to provide a culminating experience which requires the preservice teachers to reflect on and relate professional knowledge to their classroom practice. Students are required to identify and resolve a classroom problem using a structured format called the "Situation Analysis Guide." This action research format indicates how well students (1) understand and resolve their teaching problems while explicitly following a problem-solving model, (2) draw on theory and research based knowledge, and (3) reflect on the normative as well as technical aspects of teaching in their problem resolution (Valli, Blum, and Taylor, 1986).

The students have a set of observational activities and are taught a problem-solving mode of reflection. They keep journals about events which seem important, interesting, or troublesome. Students then select a situation and work through a series of activities to improve it. This process involves data gathering, analyzing, redefining, solution generating, implementing, and evaluating. At the end of the semester, the student teachers submit an extensive report of all aspects of the process and the changes effected by their interventions. This report then forms the basis of the comprehensive examination, an integrated paper with three major sections: a summary of the situation analysis; a review of literature relevant to the situation; and a retrospective analysis of their experience. In this last section, students are asked to put into perspective the action research project and their entire student teaching experience by reflecting on their thinking and actions, discussing how or if their thinking about teaching changed as a result of the experience, and describing their projected role in establishing an ideal learning environment.

Practicum. In 1989 an additional effort to facilitate transfer of learning from the university to the classroom was introduced by requiring journal writing during the practicum. Even though the research linking the effectiveness of journal work to reflection is inconclusive (Zeichner, 1987) some studies (Holly, 1984; Yinger and Clark, 1981) argue that journal writing can foster higher levels of thinking and increase awareness of values and implicit theories through which one processes experience. During the junior year the elementary and early childhood students spend one full day a week in a classroom working with children under the supervision of a cooperating teacher. This first long-term, regular experience in a classroom provides the context for completing assignments and activities related to the three methods courses taken each semester in the junior year. Besides the specific assignments related to particular classes, preservice teachers maintain weekly journal accounts of their efforts both to plan for and reflect upon weekly events.

Students are encouraged to confer with their cooperating teachers and then develop some projected goals in the planning section of their journals. Students are prodded to go beyond organizational objectives which facilitate order in the classroom to develop goals based on professional knowledge which address other issues, such as deciding on which instructional activities or motivation strategies are appropriate in light of the developmental needs of the children and the philosophy of the school.

In the reflection section, students write about their personal thoughts and reactions to the experience of the day. They are urged to share their "triumphs" as well as their "defeats" and to look at each situation or problem as an opportunity for growth. They are challenged not only to relate their personal viewpoint, but also to analyze the situation from the perspective of their pupils. Finally, preservice students are expected to articulate their thinking processes as they react to situations and to relate their decisions and reactions to the problems. For instance, one student explored the problem-solving strategies she used to adjust the pace and type of questioning for different reading groups.

This journal is submitted in triplicate to the professor of the general methods course: Teaching and Learning in the Elementary School. One copy containing feedback in the form of questions or comments is returned to the student. A second copy is given to the university supervisor and used as the basis for discussing specific pedagogical issues with the student. The department professors, who are concurrently teaching the professional methods courses, have access to a copy and frequently use examples from the journals to illustrate the issues being discussed in class. The dissemination of the journals among all actors having academic and supervisory responsibilities for the preservice teacher has provided a potential tool for integrating theory and practice.

Creating Conducive School Environments

Department faculty began revising the program with the conviction that one way to address the problem of transfer was to develop collaborative agreements between university and field personnel on program goals and expectations regarding curriculum, instructional methods, and management strategies. Collaboration would provide a context for discussion and clarification of the central knowledge and skills that the university expected of the teacher education graduates. Another purpose for collaboration was to provide leadership in developing a process which would help effect change in each of the cooperating schools.

School based problem-solving groups. During the 1986-87 school year teachers, university faculty, supervisors, and preservice students met in school based task forces. The emphasis was on concrete school problems since their resolution would provide real benefits to the teachers. Participation in problem definition and resolution would also enhance teachers' collaboration and growth as professionals. The teams worked cooperatively to identify issues of concern to preservice teachers in their initial field experiences and used problem-solving strategies to develop and implement various improvement activities within the school such as addressing school morale problems through communication and curriculum revision. These task forces decided to disband in 1988. Reasons for this decision will be discussed later in the chapter.

Student teacher placement. To facilitate better communication between the university and the schools, care was taken during the 1986 school year to place student teachers in groups and to assign them only to schools participating in grant activities. This decision was made so that the student teachers would be in environments orientated to CUA's program. Teachers in those schools would be better able to provide experiences and model interactions consistent with the reflective orientation of the program, thereby enhancing the possibility for transfer of learning. Assigning students in groups would enable them to act as a support group for each other and provide an opportunity for them to engage in problem-oriented activities such as peer coaching. A further benefit would result because the university could provide more intensive supervision by reducing the number of schools in which students were placed (Valli, 1989b).

Supervision. Throughout the revision of the program, orientation activities presenting a problem-solving perspective have been provided to university supervisors, who are usually doctoral students, and to cooperating teachers. Course content and teaching strategies recommended for the preservice teachers are discussed. Cooperating teachers are asked to encourage student teachers to draw on professional knowledge in their planning and practice. In addition, all participants are provided with a copy of the department's *Teacher Education Program Handbook* which contains the university's goals and expectations for student teachers and other explicit policies pertinent to the program.

In 1987 a grant funded workshop was held in which cooperating teachers, university supervisors, and faculty met to focus on models of supervision which encouraged problem-solving strategies (e.g., Glickman, 1990; Goldhammer, 1980). Participants were introduced to supervisory styles which promote reflection. They were encouraged, for instance, to begin postobservation conferences with questions to elicit the preservice teacher's thoughts and assessment of the lesson. This strategy was to counteract a common protocol in which the supervisor passes initial judgment on the success of the lesson. Time was also provided for participants to share their successes and problems with supervising, and to brainstorm ways to organize and implement a more reflective supervisory style. One idea which surfaced was the need to make time in the daily schedule to discuss the problems and to help students make connections between prior learning and current experiences. Subsequently, each fall, sessions are provided to orient cooperating teachers and university supervisors to the university expectations for field experiences. Additional training in the use of problem-solving strategies as a supervisory method is also provided to university supervisors as needed.

Conceptual Framework

After the first year of the grant it became apparent that our conceptualization of problem solving was inadequate in fostering reflection which critically examines goals and assumptions. Preservice teachers still had difficulty in using professional knowledge in classrooms. They frequently fell prey to a prevailing mentality which justified using any management or survival strategy as long as it "worked." Students were not thinking about principled action or the ethical issues of schooling. To overcome these shortcomings a conceptual framework was developed for the program to guide and expand thinking as students engaged in problem solving and other reflective activities (Valli and Blum, 1987).

Frameworks, similar to scaffolding, provide a skeleton upon which to hang ideas and develop connections (Perkins, 1987). The conceptual framework is presented to help students integrate professional knowledge across courses and to use appropriately this knowledge in the field. The framework provides the faculty with a common language which, when employed across classes, supports and reinforces students' understanding (Valli and Taylor, 1988). The framework also provides a vehicle for supervisors and cooperating teachers to explain and discuss underlying specific classroom situations and decisions. In general, the framework is meant to encourage a view of schooling and teaching from multiple perspectives; to stimulate students to make explicit the ethical, moral, and political ramifications of routine classroom decisions; and to consider thoughtfully the consequences of their actions (Valli, 1990).

The conceptual framework has three dimensions: Schwab's (1973) commonplaces of education, Berlak and Berlak's (1981) dilemmas of schooling, and van Manen's (1977) levels of reflection.

Commonplaces. Schwab notes that each teaching situation has four aspects or commonplaces: the student(s) who are taught, a teacher who instructs, subject matter which is presented, and the context in which the action takes place (Posner, 1988; Schwab, 1971). The commonplaces taken together provide foci for reflection. The aim is to promote concurrent analysis of these four aspects of the teaching-learning situation in order to develop comprehensive and integrated understandings. The commonplaces are intended to broaden the range of information used in decision making.

Dilemmas of schooling. The dilemmas of schooling proposed by Berlak and Berlak (1981) compose the second dimension of the framework. These dilemmas provide issues for reflection arising within the commonplaces. They push preservice teachers to realize that educational decisions often involve choosing between or among competing goals. The dilemmas address the spectrum of actions possible in decision making that may result in diverse and possibly divergent educational outcomes. The Berlaks place the dilemmas into three categories: control, curriculum, and society.

Levels of reflection. Composing the third dimension of the framework, van Manen's (1977) three levels of reflection (technical, interpretive, and critical) help students ponder the commonplaces and dilemmas through various approaches to knowledge.

At the technical level, educational knowledge and basic curriculum principles are approached through "how to" questions. Teachers can address curriculum, instruction, as well as diagnostic and control issues through this mode of thinking. At the interpretive level, educational decisions are based on understanding personal and cultural experiences, assumptions, and perceptions. Communication is fostered by asking questions such as "What does this mean for . . . ?" Teachers thus become attuned to ways students, parents, and colleagues interpret their words and actions. The critical level of reflection looks at questions of worth and the nature of social conditions. The salient question is "What ought to be" in terms of what liberates from oppression and provides just and equitable conditions for all.

Figure 6.1 illustrates the conceptual framework. The critical level is placed first to emphasize that questions of meaning and technique should always be addressed in the context of ethical goals and values.

This framework is the integrating principle for all aspects of the teacher education program. In particular, it is meant to shape the way the curricular content is presented in each professional education course. For example, in a unit on inappropriate behavior in Classroom Management, preservice teachers might deal with questions at the three levels of reflection which focus on the student and deal with the control

FIGURE 6.1
Conceptual Framework for Reflection[1]

Common-places	Levels	DILEMMAS		
		Control	Curriculum	Society
Student	Critical	1		
	Interpretive	2		
	Technical	3		
Teacher	Critical			
	Interpretive			
	Technical			
Subject Matter	Critical			
	Interpretive			
	Technical			
Context	Critical			6
	Interpretive			5
	Technical			4

dilemmas. (1) What norms and values should govern my choice of disciplinary strategies? How will they benefit the student? (2) What will it mean to a student if I use a certain disciplinary strategy (e.g., call home, discuss the situation, cancel recess privileges?) (3) How will I handle disruptive classroom behavior? Similarly, during school observations in Foundations of Education, students might reflect on tracking issues. (4) How does the school group students? (5) What impact do grouping practices have on students' self-image, school attitudes, and so forth? (6) What criteria should a school use in making decisions about tracking or grouping students? Although this issue impacts all the commonplaces, it primarily deals with the school context and the societal dilemma of allocation of resources.

The purpose of encouraging all three levels of reflection is to prod professors, students, supervisors, and cooperating teachers to expand thinking beyond efficiency-oriented concerns of survival. Student teachers are asked to weigh the meaning of actions to gain empathetic insights and to ponder long-term consequences of their conduct. They are prompted to assess goals and activities to determine their desirability in light of values such as equality and justice. To varying degrees, each professor employs the language of the framework to organize and encourage reflective inquiry and problem-solving activities related to the course. In general, the progression of the professional courses is aimed at enhancing reflective problem solving so that eventually preservice teachers will internalize reflective habits which bring personal experience and research knowledge to bear on the ethics of their everyday practice. Thus the framework itself becomes the overarching instructional strategy for the program. It represents a way of viewing the act of teaching, structures student assignments and reflection, and helps faculty situate the questions of the particular disciplines (Valli and Taylor, 1988).

Although the professional sequence did not change, each course was examined and modified so that within the sequence students would systematically be introduced to reflective problem solving through application of the framework to course content.

EVALUATION PROCEDURES AND RESULTS

Two evaluation studies have addressed the progress of students in becoming more reflective while one other study has looked at faculty implementation of the framework.

The first evaluation effort was aimed at assessing students'

progress in reflecting on their practice rather than just focusing techni-
cally on how to do things the one "best" way in the classroom. Students are pushed to expand their thinking beyond the typical concerns
of the teaching-learning process to consider social, political, and ethical
principles underlying teaching (Valli, 1989a).

Student teachers from the 1987 and 1988 cohorts who graduated
before the inception of the conceptual framework completed a ques-
tionnaire assessing the value of the action research project begun while
student teaching and completed as their comprehensive examination.
Their responses were analyzed for evidence of reflective orientations
(Valli and Taylor, 1989).

Two themes emerged from these self-reports which suggest student thinking was affected: context awareness and organized thinking.
Students reported that the activity helped them become aware of multiple factors associated with their problems and helped them to see the
relationships among factors. Because students became increasingly
aware of the complexity of the classroom environment, they seemed
to value the action research project in helping them consider these phenomena in a systematic manner. Written reports of their action research
projects and supervisor feedback corroborated these claims of reflective
outcomes. Supervisors reported that the project enabled the students to
look at the complex environment of the classroom in a structured way
which helped them manage the "monumental" demands of student
teaching without becoming overwhelmed (Valli and Taylor, 1989).

Three additional themes indicated that the scope of students'
reflections was expanded by the action research project to include teaching goals, moral responsibility, and the need to challenge taken-for-
granted practices (Valli, 1989a). However, these themes were relatively
weak, surfacing only from a small percentage of students.

The focus of the evaluation on the 1989 cohort was the relationship
between teaching skill and the quality and scope of reflection. Student
teachers were rated by their supervisors and by the student teaching
coordinator as having an easy or difficult time, first, with the teaching
experience and, then, with completing the action research project. Student teachers were asked whether the conceptual framework was valuable to them in their actual teaching and in their research projects. Student teachers rated by their supervisors and the coordinator of student
teaching as having an "easy" time with both teaching and the reflective
project reported seeing much more value in the framework for teaching
than those student teachers who were rated as having a "hard" time
with both the teaching and the research project. The latter group rated
the framework as more useful for the project but much less useful for

teaching. Even though the action research project focused on an aspect of teaching which students encountered every day, the reflection imposed by the problem-solving activity did not carry over to teaching for the group of teachers who had difficulties. Analysis of the relationship between reflection and skill indicates that most students were simultaneously high or low on both dimensions. A few were rated high on teaching and low on reflection. No one was rated low on teaching and high on reflection. It would seem that basic teaching skills are a prerequisite to reflective teaching, but that one does not have to be an experienced teacher prior to the development of reflective abilities (Valli and Taylor, 1989).

Throughout the revision of the program a premise has been that reflection is best taught by infusing it within each aspect of the program, particularly by providing students many opportunities to articulate their reasoning and to practice reflective problem solving. The graduating class of 1990 is the first cohort of students who were introduced to the framework and reflective problem-solving activities from the beginning of their program. Therefore the program may now be summatively evaluated. Longitudinal data have been collected on this cohort beginning with biographical survey and interview data to assess their entry level capacity and inclination to be generally reflective. Exit interviews and surveys as well as their action research projects and data collected over the years from their supervisors will be used to analyze growth in both quality and scope of reflection, the development of their professional knowledge, and their attitudes about teaching.

Another evaluation concern, because it affects student outcomes, is the degree to which the faculty actually implements the framework within their individual courses. Data were collected by asking the faculty to specify how the framework was addressed in their courses. Three sources of variation surfaced. First faculty differed in valuing reflection as a goal because it had a potential of limiting the amount of content covered in a course. Faculty struggled with their desire to provide core knowledge while allowing the time needed for students to engage in process-oriented activities and assignments designed to promote reflection. Second, faculty varied in the degree to which they were committed to an infused model and the idea that the framework could help students organize information. The faculty was committed, in concept, to encouraging reflection and to having a united program focus embodied through the framework. But the actual implementation of the framework often entailed redesigning entire courses. Needless-to-say, not all faculty enthusiastically appreciated this. Third, the faculty varied in their degree of understanding and acceptance of the broad, critical focus of the framework. Most faculty agreed with the goal of developing multiplicity in thinking but have more difficulty with the social and critical aspects of reflection (Valli and Taylor, 1989).

DIFFICULTIES, CONSTRAINTS, AND PROBLEMS

Developing habits of reflection takes patience and a substantial investment of time. Reflection is seldom mastered without conscious practice and consistent encouragement. Many faculty concerns relate to the issue of time and the energy required to sustain reflective efforts. All faculty agree that focusing on developing reflection tends to be time consuming for both the instructors and the students. Some wonder if it is necessary to insist that every student become reflective. If it is necessary, what implications does that have for faculty work load especially as enrollment increases? What are the minimum essential activities which will encourage and develop reflection? Keeping momentum and interest among faculty in the face of the additional "burden" an ambitious program puts on them is a challenge.

Specific problems also arose in trying to implement some of the original goals of the program. One goal was to develop educational environments knowledgeable of and conducive to reflection. The school-based task forces were conceptualized and implemented to support collaborative efforts between the university and the schools. Originally, the schools agreed to participate in school-based problem-solving meetings in order to model a reflective environment for the preservice teachers. Even though the teachers went along with the project, they tended to see the process as another set of meetings to attend rather than a vehicle which had the potential to facilitate change and improvement. They never really owned the concept so when the option to continue was offered they declined. At that point the task forces were disbanded. So the department abandoned the practice of placing students only in schools which participated in the original OERI grant. Instead, efforts have shifted to looking for placements having two or more teachers interested in the goals of reflective teaching and willing to support the requirements of the field placement. The effort spent in developing positive, professional school-university relationships was partially rewarded. But stability has never been achieved since over the years the program has been plagued with high turnover of cooperating teachers and administrators (Blum and Valli, 1988). Although full scale institutional participation has been unstable, positive and professional relationships with some schools have been maintained.

Another ongoing problem is assuring that university supervisors and cooperating teachers possess adequate understanding and appropriate skills to foster the goals of the program. Some university supervisors and cooperating teachers have a tendency to give feedback which rewards technical efficiency instead of critical reflection. Such feedback does not encourage the student to make the extra effort to be reflective and creates mixed messages about our expectations. Careful selection of cooperating teachers and ongoing staff development address this concern.

FUTURE PLANS FOR RESEARCH

No research has yet been completed on whether the program orientation carries into the first years of teaching or if students can continue the same type of reflection without guidance and feedback. Because in the past, most of the graduates moved away from the area after graduation, follow-up efforts have been only marginally successful. However the majority of the 1990 graduating class found teaching positions in the metropolitan area surrounding the university so prospects for systematic data collection and comprehensive assessment are now feasible.

The conceptual framework developed for our preservice teachers is also useful in guiding our own inquiry about the effects of the program. At the critical level we can ask if every child is best served by a reflective teacher? Are our graduates more conscious of the ethical implications of their actions? From an interpretive perspective concerns about the implications of reflection surface. Does reflection on the part of the teacher encourage their own students to be reflective? How do students, co-workers, and administrators view reflective teachers? The technical issues of interest are questions relating to the general context of the teacher's "world" and particular school effects. How do new teachers cope with the bureaucracy? Will the new teachers' efforts at reflection result in improved student outcomes?

Some questions of interest also concern program applicants. For instance: What influences outside the program might contribute to a student's penchant for reflection and divergent thinking? What are the entering characteristics of students who seem to be most successful in developing a reflective orientation? What measure(s) might predict the student who will be successful in this type of program? How long does it take to develop reflection? Are three years sufficient? Should reflection even be a required goal?

These are the questions which continue to disturb our equilibrium. They prompt us to collaboratively (and sometimes conflictually) reflect on our own teaching practice in much the same way we encourage the students to reflect on theirs. We have learned that the process is not easy and the answers are seldom clear. But we are not discouraged because we are convinced of the ethical implications of our efforts.

RENEE T. CLIFT
W. ROBERT HOUSTON
JANE McCARTHY

7

Getting it RITE: A Case of Negotiated Curriculum in Teacher Preparation at the University of Houston

As this book illustrates, teacher education is undergoing a period of change. Many of the changes are a result of reform recommendations, others are in response to legislative mandates. In writing this chapter, we are unable to fully describe the future status of the Reflective Inquiry Teacher Education (RITE) program at the University of Houston. One reason for the fluctuating status of our program, which may not be typical of all programs, is that recent changes mandated by the state legislature have not been fully implemented, therefore it would be inappropriate for us to project the ways reflection is implemented while still in the process of redesign. The primary reason, however, for our reluctance to present our program as a completed product is that we have come to realize that programs in teacher education are not static entities, but are continually being modified by such curriculum developers as administrators, department chairs, professors, adjunct professors, students, school district administrators, teachers, and state and national level policy makers.

This case is presented as one which is not, and never will be, closed as are cases in law or medicine. Rather, we describe what RITE was intended to be, what it began to be once the intended curriculum became operational, and what the future appears to be at this time. The central thesis of this chapter is that what began as an attempt to follow a rational course of curriculum development quickly began to exemplify the phenomenon of a negotiated curriculum. The three chapter authors were directly involved in one or more stages of the development of the RITE curriculum. This chapter represents our collective reconstruction of experiences that span the past six years.

CURRICULUM THEORY AND TEACHER EDUCATION

The recent Holmes proposal (1986) for the reform of teacher education did not focus on the curriculum for preparing teachers, but rather on the university and school structures that might support a teacher preparation curriculum. Curriculum study in general has tended to elaborate upon the K-12 curriculum, and to ignore the university curriculum that prepares teachers to implement, consciously or unconsciously, the assumptions embedded in the curricula they are expected to implement once they enter into a teaching contract. While it is not our purpose to propose a theory of teacher preparation curriculum in this chapter, we do find it necessary to place our case study within a broader frame than that provided by recent discussions of reflective practice.

Walker (1987) identified four conceptions of curriculum theory that help to provide such a frame: (a) theories that propose a program, and debate the content, aims, and approaches to education such as Allan Bloom's (1987) indictment of undergraduate studies; (b) theories that rationalize a set of procedures for curriculum construction, exemplified by Tyler's (1949) four basic questions for curriculum planners; (c) theories such as those discussed by Dewey (1904) that provide a conceptual frame for thinking about curriculum development, and prioritize areas that must be addressed if the curriculum is to meet the needs and abilities of students; and (d) theories such as those elaborated by Eisner (1985) that attempt to explain the process of curriculum development, implementation, and change without prescribing desirable curriculum practice. The first three theoretical approaches can be found in recent accounts of teacher education programs, the fourth is noticeably absent.

The programmatic focus is exemplified by Michigan State University's planned variations in both elementary and secondary teacher preparation. In their case studies of teacher education programs, Howey and Zimpher (1989) carefully document this concept of planned variations and highlight one of the thematic variations, the Heterogeneous Classrooms program. The content of the program, both in course work and field experiences, emphasizes cultural differences and individual differences among students in all classrooms. The aim of the program is to promote awareness of individual differences in the program, with special attention paid to the themes of equity and diversity. The approach to education, therefore, is to have students participate in a sequence of experiences designed to deepen their initial commitment to working in schools where students are academically and socially at risk. At the same time, courses are designed to provide a knowledge base focused on the learners in potentially at-risk situations.

The rational approach to curriculum planning is exemplified by the competency based teacher education design. Hall and Jones (1976) described such programs rooted in the conception of mastery learning wherein learning objectives are defined and instructors are obligated to work with students until the objective is obtained—no matter how long it takes. In Competency Based Teacher Education (CBTE) skills, behaviors, and demonstrable knowledge are identified and stated such that student learning can be assessed through direct observation. Experiences that promote competency acquisition are identified and sequenced appropriately. Students then complete the experiences and demonstrate proficiency by completing the evaluation experience for a given competency.

Currently there is an interest in programs providing a conceptual lens for teacher education curriculum. This interest has been manifested in settings that provide prospective teachers with an opportunity to become more reflective about their teaching, including the moral and ethical effects of their teaching as well as the more technical execution of teaching skills. The range of approaches to encouraging reflective teaching have been documented in several recent volumes (e.g., Grimmett and Erickson, 1989; Clift, Houston, and Pugach, 1990; Schön, 1991), including this one.

While it is not typical of teacher preparation programs to explicate the process of curriculum development and change, the critical movement in teacher education comes closest to exemplifying this fourth theoretical approach. We note that it also shares features of the first approach in that desirable goals/ends are specified by critical theorists. Zeichner's (1981-82) discussion of a seminar designed to help student teachers, "resist the slide into the routine," (p. 17) presents an argument for teacher preparation as critical study of the status quo. He argues that one factor in this resistance is the ability to analyze the rationale for school's curriculum and to raise questions about curriculum decisions in terms of their impact on students. Another factor is for prospective teachers to raise questions about their own socialization and to understand how their experiences in schools shape their current conceptions of classrooms.

While we do not represent a critical perspective on teaching or teacher education, we do take the view that teacher education curriculum is best understood through thoughtful examination of the process participants undergo as they begin to design and implement teacher education programs. We assume that curriculum development in teacher education is inherently a social and political process during which all who come in contact with teacher education have the opportunity to modify the program overtly through course requirements or covertly through modifying such requirements to individual needs or purposes.

To our knowledge, such a conception of teacher education has not been articulated, although it has been alluded to in discussions of colleges of education (e.g., Clifford and Guthrie, 1988), histories of teacher education (e.g., Borrowman, 1956), and case descriptions for teacher education programs (e.g., Howey and Zimpher, 1989). We believe that in the case of RITE, political and social forces operated at the college level throughout program development, at the classroom level once the curriculum became operational, and at the state level once forces beyond university control legislated teacher education curriculum policy. At all levels, negotiations regarding the content, instructional process, and evaluation of the curriculum continue to shape the meaning of RITE.

Curriculum as a Negotiating Process

Two bodies of literature refer to curriculum negotiation. The first is an ongoing debate over how much control students, particularly college students, should exert over their own degree plans, course syllabi, and activities. The second is a description of the relationship between curriculum policy making and curriculum writing. Both are relevant to the case of the RITE program and to conceptions of preparing reflective teachers.

During the late 1960s and early 1970s university student activism in the United States challenged exclusive faculty rights to curriculum development. While students' motives, responsibilities, and expertise were debated, their demands for participation could not be ignored (for examples of such debates see Rooker, 1981; Kridel, 1983). In the 1980s student participation in curriculum development was advocated for adult education in urban universities (Jones, 1982; Niemi, 1985) to encourage student ownership of the educational process. Descriptions of such programs describe discussions between professors and students as themes are determined, course syllabi are structured and contractual arrangements for student products are agreed upon (e.g., Brace, 1984; Sparrow, 1986).

Such negotiations are inherently personal. That is, all parties are encouraged to share individual interests or wishes and to disclose their own feelings and opinions. The emphasis is on the process of developing arguments that justify one's position and developing skills in consensus building. Themes, activities, and materials are identified only after attaining consensus among all negotiating parties. The result is a curriculum developed locally, as opposed to a policy mandated course of study.

But curriculum policy mandates are also subject to intensive negotiating processes. At the state level, laws and regulations are developed by state legislatures, state education agencies, organized lobbying groups, and the courts. These are then reinterpreted by state regulatory agencies, local school districts, and classroom teachers. As Walker (1990) noted, policy is fundamentally political, not technical. While the concept of curriculum policy challenges the tradition of local control in principle, in practice, educational issues are increasingly becoming important topics of national policy councils. The same can be said for curriculum policy that affects teacher education.

THE DESIGN OF THE RITE PROGRAM

Designing RITE, as with almost any other teacher preparation program, was accomplished among a group of people who brought their own visions of teacher education and their own personal histories of what can and cannot be accomplished with a preservice program. In this particular instance, each of the designers also brought with them their own conceptions of reflection and reflective teaching. Furthermore, as participants began to work within the program, to read others' views of what it means to be reflective, and to interact with other teacher educators across the country, notions of both reflection and teacher education were modified. In this section we describe the dynamic and interactive nature of program design, beginning with the university's transition from a product orientation to one of process.

Identifying Competencies

During the 1960s the University of Houston became internationally known for implementing a competency-based teacher preparation program. The second author of this chapter is generally acknowledged as a leading figure in the national competency-based movement, and many of the faculty members who began were asked to participate in identifying competencies for a new program in teacher education in 1983 were advocates and participants in the competency movement. Some, including the first author of this chapter, were not. Discussion of a new program in teacher education to replace CBTE began in 1983 as a result of a new Dean's desire to stimulate renewed interest in teacher education by the College of Education faculty accompanied by new state standards which lengthened the number of semester hours required for certification.

Task Force I met for over a year to identify "competencies" for a new teacher education program. The task force was originally convened to answer the first question posed by Ralph Tyler (1949), "What educational purposes should the school seek to attain?" Representatives for each of the four departments in the College of Education debated a list of competencies which seemed to grow daily. As the task reached completion—competencies had been identified—but they were no longer labeled competencies. The group of participants who had not been identified with CBTE argued successfully that this "new" program should eschew the earlier terminology as well as the accompanying philosophy. Both CBTE and the Tyler rationale were under attack. The competencies were relabeled "knowledge, skills, and attitudes" and it was agreed that the program would be designed and delivered by an interdepartmental team of faculty members.

Once knowledge, skills, and attitudes were agreed upon and written they were disseminated to the faculty along with the recommendation that all general course work in teacher preparation be subsumed under an education prefix as opposed to departmental prefixes. While the recommendations for content were never debated, the absence of department ownership was hotly contested when first introduced and is still contested (although with less vigor and violence) today. Following endorsement by the entire faculty, a second task force was convened to design a conceptual framework for the program. At this point, the theory underlying the development of the curriculum shifted from a rational model to one more focused on the conceptual orientation of the program to be.

The RITE Idea

Task Force II specified five assumptions that should undergird teacher preparation "to produce teachers who":

a. are liberally educated;
b. have a scholarly command of the disciplines; i.e., understand the purpose, structure, and methodology as well as the information of a subject field(s);
c. teach effectively, integrating the affective and cognitive flow of experience in learning;
d. reflect on and inquire into teaching practice in ways which foster continuous professional growth;
e. can work effectively in cross-cultural settings with children of diverse ethnic backgrounds" (Redesign Task Force, 1985, pp. 2-3).

The task force, comprised of professors from all four departments, made a number of recommendations concerning program structure, sequence, and characteristics, but never prescribed the content, organization, or evaluation of learning experiences. Throughout the recommendations were emphases on understanding the complexities of teaching through inquiry, accompanied by reflection on the process and the outcome of such inquiry. It was suggested that complex problems in teaching be simulated through focal problems, while field work and clinical training would "orient students toward an analytic approach to teaching" (p. 3). Training in stimulated process recall would be one of the major tools of inquiry, but generic tools would be adjunct to instruction by faculty specialists in pedagogy. The task force also recommended continual reflection and inquiry by faculty members through research into "the characteristics of effective teachers, schools, and teacher training practices" (p. 3).

Naming the program summarized all that the task force considered important.

The task force took quite seriously the responsibility to recommend a name for the new program. Believing that the University of Houston College of Education teacher education program will become a symbol of quality in the profession, the task force wanted the name to reflect the program's essence. The task force recommends that the College of Teacher Education Program be named: The Reflective-Inquiry Teacher Education Program, The RITE Program (pp. 18-19).

The task force's report was shared with the faculty and then given to an implementation team (Implementation Team I). While team members included participants in Task Force I, there were no members from Task Force II on the Implementation Team I. Thus, team members were not always sure of the meanings that underlay the document produced by Task Force II. In addition, prior to implementation, another set of negotiators entered when RITE applied for and received funding as a demonstration project through the United States Department of Education, Office of Educational Research and Improvement (OERI). OERI's request for proposals specified that universities and school districts must work together to meet the joint needs identified by both parties.

Up until this point, the development of RITE had been strictly a local effort controlled by professors of education. With the addition of the OERI requirements, the design was modified to meet both local and national interests. Student interests and demands were not a part of the process—until the curriculum became operational.

Curriculum Implementation and Subsequent Renegotiation

A program design team was formed during the summer of 1985 and charged with implementing the recommendations of Task Forces I and II, plus the requirements of the OERI contract. By this time, teacher education administrators had suggested a desirable sequence for the program content and Task Force I had suggested an instructional form that utilized differentiated staffing. The team was given one summer to have Phase I of RITE in operation by Fall 1985.

The team began by agreeing that they could not possibly meet all of the requirements suggested by earlier efforts. They also agreed that it would take at least one year to have the introductory course completely in place. Therefore, the first year would be a year of experimentation, maintaining an interdepartmental instructional approach, an orientation to reflection and inquiry, and school-university collaboration. Implementation Team I adopted an action research frame on their own efforts, encouraging student feedback on all aspects of the course throughout the semester and examining the results of student progress as an indication of curriculum efficacy.

A six-hour course entitled "Introduction to Teaching" (Phase I), which attempted to synthesize social, psychological, and curricular foundations, was taught that fall. The course included three hours of lecture and two hours of small group instruction. During this semester and the following semester, course instructors worked with one another and with the students in Phase I to establish a reasonable workload for students, to designate which areas of instruction was the province of which faculty members, and to define the respective team roles played by full professors, associates, assistants, and graduate students. At this time students became active participants in the process of negotiation through informal feedback on course events and formal recommendations for changes in university-based assignments and field assignments. Although the primary curriculum developers were still faculty members, the students were actively encouraged to attend curriculum meetings, to rewrite assignments, and to make recommendations.

Negotiating the Field Component

The RITE program was designed to integrate field experiences throughout course work. The original task force which designed the program (Task Force II) recommended more than sixty-five hours of field experiences be included in the first two phases of the program. To implement this recommendation, teachers from nineteen cooperating schools in three different school districts were asked to meet during the summer to plan collaborative educational experiences. During these summers the teachers emphasized the importance of practical, hands on experiences with teaching, while the university faculty emphasized the importance of considering the meaning of such activities for students. The teachers expressed their concerns that time precluded long discussions between the cooperating teachers and the RITE students, and so discussions were defined as the province of university faculty members during regularly scheduled course meeting times.

One result of the summer work sessions was a syllabus containing readings and activities that were directly related to the teaching activities the RITE students would be observing in the field week by week. The teachers agreed to serve as field guides for the RITE students, to be open to discuss observations when time permitted. In the first two years of operation, when most of the collaborating schools had been workshop participants, there was a high degree of fidelity between the negotiated field experiences and the actual experiences as reported by the students. In those schools which did not attend the summer sessions and, over time, as new schools and a fourth district were added to the collaborative network, the fidelity began to break down.

After the summer sessions ended, there was no formal structure in place to renegotiate the conception of the field experiences, much less to discuss the power of the field experience to promote reflection among prospective teachers, practicing teachers, or university faculty members. Thus, reflection on experience occurred only in the students' journals and in campus discussions with the sole exception of those instances in which a teacher provides the RITE student with feedback on demonstration lessons.

The Intended versus the Operational Curriculum

Task Force II had envisioned an instructional pattern in which all faculty members involved in teacher preparation would be involved with the RITE program. The formal structure for such participation, however, was left to the work of the implementation teams. In the absence of such structure, faculty members struggled to create time to reflect among themselves. Team meetings were scheduled, working papers were drafted, and discussions ranged from the meaning of reflection to the role of the faculty monitoring basic literacy of students. The value of such meetings varied with the individual faculty member's other commitments and general tolerance for discussion. In a second summer planning session (1986) faculty in educational psychology decided to withdraw from the interdepartmental team concept. They expressed the view held by others outside of their department that curriculum content should be determined by content specialists and was, therefore, non-negotiable.

The remaining three departments decided to continue an interdepartmental team effort. They devoted the remainder of the summer work session to redistributing course content across the first and second semesters (Phases I and II) of the program. At this time the concept of organizing around focal problems was integrated into the curriculum, although such integration differed between phases. RITE became operational in the fall of 1986, although it was not exactly what any task force or implementation team had envisioned. Rather, RITE is best described as a thoughtful and practical compromise among strong willed faculty members and active, concerned students.

Programmatic Definition of Reflective Inquiry

Zeichner and Liston (1987) described four goals of their reflective teacher education program as: (1) the acquisition of technical competence; (2) the ability to analyze one's own practice and the practice of others; (3) the awareness of ethical and moral choices inherent in the activity of teaching; and (4) sensitivity to the diversity of students' backgrounds, characteristics, and abilities. We came to agree with these goals and decided our program must begin with early classroom and other pre-student teaching experiences that promote reflection and inquiry, with follow-up throughout the professional education sequence. Therefore, the RITE implementation teams adopted a spiraling approach in which concepts and processes are introduced early in the program and are elaborated throughout course work and field experiences. We emphasize that reflection as a concept does not mean the same things to all of the instructors within RITE (McCarthy et al., 1989). Additionally, the contexts of reflection, as well as the content, is seen to require differing reflective responses. As with all other aspects of RITE, conceptual underpinnings are also open to negotiation. The following description, therefore, is illustrative of the activities and settings which encourage reflection, but the reflective process, as well as the topics under discussion, will vary with the individual instructor.

Types of Reflection

Our program begins encouraging the students to reflect on the nature of teaching and the experience of being a student in public schools by helping them understand that their own educational experiences may not be universal. We endeavor to do this by placing students in two very different Houston Area schools and by having them conduct a detailed community study of the area surrounding the school which is most unlike the school(s) in which they were educated. This first level of awareness of community context is followed by a second level in which students begin to inquire into the factors that lead to diverse educational paths for groups as well as for individuals within these communities. Some of this inquiry is guided by readings, guest lectures by local educators, and by class discussions. Much of the inquiry is accomplished through a community study in which students interview residents and business people concerning their opinions on the present experiences and the possible futures of the children in the community.

A second project, the study of the organization and support structures in one school, enables the students to raise questions about the function of the school as the facilitator for educational, social, or other changes in groups or individuals. This study is conducted within schools which collaborate with the university and wherein the faculty and the administration take an active role in the educational process. In class discussions students compare notes across schools and check their observations against those of sociologists and researchers of school effectiveness.

Students are then introduced to technical knowledge that will enable them to work effectively in many classroom settings. They begin with observations of diverse classroom management styles through an analysis of teacher time allocation and through recording student on task behavior. They also record student-teacher interaction patterns using a seating chart and a series of interaction categories developed by Stallings (1986). At this time students are encouraged to practice basic skills in lesson planning and instruction and to examine their assumptions about their own teaching and planning. In microteaching settings the students work together to analyze their lesson plans and their teaching behaviors. In field settings the students work with an experienced teacher (known as a school based teacher educator) to analyze interactions with students.

In a fourth type of reflection, students begin to consider the moral and ethical choices that are inherent in the application of technical knowledge. They consider different alternatives in classroom management and the assumptions that accompany those alternatives. They also begin to develop a description of their own philosophy of teaching as they discuss what an educational philosophy means for teaching students.

This leads to the fifth type in which students begin to consider teachers' abilities and dispositions to control the application of technical knowledge and the implementation of a personal philosophy of teaching. Questions about a teacher's responsibility to society, to the profession, and to self are raised, but are often left unanswered because the students and the faculty expect responses to change over time.

In our three semester curriculum, students are continually offered opportunities to reorganize prior experience in light of new information and are challenged to defend their choices as they consider the effects of those choices. Therefore, for us, reflection is defined as the disposition and ability to consider education as the result of many social, political, and individual factors accompanied by an understanding of the need to base subsequent action on careful analysis of the results of such inquiry.

Course Structure

Course work is organized into three phases, each of which occurs during one of the four semesters normally devoted to teacher preparation courses. In Phase I elementary, secondary, and special subject area students are introduced to the profession of teaching, including the constraints and the opportunities teachers deal with as they work within schools. They are also introduced to some of the basic technical skills of teaching such as lesson design and concepts from research on the use of instructional time. Most of the students' time is spent in small groups of twenty to twenty-five with an instructor who is also a faculty member or, in rare cases, an advanced doctoral student. Large group lectures allow students and instructors to hear from local experts on educational matters related to their experiences, such as school superintendents, state legislators, community leaders, and elementary and secondary teachers and students.

Phase II emphasizes learning to teach by teaching and then reflecting on the nature of that teaching experience. Assignments encourage students to explore the teaching-learning process and the factors which contribute to the effectiveness of the process. Students complete at least two microteaching assignments and two classroom teaching assignments. Once again, faculty members serve as instructors for small groups of students. This semester strives to bind together knowledge, theory, and actual teaching experiences into a meaningful whole. Students begin to integrate basic teaching and managerial skills into a working, effective repertoire.

FIGURE 7.1
The Sequence of the RITE Curriculum

Phase I	*Phase II*	*Phase III*
Decision Making:	Skill Building:	Application:
Do I want to teach? What settings are best for me?	What is the knowledge base of teaching and learning?	
Introduction to social, culture, and practical issues in teaching. Reflection on the internal and external factors affecting teaching and learning.	Introduction to research on effective teaching. Practice in teaching skills. Reflection on cognitive and affective issues in teaching and learning.	Supervised practice teaching. Reflection on the content of Phases I and II as they apply to practice.

In the first six hours of their program (Phase I), students complete detailed community study projects that take them into the residential and business areas surrounding selected Houston area schools. As they complete the tasks within the project they meet and interview parents, police workers, librarians, real estate agents, and other people who are not directly affiliated with the school. They observe living conditions, recreational opportunities, and identify community support services. From these projects they raise questions about community factors that might affect students' attitudes toward school and their performance in school.

A second project focuses on school contexts and their influence on the practice of teaching. Students are introduced to research on effective schools with a particular emphasis on the role of the principal (or other instructional leaders) in creating a climate that is conducive to learning. Additionally, they examine at least four different classrooms and compare the organizational patterns and the ways teachers organize instructional time. Once again, they are encouraged to raise questions—this time focusing on school level factors that enhance or diminish a teacher's ability to work with children.

Once students have completed projects in which they demonstrate a knowledge of selected contextual factors that directly and indirectly affect the conduct of teaching, they are introduced to an overview of research on classroom management, direct instruction, cooperative learning, and the effective use of time. In other words, technical skill building is not taught apart from a consideration of the environment in which those skills may be used. The students' projects at the end of their six hour introduction examine the skills of one school-based cooperating teacher, including patterns of interaction between the teacher and students as well as the diverse ways instructional time is used. They also analyze their own teaching, first in a microteaching laboratory assignment and then in an actual teaching assignment in the classroom. Students are expected to raise questions about their own planning, their interactions with the students, and their assessments of the instructional decisions that were made during their teaching.

The following excerpt from a student's final project demonstrates the awareness of contextual factors.

> I never gave it much thought that I would be teaching students who don't get three balanced meals and nice, warm clothes in winter . . . I didn't think of the fact that I might be expected to teach students who couldn't read, write, or speak English . . . I just hope I'm ready for whatever challenge is ahead of me and I hope I'm ready for whatever turn I take.

This beginning level awareness is elaborated and strengthened in the six hours following the introductory course. Once again, students are placed in a collaborating field site in which they become aware of contextual factors. Here they are also introduced to individual differences among students due to ability, development, social skills, and prior experiences with schooling. Research on learning *and* research on teaching effectiveness are emphasized as the prospective teachers practice their skills in microteaching assignments and in their field classrooms.

These assignments include an analysis of lesson design prior to implementation and an analysis of the actual teaching. The school based teacher educator (SBTE) encourages the prospective teacher to assume responsibility for teaching at least two lessons. Both the student and the SBTE review the lesson and analyze the presentation and the content.

Frequent meetings with teacher education instructors (twice weekly) and journal entries provide avenues for students and faculty to discuss the problems individuals face as they confront new material and as they work through instructional management issues. By the end of the second semester the students have both declarative knowledge of and experience in working with time management, classroom management, lesson design, direct instruction, and three additional generic teaching strategies. They are also acutely aware that their instruction will need to be modified based on factors that are external to the classroom as well as those that are operating within the classroom. They are also aware that they need to continue studying their content area and to continue developing their technical skills. They have not been able to develop routines or structures that will help them implement their knowledge, although they observed successful routines and unsuccessful routines. They are aware of classrooms as social systems and the teacher's role in organizing the system to enable learning to take place. Developing such organizational skills—or sustaining routines that are already in place—occurs in student teaching.

Phase III, student teaching, never became fully operational. Before that implementation team began to meet, state legislative actions diverted faculty attention from implementing RITE to revising teacher education completely. At this time, the "new" program is being implemented and Phase III is scheduled for major revision beginning in 1991.

An Attempt to End Negotiations

Teacher education is highly regulated in Texas, and because of that, strongly influenced by political events. Dozens of bills are passed in each legislative session, many in the waning days of the session without careful review of their consequences (or more appropriately, unanticipated consequences). Two agencies are responsible for regulation at the state level, the State Board of Education and the Coordinating Board for Higher Education. Each has its own agenda that only peripherally includes the education of teachers; each has its own constituencies, and its own regulations.

Individual universities have their own requirements as well, often responding to national agencies which may or may not agree with state regulations. The University of Houston is affiliated with the National Council for the Accreditation of Teacher Education (NCATE) and the Southern Association of Colleges and Universities. Both review and accredit programs on the basis of their own standards. In addition, the College of Education is also a member of the Holmes Group. With often conflicting demands and requirements which are changed regularly, but seldom predictably, teacher education is buffered by events over which it has no control nor input. And so it is with the current status of RITE.

The Commission on Professional Standards was established in 1978 to oversee teacher education for the State Board of Education. A seventy-four page set of regulations was developed and approved as the 1984 Standards, the impetus for Task Force I. Before these standards (and therefore RITE) could be fully implemented, a firestorm erupted between leaders in the state legislature and the State Board of Education. A state commission, headed by billionaire Ross Perot, made major recommendations for changes in every aspect of public schools. These were enacted in House Bill 72 and passed in 1985. Radical changes in curriculum, extracurricular activities, student testing, teacher salaries, teacher evaluation, and career ladders affected practice; the replacement of a twenty-three member elected Board of Education by a fifteen member appointed Board affected policy. Policy was again affected two years later when the appointed board was replaced by a fifteen member elected board.

Following a second study, this time of higher education, the legislature passed Senate Bill 994 in 1987. In addition to many other provisions, three are of major concern here. The first required all prospective teachers to have a bachelor's degree earned in a noneducation major. The second limited course work in professional education to eighteen semester hours, plus six hours in reading for elementary teachers and three hours of reading for secondary teachers. The third provision created a one-year of induction programs for teachers that were to be jointly operated among school districts and universities, but no funding accompanied this requirement. All provisions were to be implemented by September 1, 1991, with no exceptions.

The State Board of Education approved a modified set of 1987 Standards that incorporated the legislative changes. Even though the scope of teacher education had been drastically reduced, the 1987 Standards maintained the same general requirements and specific regulations. These included a minimum of sixty semester hours in general education, forty-eight for which the content was specifically identified. Elementary teachers were required to have a minimum of thirty-six hours in an academic specialization, while most secondary teachers were required to take forty-eight hours. The maximum number of hours in professional education was set at eighteen plus the mandated reading courses.

The twelve hours of professional education content plus the six hours of student teaching was rigidly defined. Six hours were to include experiences in the teaching-learning process, measurement and evaluation of students, human growth and development, special education (including gifted and talented education), multicultural education, legal and ethical concerns related to teaching, school organization and management in Texas and the United States, and instructional media and technology. The remaining six hours was to be devoted to instructional methods, lesson design and evaluation, curriculum organization (including scope and sequence), and classroom management. Students were also expected to spend forty-five clock hours in schools. Student teaching was to be reduced to eight weeks for most students, twelve for those seeking dual certification.

The Coordinating Board further restricted teacher preparation by requiring all state institutions to offer a baccalaureate degree teacher education program in which requirements were limited to one hundred thirty-nine total semester hours. While prospective teachers were expected to complete degree requirements comparable to those for all majors, the eighteen hours of professional education could only carry undergraduate course credit. This leads to conflict expectations between the two regulatory agencies, either of which could refuse to approve a teacher preparation curriculum. For example, a forty-eight hour degree requirement in interdisciplinary studies that might be completed by a prospective elementary teacher did not meet both Coordinating Board requirements for comparability and Texas Education Agency requirements for a thirty-six hour certification program.

Additionally, the University of Houston had implemented undergraduate core requirements that further limited teacher preparation programs. Although the university's requirements often agreed with those of the Texas Education Agency, courses that satisfied a knowledge integration requirement could not be taken outside of an approved minor or without a prerequisite or co-requisite course. Add this to recommendations from the Holmes report and to requirements for NCATE accreditation and the competing demands move from the realm of negotiation into a Kafkaesque insanity.

Faculty Perceptions of Reflection in Teacher Education

We have described the content and process of curriculum development through 1988. At that time faculty who had participated in the process were interviewed concerning their perceptions of what it means to prepare reflective teachers (McCarthy et al., 1989). Three of the faculty members interviewed expressed general dissatisfaction with the programmatic theme and virtually everyone had suggestions for revising and modifying the RITE curriculum two years after it became operational. In addition, the faculty held diverse views on the nature of reflection itself. Four different perspectives were identified: technical, strategic, social, or personal.

The technical perspective is similar to that described by van Manen (1977) as coming from an empirical-analytic tradition in which the central issue is the way in which knowledge can improve one's effectiveness. The strategic perspective is derived from Dewey's (1904) conception of reflection and data collection is an important component in resolving the dilemma of practice.

The social perspective is the view closest to the critical view discussed by Zeichner (1987) cited earlier, but differs from a critical perspective in that the faculty members who expressed this view sought to have students understand the relationship between classroom teaching and broader social issues, but did not advocate teachers as transformers of society. The personal perspective represented emphasizes the interpersonal nature of teaching and the importance of reflection on the deeply personal nature of the enterprise using a process of interpersonal process recall (Kagan, 1980). While the strategic perspective was most frequently represented, it is important to note that the combined total of the other views represented 50 percent of the total responses. This leads us to conclude that the thematic foundation for the RITE program would continue to be a point of negotiation even if external forces had not intervened.

PROGRAM EVALUATION?

When designers write about program evaluation, it is usually as a systematic process similar to that described by Tyler (1949). Evaluation, whether formative or summative, is considered to be a logical process, and an extension of program development. Feedback loops modify program components.

This theoretical construct falls apart when conditions such as those described in the preceding sections prevail. In our case, the program based on 1984 standards had not been fully implemented before a new set of requirements imposed a completely new cycle of curriculum development. In this case, systematic evaluation is less than feasible. As one of our colleagues in another university expressed it, "Change is occurring too rapidly for us to study the impact of our programs."

We were able to evaluate a few of the components, however. As previously discussed, action research enabled the Phase I team to monitor student perceptions of the program and to revise the curriculum based, in part, on the responses. Forms of feedback during student teaching and affective changes in students were documented (Waxman et al., 1989). These results are more of a formative than a summative nature, however, because a comprehensive evaluation of the program was neither feasible nor desirable given that the program students completed one semester was not comparable to prior or subsequent semesters.

This leads us to speculate on the nature of evaluation in rapidly changing educational environments and the relationships between evaluation, curriculum negotiation, and the nature of reflective practice in teacher education.

SUMMARY

We have described the evolution of RITE as a process of negotiation primarily within a university setting, although subject to external factors. This discussion has been illustrative of one organization's struggle to obtain consensus regarding teacher education. Committees and the practical demands of specific instructional situations have continually modified the content and delivery of RITE. In addition, there have been internal and external challenges to the assumptions underlying the program. Consensus has often been difficult to achieve; it has been impossible to retain. Perhaps we were asking the impossible. Perhaps our collective thinking was product oriented, not process oriented. In other words, we sought to build a program that encouraged reflection in our students, but have not yet created university contexts that facilitated ongoing reflection and inquiry among our colleagues. If we accept curriculum negotiation as a norm, then how might we develop curriculum developmental processes that encourage all partners in teacher education to participate in reflective conversations?

The assumption underlying the question is that teacher education is inherently a group process and that a notion of reflection involves commitment to dialogue within a community of teacher educators. This notion runs counter to current university structures that encourage departmentalized funding, individual as opposed to collaborative ventures, and publication in refereed journals over curriculum development and redesign. Still, we feel that it is a question that is worth asking if we are serious about teacher learning and the education of all educators, including ourselves.

What began as an attempt in rational planning with Task Force I evolved into an attempt to organize a curriculum through the conceptual frame of reflective inquiry with Task Force II. The curriculum that now exists is the result of a negotiating process among diverse, and important, groups of people who are stake holders in the education of teachers. The concept of program as a fixed entity does not apply in our case. This, we feel, is the most important lesson that we have learned from the past seven years. After struggling through what reflection and inquiry might mean for our students, we have come to the understanding that such a conception is meaningless if we do not enact the concept ourselves.

Reflective, inquiry-oriented teacher educators can not—and probably should not—attempt to reach closure on the scope, content, or structure of teacher education. In our experience, closure was not possible. With hindsight we realize that it is not desirable. Rather we should seek to create structures that encourage reflective conversations, action oriented experimentation, debate, and ongoing program revision. We conclude this case with an invitation to our colleagues to work with us as we focus on making the teacher education curriculum better instead of trying to get it right.

PART II. CRITIQUES OF REFLECTIVE TEACHER EDUCATION

8

The Role of Reflection in Learning to Teach

A teacher education program is typically the product of a wide range of influencing factors, including historical and organizational features of the institution, the expertise of individual members of staff, and regional or national policy restrictions. Surprisingly, teacher education programs seem rarely to be influenced, to any substantial extent, by an understanding of how student teachers learn to teach. This may be partly attributable to the priority given, in their formation, to policy and organizational constraints, but also to the partial and limited nature of the available theory or empirical research on teachers' professional development. We know that learning to teach is a complex process, involving affective, cognitive, and performance factors and there are various psychological and sociological theories that shed some light on particular aspects of learning to teach and how this learning might be facilitated. Theories of socialization, for instance, have been used to interpret many of the beginning teacher's encounters in school (Lacey, 1977; Tabachnick and Zeichner, 1984), and theories of counseling have been used to guide the supervision of some field placements (Handal and Lauvas, 1987). As yet, however, no coherent theoretical framework is available for understanding the professional development of student teachers, and for informing the design of professional training courses.

These constraints and impediments are clearly evident in the accounts provided in this book. The authors both describe the sometimes quite powerful organizational and institutional influences on the development of their programs and also indicate the considerable uncertainty about how best to prepare students for reflective teaching and the need to trial various approaches. In spite of these difficulties, however, what characterizes these accounts is an attempt to change quite radically the nature and effects of teachers' initial training and to examine and evaluate their impact on student teachers. In each of the papers, the authors describe their particular teacher education programs for reflective teaching, outlining the beliefs that shaped their innovative work, the difficulties they have encountered, how their programs have evolved over time, and the particular activities that they employ to promote reflective practice.

CONCEPTUALIZING REFLECTION

From these accounts it is apparent that the authors' conceptions vary not only with respect to the nature of the reflective process, but also concerning what it is teachers reflect about, and how student teachers might become reflective. Ciriello, Valli, and Taylor, for instance, view reflection as a deliberative process concerned to a large extent with the consideration of values implicit in alternative practices. They suggest an important aspect of deliberation is for teachers to consider the ethical implications of their work, and student teachers are encouraged to become more reflective through documenting their observations and experiences and to make explicit the ethical, moral, and political implications of routine classroom decisions. McCaleb, Borko, and Arends, on the other hand, view reflective teaching more in terms of the utilization of a professional knowledge base. Critical thought is seen as relying on a sophisticated understanding of classroom processes, and therefore a major component of becoming a reflective teacher lies in developing a language, and way of thinking, about teaching and learning which can be achieved through the critical examination of empirical research studies. Ross, Johnson, and Smith view the reflective teacher as one who holds a personal philosophy of teaching. Becoming a reflective teacher is considered to be a matter of critically examining one's own and other's educational beliefs, and developing a coherent, articulated view of teaching and learning. Despite the differing emphases in these conceptions of reflective practice, there is, nevertheless, some general agreement that the reflective teacher is one who is able to analyze their own practice and the context in which it occurs; the reflective teacher is expected to be able to stand back from their own teaching, evaluate their situation and take responsibility for their own future action. The extent to which reflective teachers are expected to take into consideration personal, organizational, social, ethical, and political factors in their deliberation, however, differs from one teacher education program to another.

PROMOTING REFLECTION

While there is some variation in the defined goals of these programs, there is probably even greater divergence on how these goals might be achieved. Is it more appropriate, for instance, for student teachers to start their teacher training by looking at the wider context of teaching and the educational values within the community served by a school, as suggested by Clift, Houston, and McCarthy, or to start by examining the diverse assumptions about teaching, learning and the curriculum that student teachers themselves start out with in training, as proposed by Ross, Johnson, and Smith? Is the training course for reflective teaching better oriented towards engaging students in the processes of reflection or should it focus more on the substance, or knowledge base, that might inform reflection? The difficulty with such questions is that they are probably unanswerable in any general way. We know that student teachers approach teacher training with different ideas and expectations about their own professional development (Book, Byers, and Freeman, 1983; Calderhead, 1988; Korthagen, 1988). Many, for instance, expect to be told how to teach either by their college tutors or by teachers in school, some expect to learn from their own trial and error, others expect to model their practice on a teacher familiar to them, a few regard learning to teach as completely unproblematic, it is an activity that everyone can do and there is little need for training.

Student teachers also start out their training with diverse views about the nature of teaching, learning, and the curriculum. Teaching and learning may well be regarded in basic terms of teachers showing or telling, and children memorizing, and different subject areas may be viewed in terms of particular techniques, skills, or knowledge. Wilson and Wineburg (1988) for example demonstrate how beginning teachers can hold quite different conceptions of history. Brickhouse (1990) demonstrates how alternative views of science amongst teachers can lead to quite different practices. Contrasting views of scientific theory as truths or as tools to solve problems, for example, were found to be associated with different educational goals and activities valued and practiced by teachers.

Various methods nevertheless are suggested for how reflective teaching might be fostered among student teachers. Journals and learning logs are frequently incorporated into the programs, and ways of working collaboratively with other students, teachers, and tutors in such a manner as to foster the criticism and sharing of ideas are described. Think aloud protocols and microteaching are suggested as means of focusing analysis on particular aspects of teaching. Writing about one's own beliefs and contrasting them with alternative beliefs in the literature is viewed as a way of encouraging awareness and reflection, as are studies of schools and their communities, or action research studies focusing on the classroom.

TAKING ACCOUNT OF INDIVIDUAL DIFFERENCES IN LEARNING TO REFLECT

These methods, employed in various combinations, aim to develop skills of critical analysis, knowledge related to teaching and its context, and attitudes of openness and self-awareness. Their actual effects upon students, however, are obviously less predictable. Because student teachers approach preservice training with different knowledge and perspectives, they may progress towards reflective teaching in different ways. They will inevitably learn in diverse ways and take different meanings from the experiences that are offered to them. Some students, for example, may have the appropriate attitudes, knowledge, and skills to analyze and appraise their entering conceptions of teaching, while others may need considerable and varied experience of classroom observation and teaching before they are able to identify their own preconceptions. Yet others may need to acquire confidence in themselves as teachers before they can begin to look critically at their own ideas or practices. It can be a highly frustrating and apparently futile task for some students who have come to preservice training with the expectation to be told how to teach, to be asked to reflect on their own experience or make explicit their own beliefs; and students who expect to learn by being told may find quite different experiences to be professionally enriching from those that are appreciated by students who are oriented to learn from their own action. Similarly, for tutors, it can be highly tempting, when observing a student in difficulty with their teaching, simply to tell the student what they appear to need to know, rather than encourage the student to analyze the difficulty and evaluate their own solution. Obtaining appropriate behavior from the student may at times be at the cost of encouraging reflection. The implication of this is that in order to promote reflective teaching, teacher trainers must be aware not only of the attitudes, skills, and knowledge that they wish to encourage, and how these might be facilitated, but also of the many alternative routes and ways in which students' professional development might progress.

IMPEDIMENTS TO REFLECTIVE TEACHING

Developing reflective practice, in fact, places heavy demands upon both tutors in college and supervising teachers in schools, requiring them to develop a complex conception of student teachers' professional growth, and monitor the various changes in the students they supervise. Teachers and tutors encounter at least two major impediments in carrying out this task, both of which are implicit or explicit in the accounts provided in the earlier sections of this book. The first impediment is the general lack of knowledge about student teachers' professional growth. Relevant theory and empirical research is sparse, and as indicated in several of the papers, there is little to guide the practice of teachers and tutors involved in programs aiming to promote reflective teaching. For example, Ross, Johnson, and Smith are able to draw upon research on teachers' images and metaphors to devise some initial training activities for student teachers on personal theories of teachers. But such activities are experimental and teachers and tutors learn to manage such activities through their own trial and error involvement, and develop their own understanding of student teachers' professional growth in the process.

A second major impediment arises when teachers and tutors find themselves in institutions, where typically the values, expectations, and accepted practices do not support their role as facilitators of reflective practice. For example, teacher training institutions are frequently reported to enshrine a "technical skills" ethos of training (Lanier and Little, 1986). The teacher educator is viewed as expert teacher and trainer who possesses the required expertise to be passed on to trainee teachers. This may well foster a closed rather than open-minded attitude within the institutions, suggesting that good practice is widely agreed, accepted, and available to be modeled and learned, rather than open to question, analysis, and individual development. Similarly, schools frequently do not present an environment in which experimentation, innovation, and reflection are supported (Goodlad, 1983). Teachers are viewed as trained practitioners, working alone, responsible for their own classes, with little need for reflection or discussion. As a result of these various constraints, teachers and tutors can experience frequent dilemmas in how most appropriately to help their students.

For example, when faced with the expectation that they act as assessors of students and guardians to the profession, how do teachers and tutors reconcile this with an ideal of developing reflection and self-empowerment? How can one facilitate the development of a student teacher's own values when one knows they conflict sharply with the values generally accepted within the profession itself? How can one prepare student teachers for the real world of teaching where action is often valued more highly than reflection, and decisiveness more than evaluation?

These roles are difficult though not altogether incompatible. Any professional group has standards of behavior and practice that are expected to be upheld in order to maintain membership of the group, and part of learning to be a teacher is to appreciate where the boundaries lie and where and where not they might be manipulated. Consequently, while teacher educators may wish to encourage students to examine critically accepted beliefs and practices, they must also consider introducing students to the social and political realities of teachers' work. This dual task of the teacher and tutor—to help students develop informed self-direction and responsibility for their own professional development and at the same time to appreciate the demands within and beyond the profession—nevertheless presents many individual difficulties and dilemmas in the process of supervising and developing reflective practice. These difficulties also emphasize the need to consider the social and professional context of learning to teach in developing a reflective teacher program, a point well taken up by Oja et al. who attempt, in their program, to develop a culture of collaboration and "co-exploration." If beginning teachers are to develop critical reflection, they will need support in these activities from the schools in which they are placed, and reflective teacher education programs clearly need to give consideration to the social factors influencing student teachers' professional growth.

In short, teachers and tutors must themselves become reflective practitioners working in a complex and value laden area with many competing beliefs about good practice and with many values implicit within the taken for granted practices and procedures of their institution. Part of being a tutor for reflective teaching is being able to evaluate competing demands and consider the effects of alternative tutoring strategies. And due to our lack of knowledge about learning to teach, and the inevitable need for experimentation, there is a need for constant evaluation and development to monitor and adjust the form that these innovatory programs take. The burden of this task falls very heavily on tutors and supervising teachers.

DEVELOPING REFLECTIVE TEACHER PROGRAMS

Consequently, while the ideals of reflective teaching may be relatively well described, the processes of implementing these are not so clear cut. There are few well-established ground rules for teacher educators in this new area, and as a result tutors and supervising teachers are required constantly to examine what they are doing and where they are going. Teacher educators have set themselves some ambitious aims in reflective teaching and it is as yet uncertain what is actually achievable in the context of a preservice training program. Van Manen, for example, whose work is drawn upon in several of the preceding papers, defines reflection at three different levels: technical rationality, which is concerned with the efficient application of knowledge to achieve accepted goals; practical action, which involves consideration of the values implicit in alternative actions and their consequences; and critical reflection which concerns the ethical and moral dimensions of educational practices.

But is it possible, or reasonable, to have students graduate from preservice training able to engage competently at all three levels? Or is this, in fact, a more realistic target for a teacher ten to fifteen years into a teaching career? And can we expect all teachers to reach these levels or are they ideals only likely to be attained by a few? And to what extent is it reasonable to hold out these ideals for individual teachers, or is it more reasonable to acknowledge that reflective practice is most likely to occur within communities of reflective practitioners who can support one another, and create an ethos in which reflection, analysis, and evaluation can thrive? Ought we to be thinking much more of reflective practice as a long-term aim referring to communities of teachers working together, rather than a short-term aim for individual teachers?

These questions can only be answered through the experience of teacher educators, and the evaluation of that experience, in developing teacher education programs for reflective practice and in promoting our understanding of professional growth. In the process of developing reflective teaching as a goal of preservice education, there is a need to develop our own knowledge about reflective teaching and how it is facilitated. In particular, we clearly need to know much more about the ways in which student teachers learn to become reflective practitioners. We need to know how the individual characteristics of the student teacher, the demands of the alternative training activities we present to them, and the contexts in which they work in schools interact. We need to develop much greater knowledge of what reflection involves, and the different ways in which relevant knowledge, skills, and attitudes are developed. This can only come through a thorough evaluation of the types of experimental programs described in this book: evaluations which examine in some detail how student teachers are learning to teach, and how their learning is influenced not just within the program but in later years of professional life, for preservice education may well only be able to initiate certain reflective processes that need further nurturing in teachers' later careers. In addition, if we are seriously to pursue the goal of reflective teaching for a substantial number of teachers in schools, we need to place the issue of teachers' own professional learning much higher up the agenda of teachers' in-service training needs. Teachers in school who supervise student teachers have to become aware of how their own and other teachers' professional development occurs, and the ways in which they might facilitate its growth. A greater focus in in-service training is needed on how to foster reflective schools that are facilitative of the professional growth not only of new teachers in school but of those already there.

This may well in fact represent the greatest obstacle to the dissemination of reflective practice. Before we can have reflective teachers, we need reflective schools and reflective teacher educators. Programs of reflective teaching, like any form of preservice training, cannot be viewed as isolated experiences that on their own prepare student teachers for a career in the classroom. They are part of a continuous, life-long process of professional development. As teacher educators we need to improve our own understanding of that development and the professional needs of teachers at all levels.

9

In the Eye of the Beholder: Cognitive, Critical, and Narrative Approaches to Teacher Reflection

The exact meaning of the term "teacher reflection" is difficult to pin down. Most who use the term would probably agree that the opposite of reflective action is the mindless following of unexamined practices or principles. But within that agreement, there is quite a range of opinion regarding what reflection is and what it looks like in action. Thus, reflection has no one definition; it is perceived in the eye of the beholder.

This chapter presents three approaches to understanding teachers' reflective thinking. The first is the Cognitive Approach, which includes studies of teachers' information processing and decision making. The second, the Critical Approach, has its roots in ethical and moral reasoning. The final approach to reflection, the Narrative Approach, refers to teachers telling their own stories through problem framing, naturalistic inquiry, and case studies. The chapter concludes with an analysis of how the seven programs presented in this book fit into the three approaches to reflection.

THE COGNITIVE APPROACH TO REFLECTION

The cognitive approach to teacher reflection focuses on the knowledge and processes involved in teacher decision making. Shulman (1987) has described six categories of knowledge: content; pedagogy; curriculum; characteristics of learners; contexts; and educational purposes, ends, and aims. The idea of "pedagogical content knowledge," which encompasses the first three categories, refers to how teachers portray important ideas specific to their content. These representations or metaphors enable the teacher to convey complex ideas in ways that bring meaning to students.

Most cognitive researchers have not delved deeply into the last two aspects of the knowledge base—contexts and educational purposes, ends, and aims. They tend to stick with what van Manen (1977) might call the technical level of reflection where the purposes often remain unexamined. We will see later, however, that the narrative approach to reflection stresses the consideration of context factors, while the critical view emphasizes the questioning of the purposes, ends, and aims of education.

Another focus of cognitive research is how the knowledge base is organized. Cognitivists think of information as organized into a network of related facts, concepts, generalizations, and experiences. These organized structures, called *schemata*, constitute the individual's comprehension of the world and allow a large body of information to be stored and accessed with enormous speed (Anderson, 1984; Berliner, 1986). Studies of novice and expert teachers' interpretations of classroom events have indicated that experts have deeper, more richly connected schemata to draw upon when making a decision. In contrast, novices tend to have leaner, less developed schemata, presumably because of a lack of experience (Leinhardt and Greeno, 1986).

Carter and her colleagues (1988) studied how experts, novices, and aspiring teachers perceive visual information about classrooms. She observed that experts were "better able to weigh the import of one piece of visual information against another, to form connections among pieces of information, and to represent management and instructional situations into meaningful problem units" (p. 25). This ability was attributed to the experts' more elaborate, complex, and interconnected schemata. These schemata first help determine which events merit attention, and second, trigger other relevant information from memory so the teacher can determine an appropriate response.

Schemata do not automatically appear in a teacher's mind; they are constructed through experience. Constructivist theory (Clark and

Peterson, 1986) indicates that individuals are constantly constructing their own meaning out of what is perceived. This is a dual process of assimilation (fitting the new in with the old) and accommodation (changing the old mental organization to incorporate the new) (Piaget, 1978). Therefore, the experiences, values, and beliefs stored in memory have a major influence on how a new piece of information is perceived and interpreted. Such "culturally based filters" have been investigated by Hollingsworth (1990) and others (Ross, 1990), with the result that teacher educators are now giving more attention to how preconceptions about the aims of education can influence what college students do (and do not) learn from teacher education programs.

Lampert and Clark (1990) believe schema theory may give too little importance to context factors. They refer to "situated cognition," which suggests that knowledge is constructed through the interaction between the mind and the context surrounding the problem. Thus, rather than apply a generalized schema (learned rules, principles, or concepts) to a problem, teachers may make a case-by-case response to the particulars of a problem. If this is true, then greater opportunities need to be provided for future teachers to "anchor" their knowledge and experience in rich educational contexts.

One conclusion some have drawn from the cognitive research is that we should teach novices the schemata of experts. But, this would be ignoring the lessons learned from constructivism (we each must construct our own meaning) and from situated cognition (expert teachers probably draw on their own contextually developed knowledge and prior case-experience to develop their own wisdom of practice.) The development of professional judgment might also be short-circuited. While research can inform one about how complex and uncertain teaching is, it "cannot describe the sorts of decisions teachers should be taught to make in any particular situation" (Lampert and Clark, 1990, p. 29).

THE CRITICAL APPROACH TO REFLECTION

While the cognitive approach emphasizes *how* teachers make decisions, the critical approach stresses the *what* of those decisions by examining the experiences, values, and goals of teachers in terms of their sociopolitical implications. The literature on critical reflection derives mostly from the philosophical base of critical theory (McLaren, 1989; Tom, 1985). These views have enriched current views of teaching by highlighting the importance of teachers' thinking about the dilemmas of teaching and the social outcomes of education (Smyth, 1989).

Many who use the term teacher reflection think of it in terms of critical pedagogy. McLaren (1989) stated that "critical pedagogy attempts to provide teachers and researchers with a better means of understanding the role that schools actually play within a race, class, and gender-divided society" (p. 163). When teacher educators refer to helping teachers examine the ethical, moral, and justice issues in education, they refer to opening up a discourse about the role of schools in a democratic society. Students are urged to question common practices such as tracking, ability grouping, competitive grading, and behavioral control. They are encouraged to clarify their own beliefs about the purposes of education and to critically examine teaching methods and materials for hidden lessons about equity and power.

Critical theorists see knowledge as *socially constructed*, that is, constructed symbolically by the mind through social interaction with others. This knowledge is determined by the surrounding culture, context, custom, and historical era (McLaren, 1989). While cognitivists also view knowledge as socially constructed, the critical approach places more importance on life values and morals—for example, conceptions of justice, ideas about the purpose of the individual in a democracy, ethics related to treatment of students, and so on. All of these would be heavily dependent on the social milieu in which the teacher develops.

We see in critical pedagogy a reaction against what many have seen as an antiseptic, value-free, purely rational view of teaching and learning. Ross (1990) has described five elements of teachers' thinking which combine various aspects of cognitive, critical, and narrative reflection:

1. Recognizing an educational dilemma.
2. Responding to a dilemma by recognizing both the similarities to other situations and the unique qualities of the particular situation.
3. Framing and reframing the dilemma.
4. Experimenting with the dilemma to discover the consequences and implications of various solutions.
5. Examining the intended and unintended consequences of an implemented solution and evaluating the solution by determining whether the consequences are desirable or not. (p. 22)

Element five brings us to a key thinking process in critical pedagogy (McLaren, 1989), the examination of the relationship between power and knowledge. Knowledge should be examined "for the way it misrepresents or marginalizes particular views of the world" (p. 183).

That is, many accepted facts and explanations are biased in favor of the group in power at the time when the ideas were formed. Teachers, then, need to see teaching and learning as a process of inquiry into the problematic by asking questions such as, If we use this process or content, what is the long-term effect on students' values, and thus on society? Through such questions emerges a "language of hope" for bringing about greater social equity.

THE NARRATIVE APPROACH TO REFLECTION

Cochran-Smith and Lytle (1990) wrote, "what is missing from the knowledge base of teaching . . . are the voices of the teachers themselves, the questions teachers ask, the ways teachers use writing and intentional talk in their work lives, and the interpretive frames teachers use to understand and improve their own classroom practices" (p. 2). They have stated the essence of the narrative approach to reflection. While this approach may include cognitive or critical aspects, the main emphasis is on teachers' own descriptions of *the personal circumstances under which* they make decisions.

Many terms and concepts are joined together in this view of reflection: wisdom of practice (Shulman, 1987), craft knowledge (Leinhardt, 1990), art/aesthetics of teaching (Eisner, 1982; Kagan, 1988), teacher action research (Cochran-Smith and Lytle, 1990), and narrative inquiry (Connelly and Clandinin, 1990). The common thread through all of these is the emphasis on the validity of teachers' inferences drawn from their own experiences.

The narrative view is sympathetic with Schön's (1983, 1987) notion of "giving reason" because the teachers' voices themselves comprise the story. Schön (1983) first analyzed the work of architects and other professionals to see how they reflected on their actions. Surprisingly, he found little emphasis on traditional problem *solving*. Instead of using a rational process of selecting the best solution for an agreed-upon goal, these professionals engaged in an open debate of the nature of the decisions, the value of the goals, and the ultimate implications of the actions. Schön referred to this reflective dialog as problem *setting*. He also found among teachers and others an artistic comfort with ambiguity and no-one-right-answer thinking, and a recognition of the nonlinear, uncertain complexity of professional practice.

Schön does not refer to a cognitive "knowledge base" for teaching; rather, he refers to an "appreciation system." This system contains the teacher's repertoire of theories, practices, knowledge, and values which influence how situations are defined, what is noticed, and the kinds of questions and decisions teachers will form about particular actions. While teachers acquire some professional knowledge from "packaged" educational principles and skills, the bulk of their learning comes through continuous action and reflection on everyday problems.

Schön (1987) has written extensively about the thinking processes of a reflective practitioner. To (over)simplify, as teachers describe, analyze, and make inferences about classroom events, they are creating their own pedagogical principles. These "short-range theories" (Smyth, 1989) help make sense of what is going on and guide further action. The information gained from this experience is often tacit and difficult to analyze.

In one sense, the whole emphasis on critical and narrative teacher reflection could be seen as the "bridge" into a new way of thinking about research on teaching. Since many who study the process of learning to teach were trained in the quantitative/experimental research tradition, this can be a tough leap. Yet, researchers are now truly listening and learning from teachers' stories (e.g., Huberman, 1990). The development of critical pedagogy is now being actively investigated (Zeichner and Liston, 1987). More and more examples of critical and narrative reflection are beginning to appear in professional journals. Still, we are at the uncomfortable stage where many are writing about the need for such research and too few are doing it. Further, we find little evidence that teachers are being encouraged to see their own stories as valuable and to write for publication about their experiences and beliefs.

APPROACHES TO REFLECTION IN THE SEVEN PROGRAMS

Each of the programs presented in this book has its own guiding concepts, definition of reflection, and approach to inquiry. Table 9.1 categorizes each program in terms of the emphasis placed on cognitive, critical, or narrative reflection. The programs are discussed in detail below.

University of Maryland

The University of Maryland (UM) program is predominantly cognitive in its orientation. The knowledge base upon which the program is built and the titles of the courses reflect an emphasis on research produced by educational psychologists: effective teaching, models of teaching, effective schools, quantitative research methods, and so on. There is no mention of philosophical, sociological, or historical foundations as

TABLE 9.1

Dominant Approaches to Reflection in Seven Teacher Education Programs

Program	Knowledge Base	Definition of Reflection	Inquiry Activities
University of Maryland	Cognitive	Cognitive	Cognitive
University of Florida	Narrative Critical	Narrative Critical	Narrative Critical
University of New Hampshire	Critical Narrative	Critical Narrative	Narrative
Catholic University of America	Cognitive Critical	Cognitive Critical	Cognitive Critical
Michigan State University	Cognitive Critical	Cognitive Critical	Cognitive Critical
Kent State University	Cognitive Critical	Cognitive Critical	Cognitive Critical Narrative
University of Houston	Cognitive Critical	Cognitive Critical	Cognitive Critical

part of the knowledge base, and the critical approach is seen as a "different paradigm."

The definition of reflection in the UM program is presented as problem solving through applying the information gleaned from the knowledge base: taking action, reflecting, and coming up with alternative actions. The higher level of critical thought (including multiple causes, conflicting goals, or larger moral or ethical conflicts) is only sought when no solution for the problem is reached. Interestingly, at a retreat midway through the first cycle of the program, the definition of reflection was "extended beyond technical classroom analysis [to include] . . . involvement in teachers' organizations and broader issues than the individual classroom" (p. 51). Here, we see an edging toward a critical view of reflection.

The inquiry activities at UM include guided field experiences and action research. The field experiences are in laboratory schools where students are seen as reflective scholar-teachers, rather than apprentices. The action research projects offer opportunities for more formal investigations, most of which appear to be quantitative/cognitive in nature. The one student who was using scripting and journaling to study her own thinking about how to handle call-outs during discussions provides an example of the narrative approach to reflection.

University of Florida

The PROTEACH program at the University of Florida (UF) is predominantly narrative and critical in its approach to reflection. It appears that over a period of several years the faculty have formed a common vision of the purposes of teacher education. The knowledge base used in the program draws heavily on the teacher socialization and reflection literature (e.g., Schön, 1983) which includes both the processes of reflective judgment and the ethical/moral framework used for making decisions. The program shares a view of learning as socially and politically constructed by students and teachers, clearly echoing a critical perspective.

In PROTEACH, an understanding of reflection has been growing gradually as faculty inquire into the phenomenon. The current view of reflection is based heavily on the ability to reveal and confront one's own perspectives about teaching. Two frameworks have been created, one for the components of mature reflection and one for the evaluation of reflective judgment in PROTEACH students (p. 27). While some cognitive aspects are mentioned (e.g., knowledge of subject matter), the majority of the ideas stress critical and narrative processes such as viewing teaching as problematic, monitoring the effects of actions, open-mindedness, ethical knowledge, and viewing situations from multiple perspectives.

In PROTEACH, inquiry is often seen as a critical and narrative examination of the self. For example, students explore their personal theories of teaching both at the beginning and end of the program. These explorations are made through narrative autobiographical writings about significant learning experiences, influential teachers, and so on. The students then look for "implicit beliefs" within their writing. Finally, they critique their views and judge how well their view fits with the context of their next teaching setting.

University of New Hampshire

The University of New Hampshire (UNH) program is organized around functional groupings for the purpose of support and inquiry. The program is guided by adult development theory, which stresses growth, risk-taking, and analytical thinking in safe environments. The curriculum includes philosophy of education, human development and learning, models of teaching, and topics related to public education and change. The main goal of the program is for students to develop their own personal philosophy and style which may draw on a large repertoire of justifiable alternatives. The value placed on finding a personal meaning in one's own reality echos the narrative tradition. By not relying on an "undisputed knowledge base" for the program, the UNH developers have given future teachers a chance to create their own stories of teaching.

Here we see adult developmental psychology applied to teacher preparation—a rare occurrence, at least in the programs presented here. While this lends a bit of a cognitive orientation to the program, it is not the more typical teacher-effectiveness or teacher-thinking emphasis. The critical perspective is apparent (a) in the approach to knowledge as indeterminant and eclectic; (b) in the beginning course in philosophical inquiry which stresses critical examination of one's own views and those of others; and (c) in the view of teachers as autonomous professionals who must make ethical and moral choices.

The UNH faculty have defined the reflective teacher as a decision maker who is guided by his or her own philosophical constructs to make informed choices. Students are encouraged to develop a teaching style that fits in with their own carefully examined values, interests, strengths, and abilities. These personal orientations are developed through inquiry activities conducted in courses and in extensive field experiences. Co-inquiry groups enable the students to consider and question differing and conflicting theories and beliefs.

Group inquiry conducted in classes and field activities forms the centerpiece of the program. The initial weekly field experience serves as a screening device. The students who are accepted into the program then complete courses with various practicum activities and a year-long internship. Seminars and collaborative triads help students experiment, explore, and write about their developing expertise and philosophies.

While most programs provide the classroom teacher with relatively little support, UNH has used collaborative supervisory teams to promote the professional growth of the principal, teacher, and university supervisor. At first, teams explored how varying supervisory strategies could be used with student teachers at varying developmental levels. Later topics tended to focus on teaching and learning strategies, content, or school issues. The participants gained much through actively inquiring into an issue that had been a consistent challenge to them.

The emphasis on collaborative action research in all components of the UNH program provides a fine example of the narrative orientation to reflection. Because of the importance placed on "telling one's own story," the UNH program is probably one of the strongest examples of narrative reflection in this book.

Catholic University

The Catholic University (CUA) program began with a cognitive emphasis on transfer of theory into practice. Students were encouraged to engage in "reflective problem solving" by attending to the context in which they were applying their learning. After the first year, the program developers created a conceptual framework that was more closely aligned with critical reflection. The framework includes multiple perspectives provided by: the four commonplaces of teaching (students, teacher, subject, context), three types of dilemmas (control, curriculum, and society), and three levels of reflection (technical, interpretive, and critical). Courses were redesigned to be congruent with this framework.

The CUA definition of reflection therefore draws heavily on the multiple perspectives presented in the framework. Students are expected to reflect critically on the ethical, moral, and political ramifications of their daily decisions rather than merely "doing what works" or blindly imitating another teacher's (or the book's) methods. One gets the idea, however, that cognitive problem solving has not been ignored in the move toward a more critical orientation.

As in many other programs, inquiry is promoted through field experiences and action research. Students are required to write guided journals reflecting on their field experiences. These narratives of their thoughts, feelings, and actions are completed in triplicate and shared among the professors, students (with feedback), and university supervisors. Thus, all the players in the program read the student's stories, insights, and concerns.

The action research project is structured by a "Situation Analysis Guide" which helps students follow a problem-solving model, use theories and research, and reflect on normative and technical aspects of the problem. The final integrated paper combines the above cognitive and critical aspects of reflection in its analysis of the student's learning. If written in a personal voice, the paper may well serve the purposes of narrative reflection by telling a story of how one learns to think about the dilemmas of teaching and learning.

Michigan State University

The program at Michigan State University (MSU) appears to have integrated cognitive and critical reflection. The knowledge base for the program emphasizes four functions of schooling: two cognitive (academic outcomes and personal responsibility) and two critical (social responsibility and social justice). When students prepare for teaching or analyze their teaching, they are encouraged to write justifications for each of these functions. The courses appear to move students from technical and personal competence (methods, human growth) to personal and critical competence (social and philosophical issues). In this program, knowledge is seen not as a vehicle for reproducing existing values, but as a means for transforming ourselves and society—clearly, a critical approach.

The definition of reflection includes the "interactive ability to think, understand, and act on a number of levels"—technical, clinical, personal, and critical (p. 89). The assumptions underlying the program reflect both the technical and critical orientations to reflection, with an indirect reference to the artistry of teaching—a touch of the narrative approach. The developers of the program recognize that incongruities often arise between theory and practice and that these cause discomfort. They echo Schön's perspective that not all dilemmas are reconcilable, and that accepting such uncertainties is a crucial part of reflective practice.

MSU's inquiry component includes field experiences with a concurrent Decision-Making Lab and a self-designed study of practice during student teaching. While some decision-making processes are taught during the Lab (e.g., problem solving), students also critically discuss ethical issues that arise in the field experiences. The action research study encourages student teachers to critically examine their own thinking and practice as they experiment with various teaching and learning strategies. These are presented formally at a dinner-conference.

Kent State University

The program for certification of academically talented students at Kent State University (KSU) develops multiple perspectives and cognitive complexity through inquiry activities based on psychological, sociological, and critical viewpoints. By defining educational practice as problematic, students are encouraged to challenge assumptions and question commonly accepted practices as they inquire into teaching and learning. Here we see a combination of the cognitive and critical approaches to reflection.

Reflection at KSU is defined as the development of conceptual flexibility through exploring teaching, learning, and schooling using a variety of approaches—psychological, sociological, and critical. The authors hope that the constant examination of educational information and knowledge in relationship to their own ideas, experiences, and values will enrich the cognitive complexity of students.

The inquiry activities at KSU are built around a series of discussion seminars that engage students in problem solving, critical thinking, and other complex cognitive processes. The first seminar is Inquiry into Learning, followed by Inquiry into Schooling and Research in Teaching. Field experiences are provided in the same setting throughout the program—a practice which may hamper the program goal of promoting multiple perspectives.

Action research projects are conducted during the sixteen-week internship at the end of the program. These are integrated into a "Learning to Teach Autobiography" required in the final semester. A strong narrative emphasis is seen as the students take all the data they have collected throughout the program (evaluations, journals, etc.) and discuss in writing five areas: past, present, and future career experiences; changes in self, knowledge, and learning; problems and conflicts encountered; direct and indirect learnings; and future directions. These narratives provided much of the data for the authors' naturalistic inquiry into program outcomes.

University of Houston

The RITE program at the University of Houston (UH) has been dramatically affected by local and state mandates regarding the structure of teacher education. The chapter presents a case study of "negotiated" curriculum-making in teacher education as the authors tell the story of the program's evolution and derailment by outside forces. From this perspective, the entire chapter represents a narrative approach or self-reflection by the program developers.

The RITE program as originally designed represents a combination of cognitive and critical reflection. The knowledge base provided in the courses came from social foundations (critical) and effective teaching research (cognitive). The program first taught the students a critical perspective, moved them into technical skills of teaching, and then at the end of the program combined the two perspectives as the students critically examined their technical decisions and actions.

The RITE program defined reflection as "the disposition and ability to consider education as the result of many social, political, and individual factors accompanied by an understanding of the need to base subsequent action on careful analysis of the results of such inquiry" (p. 127). The development of a personal philosophy of teaching was also stressed.

Inquiry opportunities were highly structured around field and microteaching experiences. To develop a critical perspective, students conducted a study of a school community in a neighborhood unlike their own, and began to explore the functions of schools as a facilitator of personal and social change. Technical teaching skills were developed through microteaching, structured observation with analysis of classroom data, and the use of videotapes.

While the developers of the RITE program state in their chapter that they do not represent the critical orientation, there exists a strong dose of the critical perspective combined with the cognitive/effective teaching approaches to reflective thinking. Unfortunately, because the program was stalled as of this writing, we may never find out how successful the entire program could be.

CONCLUSIONS AND OBSERVATIONS

Most of the programs presented in this book strive to develop a combination of cognitive and critical reflection. Some have encouraged students (or teachers, as at UNH) to engage in narrative inquiry, another form of reflection. Having been immersed in our own program to develop reflection at Eastern Michigan University (Sparks et al, 1990), and as a result of reviewing literature on various approaches to reflection (Sparks-Langer and Colton, 1991), I find that my own perspectives about reflective teaching are changing.

When I finished my doctorate at Stanford University in 1983, I was convinced that effective teaching research could provide some valuable insights, concepts, and "springboards" for teachers' professional decision making. After close study of teachers' implementation of these "effective" practices (Sparks, 1988), it became clear to me that experienced teachers needed to be treated as professionals, and that any "research" would have to be presented honestly, with a clear description of its sample, limitations, and findings (Sparks and Simmons, 1989). I saw the importance of encouraging teachers to question, probe, and sift through research-based teaching practices to pull out the "nuggets" they wished to pursue further. Through work with Jane Stallings, I learned the value of small, safe inquiry groups where teachers could share ideas and wrestle with dilemmas. This was a place for telling stories and constructing meaning out of the perplexing aspects of teaching.

As I observed the movement in the mid- to late-1980s from the study of teaching behavior to the study of teacher thinking, and as I became more involved with teacher preparation, I could see the crucial need to better understand how teachers develop and use professional knowledge and experience. I was inspired to think deeply about the results of the cognitive novice-expert studies. But I always felt something was lacking.

In-depth conversations with teacher friends have led me to see how incomplete our knowledge about teaching is. While the rational, cognitive processes are crucial to professional practice, I now realize more fully that teaching is an expression of the essence of who we are, and as such, must reflect our values, beliefs, and souls. Because of this, I have been strongly drawn to the critical and narrative approaches to teacher reflection. I believe these ideas are beginning to fill in our understanding of educational practice by honoring and legitimatizing the less explored but surely more essential aspects of teaching. It is, perhaps, in the eye (and the heart) of the beholder that the essence of truly great teaching lies.

10

Conceptions of Reflective Teaching in Contemporary U.S. Teacher Education Program Reforms

THE CURRENT MOVEMENT IN REFLECTIVE TEACHER EDUCATION

Along with the growing influence in educational research of cognitive psychology and interpretative sociological and anthropological perspectives (e.g., Reilly, 1989; Erickson, 1986), the subsequent and predictable growth in studies of teacher thinking (Clark, 1988) and increased interest in and respect for the practical theories of teachers (e.g., Elbaz, 1983), the term reflection has become a slogan around which teacher educators all over the world have rallied in the name of teacher education reform. In addition to efforts in the United States to make reflective inquiry the central component of teacher education program reforms (e.g., Cruickshank, 1987; Waxman et al., 1988; Clift, Houston, and Pugach, 1990; Tabachnick and Zeichner,1991), we have seen similar efforts in such countries as the United Kingdom (e.g., Lucas,

1988; Ashcroft and Griffiths, 1989; Pollard and Tann, 1987); Canada (e.g., Clandinin and Connelly, 1986; Mackinnon and Erickson, 1988); Australia (Gore, 1987; Robottom, 1988; Martinez, 1989); and continential Europe (e.g., Korthagen, 1985; Altrichter, 1988; Handal and Lauvas, 1989).

Concurrent with this rapid growth of teacher education program reforms based on the concept of reflective inquiry has been the emergence of a research literature that has sought to clarify the conceptual distinctions among proposals for reflective teacher education (e.g., Tom, 1985; Calderhead, 1989; Grimmett et al., 1990; and Valli, 1990a). One of the most notable characteristics of this emerging literature on reflective inquiry in teaching and teacher education is its ahistorical nature. Other than efforts that have been made to situate individual programs of work in relation to the broader theories and world views from which they draw their support (e.g., critical theory), there have been few attempts to either discuss the emergence of the reflective inquiry movement or to locate programs of work in relation to the traditions of practice which have characterized the field itself.[1]

Several efforts have been made in recent years to identify the major traditions of practice in teacher education.[2] Drawing on these and on the seminal work of Kliebard (1986) on the development of the public school curriculum in the United States in the twentieth century, Zeichner and Liston (1990) identified four major traditions of reform in U.S. teacher education. This framework was later extended by Zeichner and Tabachnick (1991) to address the specific issue of reflective inquiry in teacher education. Four historically based traditions of reflective teaching were discussed in this extension of the original framework. After a brief discussion of these four traditions in the section to follow, we will consider the seven cases presented earlier in this volume in relation to those traditions so that the educational and social commitments embedded in each program's use of the term reflection can be examined.

TRADITIONS OF REFLECTION IN U.S. TEACHER EDUCATION

In our examination of the development of teacher education in the United States in the twentieth century, Dan Liston and I concluded that there have been four distinct traditions of practice which have, at least implicitly, guided reform efforts. While each of these traditions is somewhat diverse (e.g., feminist and critical theory perspectives within social reconstructionism), they also each represent a common commitment to a core set of beliefs. When we examined the current literature in light of these four traditions of practice, Bob Tabachnick and I (Zeichner and Tabachnick, 1991) identified four varieties of reflective teaching practice: academic, social efficiency, developmentalist, and social reconstructionist.

Despite the differences in emphasis given to various factors within the different traditions of reflective teaching, these traditions are not mutually exclusive. In practice the traditions overlap and each attends in some manner to all the issues raised by the traditions as a group. The differences among the traditions are in terms of the emphasis and meaning given to particular factors within a tradition. Through these priorities, each tradition communicates an allegiance to particular styles of teaching and a rejection of others. With the exception of the social reconstructionist tradition, the traditions reflect a benign view of the social order.

The Academic Tradition

Prior to the existence of formal programs of teacher education, a classical liberal education was equivalent to being prepared to teach (Borrowman, 1965). As programs for the preparation of both elementary and secondary teachers became established in colleges and universities, the point of view persisted that a sound liberal arts education, complemented by an apprenticeship experience in a school, was the most sensible way to prepare teachers for their work. The academic tradition of reform in twentieth century U.S. teacher education has historically emphasized the role of the liberal arts and disciplinary knowledge in teacher preparation and, with the exception of clinical experiences, has belittled the contribution of schools, colleges, and departments of education (e.g., Koerner, 1963). This orientation emphasizes the teacher's role as a scholar and subject matter specialist and has taken many different forms.

In recent years, Lee Shulman (1986; 1987), and Margaret Buchmann (1984) among others, have advocated views of reflective practice which emphasize the teacher's deliberations about subject matter and its transformation to pupils to promote understanding. Shulman and Buchmann are unlike many others within the academic tradition, however, who have advocated only exposure to subject matter content. Their views represent a challenge to historically dominant notions of academically oriented reform. For example, Shulman and his colleagues in the "Knowledge Growth in Teaching" project (Wilson, Shulman, and Richert, 1987) have proposed a model of pedagogical reasoning and action and of the professional knowledge base for teaching which places the emphasis on the intellectual basis for teaching and on the transformation of subject matter knowledge by teachers. Their model of pedagogical reasoning identifies six aspects of the teaching act: comprehension, transformation, instruction, evaluation, reflection, and new comprehension. This framework reflects a clear emphasis in their conception of reflective practice on the content to be taught (Shulman, 1987).

While this conception of reflective teaching does not necessarily ignore general pedagogical knowledge derived from research on teaching, students' understandings and developmental characteristics, and issues of social justice and equity, the standards for assessing the adequacy of the teaching evolve primarily from the academic disciplines.

The Social Efficiency Tradition

The social efficiency tradition of reform in U.S. teacher education, has historically emphasized faith in the scientific study of teaching to provide a basis for building a teacher education curriculum. According to contemporary advocates of this view, research on teaching has, in recent years, provided a "knowledge base" that can form the foundation for teacher education curriculum (e.g., Good, 1990). Feiman-Nemser (1990) has identified two different ways in which contemporary teacher educators have interpreted the social efficiency perspective. First, there is a technological version in which the intent is to teach prospective teachers the skills and competencies which research has shown to be associated with desirable pupil outcomes. This narrow interpretation of the social efficiency view emphasizes reflection by teachers about how closely their practice conforms to standards provided by some aspect of research on teaching (e.g., Gentile, 1988).

A second and broader interpretation of the social efficiency tradition, the "deliberative orientation," is one where the findings of research on teaching are used by teachers along with other information to solve teaching problems. According to advocates of this deliberative orientation, the crucial task for teacher educators is to foster teachers' capabilities to exercise their judgment about the use of various teaching skills while taking advantage of research (including descriptive research), experience, intuition, and their own values (Zumwalt, 1982).

While this conception of reflective teaching does not totally ignore the social context of schooling, issues of equity and justice, student understandings and developmental characteristics, or subject matter, the emphasis is clearly on the intelligent use of "generic" teaching skills and strategies which have been suggested by research.

The Developmentalist Tradition

The distinguishing characteristic of the developmentalist tradition is the assumption that the natural development of the learner provides the basis for determining what should be taught to students and how it should be taught. Historically, this natural order of child development was to be determined by research involving the careful observation and description of students' behavior at various stages of development (Mitchell, 1931).

According to Perrone (1989), three central metaphors have been associated with the progressive/developmentalist tradition in U.S. teacher education: teacher as naturalist, teacher as researcher, and teacher as artist. The teacher as naturalist dimension has stressed the importance of skill in the observation of students' behavior and in building a curriculum and classroom environment consistent with patterns of child development and children's interests. Classroom practice is grounded in close observation and study of children in the classroom, either directly by the teacher, or from reflection on a literature based on such study. The teacher as researcher strand of this tradition has emphasized the need to foster the teacher's experimental attitude toward practice and to help teachers initiate and sustain ongoing inquiries in their own classrooms. Finally, the teacher as artist element has emphasized the link between creative and fully functioning persons in touch with their own learning and exciting and stimulating classrooms. One contemporary example of reflective teaching practice within this tradition is the work of Eleanor Duckworth at Harvard University. Duckworth (1987) has elaborated a constructivist view of reflective teaching that emphasizes engaging learners with phenomena, instead of explaining things to students at the onset. According to Duckworth, teachers are both practitioners and researchers and their research should be focused on their students and their current understandings of topics under study. The teacher then uses this knowledge of student understandings to decide the appropriate next steps for their learning and keeps trying to find out what sense the students are making as the instruction continues.

This developmental conception of reflective teaching has become increasingly popular in recent years with the growing influence of cognitive psychology in education. While it does not ignore subject matter standards emanating from the disciplines, research on teaching, and the social and political contexts of schooling and issues of social justice, the emphasis is clearly on reflecting about students and/or on one's own development as a teacher and person.

The Social Reconstructionist Tradition

In the social reconstructionist tradition, schooling and teacher education are both viewed as crucial elements in the movement toward a more just and humane society. According to Valli (1990a), proponents of this approach (which draws on various neo-Marxist, feminist, and critical perspectives) argue:

> that schools as social institutions, help reproduce a society based on unjust class, race, and gender relations and that teachers have a moral obligation to reflect on and change their own practices and school structures when these perpetuate such arrangements. (p. 46)

In a social reconstructionist conception of reflective teaching, the teacher's attention is focused both inwardly at their own practice *and* outwardly at the social conditions in which these practices are situated (Kemmis, 1985). How teachers' actions maintain and/or disrupt the status quo in schooling and society is of central concern. The reflection is aimed in part, at the elimination of the social conditions which distort the self-understandings of teachers and undermine the educative potential and moral basis of schooling.

A second characteristic of a social reconstructionist conception of reflective teaching is its democratic and emancipatory impulse and the focus of the teacher's deliberations upon substantitive issues which raise instances of inequality and injustice within schooling and society for close scrutiny. Recognizing the fundamentally political character of all schooling, the teacher's reflections center upon such issues as the gendered nature of schooling and of teachers' work, the relationships between race and social class on the one hand and access to school knowledge and school achievement on the other, and the influence of external interests on the process of curriculum production. These and other similar issues are addressed in part, as they arise within the context of a teacher's work (see Beyer, 1989).

The third characteristic of a social reconstructionist conception of reflective teaching is its commitment to reflection as a communal project. Social reconstructionist teacher educators seek to encourage the development of "communities of learning" where teachers can support and sustain each others' growth (e.g., Bullough and Gitlin, 1991). This commitment to collaborative modes of learning indicates a dual commitment by teacher educators to an ethic where justice and equity on the one hand, and care and compassion on the other, are valued. This commitment is also thought to be of strategic value in the transformation of unjust and inhumane institutional and social structures. Specifically, the empowerment of teachers as individuals is considered inadequate and the potential for institutional and social change is considered greater, if teachers see their individual situations linked to those of their colleagues (Freedman, Jackson, and Boles, 1986).

Generic Reflection

In addition to these four traditions of reflective practice in teaching and teacher education, there has recently been a great deal of advocacy for reflective teaching in general, without much comment about what it is the reflection should be focused on, the criteria that should be used to evaluate the quality of the reflection, or the degree to which teachers' deliberations should incorporate a critique of the social and institutional contexts in which they work. The implication here is that teachers actions are necessarily better just because they are more deliberate or intentional.

> *How* to get students to reflect can take on a life of its own, and can become *the* programmatic goal. *What* they reflect on can become immaterial. For example, racial tension as a school issue can become no more or less worthy of reflection than field trips or homework assignments. (Valli, 1990b, p.9)

One of the clearest examples of this tendency to advocate reflection in general is found in the Ohio State University materials on Reflective Teaching (Cruickshank, 1987). Drawing on the important distinction made by Dewey (1933) between reflective action and routine action, Cruickshank (1987) argues that teachers need to become more reasoned actors, without at all addressing the issues of the content, quality, and context of the reflection.

> The point is that teachers who study teaching deliberately and become students of teaching can develop life-long assurance that they know what they are doing, why they are doing it, and what will happen as a result of what they do. Foremost, they can learn to behave according to reason. To lack reason is to be a slave to chance, irrationality, self-interest, and superstition. (p. 34)

In identifying these five different orientations to reflective practice, I am not suggesting that individual programs of work can be labeled as pure examples of any of the orientations. The difficulty of doing this will become clear shortly in the discussion of the seven cases. I am suggesting though that teacher education programs will reflect various patterns of resonance with these orientations and that certain emphases and absences can be detected in any given set of programs or in the reflective teacher education movement as a whole in terms of these different orientations.

THE SEVEN CASE STUDIES

What do all of these various conceptions of reflective practice mean when we consider the reality of individual teacher education programs? Historically, although there have always been a small number of thematically oriented programs, most individual teacher education programs have lacked conceptual coherence and distinctiveness despite the existence of different theoretical orientations to teacher education in the scholarly literature (e.g., Atkin and Raths, 1974). The seven cases in this volume represent both attempts to redesign the entire effort toward teacher education at a particular institution (e.g., University of Florida) and those which sought to create small islands of coherence among a variety of typically unfocused programs (e.g., Kent State). In both cases, despite the attempts to develop program coherence based on faculty commitment to reflective inquiry, a great deal of diversity persists within programs. One reason for this continued diversity is the lack of faculty consensus. For example, in the RITE program at the University of Houston, the faculty holds four different views of reflective inquiry. At Catholic University, although the program designers set forth a vision of reflective inquiry which includes elements of social reconstructionism, many faculty misunderstood or rejected this view.

When the seven programs are examined in relation to the traditions of reflective inquiry, we can see certain emphases and absences in the programs as a group. None of the programs can be viewed as a pure example of one of the various reform traditions, but one of the most visible themes in the descriptions of the programs is a commitment to a social efficiency view of reflective practice. Although clearly rejecting what Feiman-Nemser (1990) has described as a narrow technological view (i.e., applying research to practice through rules), several of the programs emphasize helping prospective teachers reflect on the application of research (generated outside of the context of the practice under study) to teaching practice. In several cases (e.g., Michigan State University), the term "theory" is used only in reference to campus courses and "practice" is used only in relation to school-based instruction. This view of the theory-practice relationship (what Schön calls "technical rationality") is a bit odd in programs which claim affiliation with reflective inquiry. Although there is some attention in the cases to helping students develop personal and practical theories of teaching, the source of these theories is still often viewed as lying outside the reflective practice of teachers, and prospective teachers are still helped to "apply theory to practice." The relationship between theory and practice is seen as one way as opposed to dialogic.[3]

The clearest example of this social efficiency view in the seven cases is the program at the University of Maryland, which comes closest to emphasizing a single tradition of reform. This program with its "three R's of learning to teach" and "theory-practice wheels," places a great deal of emphasis on analyzing teaching practice in relation to a specific externally derived knowledge base.

> A reflective teacher who has command of the knowledge base of teaching can: (1) explain the core ideas emanating from the knowledge base and cite appropriate best practices associated with them; (2) cite key pieces of research associated with the knowledge base and provide thoughtful critique of this research; (3) execute effectively (at a novice level) selected best practices which grow out of the research in simulated and laboratory settings and in real classrooms; (4) engage in critical reflection and intellectual dialogue about the knowledge base and understand how the various ideas are connected and how they interact to inform (situationally) a particular teaching/schooling event or episode. (McCaleb, Borko, and Arends, chapter 3, p. 57-58)

Several of the other programs reflect this same emphasis on a social efficiency orientation to reflective practice although not to the same degree.

What seems to be almost absent from the programs is the emphasis of an academic tradition on the teaching of subject matter. Most of the discussion of pedagogy which is specific refers to generic teaching skills derived from research on teaching. This absence of discipline-specific discussion could reflect a view that the academic preparation of teachers is someone else's job outside of the professional education course sequence. In any case, there is a definite emphasis on knowledge, skills, and dispositions not tied to any particular subject area. The

University of Maryland, which provides the most detailed information about the substance of their curriculum, does not even mention subject matter content as part of their knowledge base. The closest thing in these cases to the academic tradition is with Kent State's focus on bringing students into their program who have strong academic backgrounds in their general education and subject matter courses.

Another tradition which receives only minor attention is social reconstructionism. Two programs (Kent State and Maryland) mention attention given in courses to radical critiques of schooling or critical theory but do not elaborate on what takes place. For example, McCaleb, Borko, and Arends (chapter 3) describe a shift in their program toward a more radical social critique of schooling and reference Giroux, Shor, and Freire. One can only wonder what this means, however, given their strong emphasis on a social efficiency perspective. Michigan State provides an example of how issues of equity and diversity are explored by students in a decision making lab. At the University of Florida we are told of increased focus on teaching "at risk" students because program evaluations showed that the graduates most likely to give up on students were those teaching a large number of such students. The University of Houston provides several examples of how students are engaged in activities to help them understand how schooling contributes to the reproduction of inequality. Clift, Houston, and McCarthy (chapter 7) distinguish this "social" perspective, however, from social reconstructionism or a critical perspective. They state that the faculty members who held a social perspective on reflection "sought to have students understand the relationship between classroom teaching and broader social issues, but did not advocate teachers as transformers of society" (p. 133).

The program in the group which gives the most emphasis to social reconstructionist themes is the one at Catholic University, but even here one cannot conclude that this perspective is what drives the program. For example, there are numerous references in the description of the Catholic University program to helping students examine the ethical, moral, and political implications of their teaching and the context of that teaching, and to helping them assess the worth of their teaching in light of norms such as equality and social justice. As mentioned earlier, however, only a small group of faculty are committed to these themes. The seven programs as a group do not prioritize the concerns raised in a social reconstructionist perspective. The cases say much about intellectual and interpersonal competence and cognitive complexity, but little about social consciousness and social responsibility. This is not surprising given the historically marginal status of this orientation in U.S. teacher education (Liston and Zeichner, 1991).

The developmentalist orientation to reflective practice is evident in these cases in several ways. First, several of the program descriptions mention efforts made to help students focus on their pupils' prior and experiential knowledge and base their instruction on close observation of their pupils. This orientation is probably the strongest in the Elementary PROTEACH program at the University of Florida where teacher educators help prospective teachers surface their entering perspectives, and reexamine them. A personalistic focus is also evident in the University of New Hampshire program where self-development (in a group context) and the development of personally meaningful teaching philosophies are major concerns.

> Because we envision teachers as reflective decision makers who work best from their own philosophical constructs, we endeavor throughout the program to provide the conditions, instructions, and communities that will enable students to develop their own coherent ways of being teachers—ways that fit and arise out of their own person. (Oja et al., chapter 1, pp. 12-13)

Both the Florida and the Kent State programs have articulated frameworks which describe mature reflection/development by their students. The Florida framework is based on the Reflective Judgment model of Kitchner and King (1990) while the Kent State framework is based on the work of Perry (1970). Other than in the Florida and New Hampshire programs though, the developmentalist tradition is not very evident in descriptions of the teacher education curriculum.

A generic view of reflection is probably one of the strongest themes in these cases. Each of the cases makes general assertions that remind one strongly of Dewey's (1933) classic statements regarding the benefits of reflective action over routine action. For example:

> We want our students to examine the fabric of teaching and be able to make reasoned choices about their own practice. (Applegate and Shaklee, chapter 4, p. 68)

A second aspect of the generic reflection theme is numerous statements that indicate teacher educators have moved beyond the technical to have their students consider "the moral and the ethical." For example:

> Students begin to consider the moral and ethical choices that are inherent in the application of technical knowledge. (Clift, Houston, and McCarthy, chapter 7, p. 127)

A third aspect of the generic theme in these cases is the desire to have students reflect about ideas and practices from multiple perspectives. The Multiple Perspectives program at Michigan State and the program at Catholic University with their elaborate conceptual frameworks are the clearest examples of this trend. All the programs though include plans for this aspect of reflective practice, plans which in many cases involve collaborative reflection among students and deliberate faculty modeling of the kind of reflection that they hope to have their students internalize.

Although each case indicates at least some of the commitments underlying reflection, we are often left with a certain degree of relativism about what it is teacher educators want students to do beyond develop their personal theories of teaching by reflecting about a specific knowledge base from multiple perspectives and from considering the moral and ethical in addition to the technical. Are these teacher educators willing to accept any action as long as their students have reflected about it in this way? What does considering the moral and ethical mean? Dan Liston and I have recently criticized our own earlier work (Liston and Zeichner, 1987) for our failure to elaborate the process of moral deliberation, and Valli (1990a) provides several different views of this process. But the program descriptions do not make clear where faculty stand with regard to different versions of moral deliberation or with regard to the choices they are willing to accept as "morally right action."

One attempt to deal with this problem of moral relativism is found in the University of New Hampshire case. Here Oja et al. identify the need to do more than merely help students construct their own philosophies of education without any restraints on the process.

> As an antidote to relativism, we call upon standard criteria for theory assessment such as clarity, comprehension, and consistency. Once we apply a full range of systematic criteria, the ground for choosing among theories becomes clearer, and the range of compelling possibilities gets narrowed. (Oja et al., chapter 1, p. 10)

Also, as mentioned earlier, teacher educators at Catholic University help students assess their practices in light of norms and values such as equality and justice. It is not evident, however, whether students are asked to consider the multiple definitions of equality, justice, and so forth, which could be employed during the reflective process (see MacIntyre, 1988). Apart from these and a few other instances where a specific moral position is articulated, what commitments to multiple perspectives and moral considerations actually mean remains elusive.

CONCLUSION

In this chapter I have attempted to describe the seven cases in relation to four traditions of practice in U.S. teacher education. Although certain emphases and absences were detected in the descriptions of the programs, in many instances the specific assumptions underlying the commitments to reflective inquiry were unclear. Although we are given access in these chapters to an impressive array of curricular and instructional arrangements and innovative program structures, the conceptual underpinnings of the programs need further articulation. A next step would be for these teacher educators to give fuller elaboration about such things as the process of moral deliberation, how specifically "critical" perspectives are dealt with in the programs which make this claim, what kinds of classroom actions are seen as acceptable and unacceptable given this deliberative process, and how subject matter knowledge fits into a program's conception of reflective practice.

One final aspect of these cases that should be noted is that by the time you read this volume, the programs will have changed in substantial ways. Most of these teacher educators have emphasized the fact that their programs are in a continual process of development. Some of these changes have and will continue to involve curricular, instructional, and structural changes within an existing conceptual position such as at the University of New Hampshire. Others, as in the case of the University of Florida, will involve dramatic shifts in the theoretical emphasis in a program.[4] I have argued throughout this analysis that stating a commitment to reflective inquiry is not a sufficient basis for defining a conceptual orientation for a teacher education program and that the theoretical perspectives associated with several of these programs remain to be articulated. We need to continue to move beyond the point where reflective teaching by itself is seen as a distinct programmatic emphasis. Building upon the work represented in these seven cases can help us toward this goal.

11

Feminist Pedagogy as a Foundation for Reflective Teacher Education Programs

During the last fifteen years, many educators have questioned the technocratic orientation that has dominated teacher education. During the 1970s this orientation became even more popularized under the title of Competency/Performance Based Teacher Education (C/PBTE) (e.g., Kliebard, 1975). Based on process/product research, C/PBTE programs listed specific skills of "good teaching" and preservice teachers were required to demonstrate their mastery of these techniques prior to graduation. Critics of this approach charged that it promoted "utilitarian perspectives" among preservice teachers (e.g., Goodman, 1985; Tabachnick et al., 1979-80, Tabachnick and Zeichner, 1985). Getting children to stay "on-task," move through the required lesson(s) on time in a quiet, smooth, and orderly fashion, and improve their scores on standardized tests became the main criteria for judging successful practice. This approach to teacher preparation implies that instructional procedures become ends in themselves rather than means towards broader educational or social purposes.

In response, several teacher educators drew from the thinking of John Dewey (1904, 1933) who suggested that the primary purpose of teacher preparation should be to help preservice teachers become "reflective practitioners." These critics called for a curriculum in which preservice teachers would become more thoughtful about the complexities of teaching and learning. The goal was to educate rather than "train," and thus empower teachers to be critical decision makers.

As its popularity grew, different definitions of "reflective teacher education" emerged. For example, Cruickshank (1981) and his colleagues took a narrow interpretation of Dewey's work by having preservice teachers merely reflect on the "success" of using specific instructional techniques to meet predetermined objectives. As Gore (1987) suggests, Cruickshank's orientation actually reinforces the previously discussed technocratic mindedness that dominates traditional teacher preparation under the guise of reflective teacher education. In contrast, other educators (e.g., Beyer, 1984; Goodman, 1984; Tom, 1984) take a broader view and suggest that teacher preparation should help preservice teachers "reflect on the origins, purposes, and consequences of their actions, as well as on the material and ideological constraints and encouragements embedded in the classroom, school, and societal contexts in which they work" (Zeichner and Liston, 1987:23).

The programs described in this book adhere more towards the broad than the narrow definition of reflection. Most authors view reflection as a cognitive and social construct. The first suggests an understanding that reflection refers to the *quality* of thought that goes into one's actions. Being reflective means thinking in more complex ways than merely memorizing specific information or instructional techniques. Several authors discuss the importance of viewing reality from multiple perspectives as an indication of "reflection." Second, these authors suggest that reflective preservice teachers become more sensitive to the relationship between schooling and society. Towards this end, several of the authors make reference to "democracy," or "critical theory" as playing a role in the development of their programs. However, in most chapters we have only a general understanding of the theoretical foundations upon which these programs are based. This is unfortunate because the most important aspect of any innovation is the educational and social perspectives of those who actually put their ideas into practice. Since teacher education does not take place in a vacuum, it cannot be reformed outside of a particular societal and historical context.

This chapter argues that, given the unique sociohistorical context of teaching in the United States, feminist pedagogy provides an ideological foundation well suited for reflective teacher education programs.

The chapter represents an effort to tease out the way in which this feminist pedagogy can lend insight and support to the work of teacher educators, such as the ones in this book.

FEMINIST PEDAGOGY

Feminist pedagogy is viewed as an area of interest within the broader field of cultural feminism. Cultural feminism emerged from critiques that early feminist work merely helped a few women gain access into a male dominated society, and that in doing so, it inadvertently reinforced the power of patriarchy. In order to gain access into "a man's world," women soon realized that they needed to learn how to "be like men." Although the struggle of these women to gain social, economic, and political access represented an important achievement, there was a subtle but powerful message that "being like a man" was the ideal that both men and women should strive towards. As Alcoff (1988: 406) states, "Cultural feminism is the ideology of a female nature or female essence reappropriated by feminists themselves in an effort to revalidate undervalued female attributes." From this perspective, the problem of patriarchy is not rooted merely in a social and economic system or in particular technocratic, hierarchical, and capitalist ideologies, but rather in a socially constructed "masculine" consciousness and set of values.[1] Feminist pedagogy then refers to an approach to education that validates a feminine way of thinking, valuing, and acting with the goal to create a more balanced world view.

Shrewsbury (1987: 6) suggests that:

> Feminist pedagogy begins with a vision of what education might be like but frequently is not. This is a vision of the classroom as a liberatory environment in which we, teacher-student and student-teacher, act as subjects, not objects. Feminist pedagogy is engaged teaching/learning—engaged with self in a continuing reflective process; engaged actively with the material being studied; engaged with others in a struggle to get beyond our sexism and racism and classism and homophobia and other destructive hatreds and to work together to enhance our knowledge; engaged with the community, with traditional organizations, and with movements for social change.

Feminist pedagogy shares many values with other critical and liberationist theories of education (Maher, 1987); however, as Leck (1987: 348) succinctly articulates, "Feminist critics . . . show that existing liberation theories have an insufficient sense of the power, presence, and importance of gender and patriarchy in schools as well as in educational theory." For instance, the technocratic rationality that is often identified by critical theorists as the dominant ideology of conventional education can be traced more accurately to patriarchy than capitalism.

Several of the authors in this book referred to their theoretical framework as "scaffolding" upon which preservice teachers and teacher educators "hang" their ideas. This scaffolding allows preservice teachers to view their own ideas from fresh perspectives, make appropriate connections, and either reaffirm or discard their previously held beliefs and ideas. As will be discussed later in this chapter, when presented appropriately this scaffolding can be particularly effective in expanding the range of preservice teachers' ideas. In addition, this scaffolding provides teacher educators with a common language with which to examine their own activities. To illuminate the way in which feminist pedagogy can serve as the scaffolding of these programs, three common areas of concern to teacher educators and preservice teachers will be discussed: teaching as an occupation, classroom dynamics, and fostering reflection.

The Work of Teaching

Perhaps the most important goal for reflective teacher education programs is to help preservice teachers examine what it means to "be a teacher." As several authors point out, preservice teachers come into their programs after completing twelve or more years of a powerful "apprenticeship of observation" in which they experienced, on a daily basis, conventional teaching (Lortie, 1975). These authors clearly hope that their preservice teachers will reconsider what they have learned from this apprenticeship and conceptualize a more substantive vision of teaching.

Feminist pedagogy offers significant insight into the work of teaching. In spite of numerous calls to develop environments in which teachers can act as autonomous and reflective practitioners, the societal demands upon teachers seriously undermine this goal. In particular, over the last two decades teachers have increasingly become "deskilled" (Apple, 1986; Gitlin, 1983; Goodman, 1988; Frymier, 1987; Shannon, 1987). This deskilling of teachers occurs when the conceptualization of instruction and the curriculum is separated from those who actually teach. Conventional teaching has become increasingly controlled through the adoption of instructional programs which come complete

with learning objectives, textbooks, assignments, tests, and daily schedule. The teacher's role is to manage these programs so that the students
finish them within the prescribed time period. Lanier and Little (1986)
conclude that opportunities for teachers to exercise informed judgment,
engage in thoughtful discourse, and participate in reflective decision
making are practically nonexistent. The implications arising from recent
national reports seem to suggest that the nature of teachers' work will
not change significantly in the near future. As Zeichner (1986: 88) states:

> Numerous analyses, conducted from a variety of ideological and
> political perspectives, have concluded that the effect of many of
> the recent policies affecting teachers has been to promote greater
> external control over the content, processes, and outcomes of
> teachers' work and to encourage teachers to adopt conformist ori-
> entations to self and society as well as technical orientations to
> the role of teacher.

If preservice teachers are to become reflective practitioners then preparation programs need to help them understand the forces that have
generated the work of teaching as it currently exists.

While bureaucratic, functionalist, and hierarchical rationalities
have influenced the work of teachers, locating the source of disem-
powerment within these rationalities presents an incomplete and mis-
leading picture. It is not possible to fully comprehend the nature of
teachers' work without addressing the role that patriarchy has played in
its development (e.g., Apple, 1986; Grumet, 1981; Lather, 1985; Tabakin
and Densmore, 1986).

One way in which patriarchy has influenced the nature of teaching is through identifying it as "women's work." Elsbree's (1939)
research indicates that during the colonial period, men did most of the
teaching. Although there was some "superficial appraisal" of one's
instruction, the community put the responsibility for educating their
children into the "hands of the teacher." Elsbree (1939:71) notes that at
this time, "the teacher was perhaps more nearly his own boss . . . than at
any subsequent period." However, by the mid-1800s, 60 percent of elementary teachers were women and by 1920 that figure had grown to
nearly 90 percent.

Due to patriarchy, as women filled the classrooms, teachers' professional status and autonomy diminished. While early proponents
(e.g., Catherine Beecher, Horace Mann, Henry Barnard) for increasing
the number of women teachers often referred to their moral superiority,
patience, and nurturing qualities, there was also the belief that women

needed to be controlled. The ideal teacher was docile and passive in the face of (male) authority. "If ever I envied mortal being upon earth, it was not the queen with realms belting the globe . . . but it was the devoted, modest female teacher, conscious only of her duties, unconscious of ambition or of earthly rewards" (Mann, 1860:85-86).

Historically, men have assumed that they have the right to dictate how women live. Even as late as the 1920s, it was not uncommon for school boards (composed almost entirely of men) to forbid their women teachers from getting married or dating, staying out past eight in the evening, smoking tobacco or drinking alcohol, wearing bright-colored clothing or less than two petticoats, and dying their hair or wearing makeup (Apple, 1986). Underneath the rhetoric of women as the natural and superior guardians of children was an unspoken belief that these young women could not be trusted in the same way as their male predecessors.

Men who stayed in education often left the classroom. The "work" of educating our children was thus divided into two camps. One group, dominated by men, conducted research, developed curriculum, and directly supervised the schooling of children. The second group, dominated by women, was expected to implement the former group's plans (Stober and Tyack, 1980). During the last decade, this division has been exacerbated as state officials now determine what schools should teach through the creation of curriculum guidelines and standardized tests. As Apple (1990:379) notes:

> This speaks to a profound mistrust of teachers, administrators, and curriculum scholars at universities. They are decidedly not part of the solution, but part of the problem. . . . The hidden gender relations here need to be mentioned. We need to remember a simple but very telling fact. Most teachers are *women* [his emphasis]. By, in essence, depowering them, by centralizing curriculum deliberation, debate, and control . . . through government intervention, we undercut the skills of curriculum design and teaching for which women teachers had struggled years to gain respect.

It is more than just a little ironic that teachers, who have had limited power to determine the education that exists in our schools and who happen to be mostly women, are the people who during the last decade have been blamed for the many failures of our schooling.

This analysis can assist preservice teachers' understanding of the complex forces which have shaped the images of teaching they bring with them to their preparation programs and the observations they make during their field experiences. The above analysis can help them avoid taking conventional notions of "teaching" for granted and grasp the way in which this occupation has been socially constructed. This analysis can help preservice teachers understand why teachers lack status and power in our schools and society. They can also begin to see the limitations of the "progress" that women have made in our society. While allowing greater access of women and minorities into traditional white, male occupations is one thing, far more difficult (and potentially liberating) is dramatically restructuring the arbitrary stratification of labor based on gender. In this manner, feminist pedagogy offers preservice teachers an opportunity to reflect on the way in which education is a form of cultural politics within a very direct and personally meaningful context.

In addition, this analysis can assist teacher educators in generating appropriate goals for their programs. For example, several of the authors in this book conceptualize their reflective teacher education programs within a context of "teacher professionalization." This orientation is similar to that taken by those who wrote the *Holmes Report* and *A Nation Prepared: Teachers for the 21st Century*. Of course, these reports are intent on making teaching a "true profession" in the tradition of lawyers, doctors, engineers, and other masculine occupations (Laird, 1988). As such, they imply that teachers should once again, be like men. That is, they should embrace the same masculine values and practices found in most male-dominated occupations such as competition, quantified accountability, individual achievement, and standardization of work/production (Tabakin and Densmore, 1986). As such, these masculine values run counter to the primary purposes for establishing reflective teacher education programs as an alternative to the C/PBTE programs previously discussed in this chapter. To the degree that reflective teaching is tied to the movement to "professionalize" teaching, it will encourage teachers to be what Grumet (1981) calls "pedagogues for patriarchy." An alternative to the image of teachers as professionals comes from Shrewsbury (1987:11) in which she encourages women (e.g., preservice teachers) to develop a sense of "feminine leadership" which is significantly more collectivist, nurturing, and visionary in nature than that promoted by advocates of "teachers as professionals." We can use feminist pedagogy to help us avoid associating reflective teacher education with movements which in the long run will undermine many of the primary purposes which originally generated this approach to teacher education.

Classroom Dynamics, Knowledge, and Learning

Another area of reflection that concerns most teacher educators and preservice teachers is classroom dynamics and conceptions of epistemology and learning. It is difficult to imagine a truly reflective practitioner who has not given considerable thought to the nature of interpersonal relationships, the conception of knowledge, or the character of their students' learning in classrooms. Here again, feminist pedagogy provides insights that can serve as a catalyst for substantive reflection.

In our society there exists a sociopsychological rationality that boys (more than girls) are socialized to embrace and vice versa. Several individuals suggest that by the time boys and girls get to middle school, they live essentially in different "worlds" (e.g., Best, 1983; Eder, 1985; Eder and Hallinan, 1978; Goodwin, 1980; Lever, 1976; Shrum, 1988; Thorne, 1986; Thorne and Luria, 1986). This masculine rationality promotes several intellectual, moral, and epistemological values such as: justice, individualism, competition, objectivity, logic, efficiency, public legitimation and standardization of knowledge, verbal articulation, the existence of absolute knowledge, the categorization of knowledge and time, and quantitative measurement of learning. This rationality is so pervasive in our society that it implies a repudiation of the values embedded in a more feminine ethos that values: caring, cooperation, consensus, intuition, creativity, subjectivity, synthesis, empathy, diversity, holistic understanding, visual or kinaestheic expression of ideas, and the legitimation of personal knowledge (e.g., Belenky et al., 1986; Gilligan, 1982; Harding and Hintikka, 1983; Janssen-Jurreit, 1980; Keller, 1985, Noddings, 1984).

Since most instructional developers have historically been men, the influence of this masculine rationality at work in our schools is not surprising. The instructional programs that have dominated classroom activity have been based primarily on principles of functional efficiency and social control (e.g., Franklin, 1986), which in themselves are reflections of masculine reasoning. As previously discussed, these instructional programs emphasize the study of utilitarian skills over substantive content or artistic talent; the sequential segmentation and memorization of knowledge over synthesis and holistic understanding; the standardized, quantitative evaluation of pupils' work over the informed, subjective judgment of the teacher; and the establishment of rules and regulations based on an ethic of justice over the creation of school environments based on an ethic of caring (e.g., Greene, 1978; Lesko, 1988; Spender, 1982; Weiler, 1988). Although the vast majority of teachers are women, they are expected to ignore the values embedded in a more feminine rationality and become "pedagogues for patriarchy." Lightfoot (1978:69-70) captures the essence of this situation in her statement that mothers and teachers "are required to raise children in the service of a dominant group whose values and goals they do not determine . . . [and they must] socialize their children to conform to a society that belongs to men."

The feminist analysis of classroom dynamics, epistemology, and learning provides preservice teachers with a rich tapestry of ideas upon which to reflect. Since most preservice teachers are drawn towards teaching as an occupation of caring and service, feminist pedagogy provides them with a vision of education and interpersonal dynamics which resonates with their inner sensibilities. While preservice teachers come to their preparation programs after an extensive "apprenticeship of observation," upon reflection, their experiences in conventional schools are often less than ideal. For example, many preservice teachers with whom this author has worked have easily recalled the boredom, frustration, and sense of isolation they felt as part of their pre-professional education. They easily recall instances in which their own voice and personal knowledge was discounted in schools. Many can recount in detail their "fears of ignorance" due to the emphasis that is placed on obtaining the "right answer" as arbitrarily defined in textbooks and on tests. They can clearly articulate their trepidation at voicing their opinion or asking substantive questions in front of their classmates and teachers. Feminist pedagogy provides an understanding of why so many preservice teachers instinctively feel alienated by what they experienced in conventional schools. The inner sensibilities of most preservice teachers concerning what makes education worthwhile is another reason why feminist pedagogy is particularly well suited for reflective teacher education programs. As Sarason (1971) noted in his sensitive analysis of schooling:

> A fair number of . . . young teachers are able to change [i.e., become more intellectually stimulating, caring, thoughtful] and sometimes dramatically so. . . . The direction in which the teacher changes (in matters of discipline, curriculum, and handling of administrative personnel) often involves doing what the teacher wanted to do but for which there was no "authoritative support."

Feminist pedagogy can provide this all important theoretical and "authoritative support" for preservice teachers. It can also serve to challenge those preservice teachers who have accepted, often unconsciously, the masculine rationality that dominates our schools and society.

Fostering Reflection

As previously mentioned, one reason for using feminist pedagogy as a foundation for reflective teacher education programs is that this discourse provides an opportunity for teacher educators to speak a common language and thus create practices that are theoretically grounded. As Schniedewind states:

> To reflect feminist values in teaching is to teach progressively, democratically, and with feeling. Such teaching rejects what Paulo Freire calls the banking system that assumes that one person with greater power and wisdom has the knowledge to dispense to others. Feminist education implies that we enter into a dialogue with our students, meeting them as human beings, and learning with them in community. (quoted in Leck, 1987:349)

When reading through the program descriptions in this volume, it is obvious that the authors have given considerable thought to the organizational structure of their programs and educational experiences they feel will foster reflection among their preservice teachers. Many of these structures and experiences are similar to those advocated by Schniedewind and other feminists who are teaching courses in women's studies programs (e.g., Bunch and Pollack, 1983; Culley and Portuges, 1985). Both groups of professors work with similar students (i.e., undergraduate women) and share similar goals; namely, to help their students seriously question the dominant values found in our culture. However, there is one aspect of feminist pedagogy which has not been sufficiently addressed and which might prove particularly useful in promoting reflective teacher preparation.

The most important thing teacher educators can do to promote reflection is to carefully consider the implications of Adrienne Rich's (1985) now classic call to take "women students seriously." This notion goes well beyond the important interpersonal dynamics of treating preservice teachers with respect.

First, it suggests that teacher preparation must provide a curriculum that is intellectually stimulating and challenging. Far too often, this author (Goodman, 1986) and others have noted the lack of substance in teacher education curriculum. As previously stated, programs that narrowly predetermine specific "good teaching skills" and a specific "knowledge base" for preservice teachers to "master," is one manifestation of this lack of respect. Teacher education curricula should help preservice teachers *construct* the knowledge needed to begin their careers, or we will continue our present practice of not taking them seriously. Many of the practices described in this book reflect efforts to mutually construct a knowledge base among faculty and preservice teachers. These efforts warrant greater consideration. However, there is one aspect of making teacher education "more rigorous" which indicates a potentially disturbing evolution of the "reflective" movement.

Recently some teacher educators seem to have succumbed to the masculine, academic practice of quantifying and thus over-specifying conceptual ideas such as reflection. Visualizing this masculine rationality at work in a number of these efforts is not difficult. First, professors define exactly what reflection means by stipulating different "levels" of it that often reflect masculine concepts of cognition such as the ability to "think logically;" then we "test" to see what level preservice teachers "are at" when they enter and leave a given program. Finally, based upon this collected data, we confidently develop curricula to "move" preservice teachers into "higher" levels of reflectivity which in itself reflects a hierarchical concept of cognitive development. Rather than predetermining specific instructional skills to master as was the case with C/PBTE programs, reflective teacher education programs will stipulate specific cognitive processes that must be demonstrated to be considered a "reflective teacher." While none of these programs give indication that they currently practice the above scenario, one can begin to detect seeds of this thinking in a number of program descriptions. From a feminist perspective, reflective teacher education programs should avoid using reflection as a measure of so called intellectual capabilities and professionalism that have their roots in a masculine ethos. Rich (1985:28) suggests that our goal should not be to teach women (preservice teachers) how to "think like men," but rather facilitate their abilities to "think like women" in a "man's world."

> Men in general think badly: in disjuncture from their personal lives, claiming objectivity where the most irrational passions seethe, losing . . . their senses in the pursuit of professionalism. It is not easy to think like a woman in a man's world, in the world of the professions; yet the capacity to do that is a strength which we can try to help our students develop. To think like a woman in a man's world means thinking critically, refusing to accept the givens, making connections between facts and ideas which men have left unconnected.

Instead of using reflection as a code word for "professional thinking" it should be used as a heuristic device through which teacher educators *and* preservice teachers can collectively construct a comprehensive understanding of what it means to teach given our current political, social, and educational circumstances.

There is more to this problem, however, than what goes on between teacher educators and their preservice teachers. Not taking preservice teachers "seriously" is also manifested in the patriarchal values found in universities. Historically, teacher education has and continues to suffer from its low status within universities (e.g., Clark and Marker, 1975; Judge, 1982). Several studies (e.g., Peseau, 1980, 1982; Peseau and Orr, 1981) document the serious underfunding of teacher education compared to other professional schools. The Normal School tradition, the lack of a specific scholarly body of knowledge, and the "simplicity" of teachers' work are reasons given to explain this marginal status. However, the most revealing reason for this low status is that schools of education, unlike other professional schools, serve a relatively powerless clientele: women and children. Lanier and Little (1986) note that the status of professional schools are directly related to the status of the groups within the society they serve. Given that the vast majority of teachers are women and that teaching has been defined as "women's work," the university's willingness to avoid taking teacher education seriously will likely continue (Judge, 1982).

While patriarchal values play a role in limiting the status of schools of education inside universities, it is important to acknowledge that these same values have an impact on the status of teacher education programs within schools of education. The closer one gets to directly serving women (i.e., preservice teachers) and their clients (children), the less prestige a professor has. It is well known that most merit systems discourage education faculty from spending most of their time working with undergraduate preservice teachers. As a result, Lanier and Little (1986:529) point out that only a small portion of faculty identify with or readily accept teaching assignments in teacher education. Even scholarship about teacher education (and thus research about women) is often "taken less seriously" within schools of education. Studies indicate that relatively few professors who regularly engage in scholarship and who teach in teacher education programs are involved in significant research related to the process of becoming a teacher or learning to teach (Guba and Clark, 1978; Howey, Yarger, and Joyce, 1978; Joyce and Clift, 1984). As a result, only a small number of faculty are more than tangentially involved (either through their teaching or as an intellectual pursuit) in teacher preparation. Judge (1982, p. 9) notes that there are strong feelings among education faculty to "distance itself [sic] from the . . . world of teacher education" in an effort to enhance their own professional status. Clearly, if we are going to develop reflective teacher education programs, then it is imperative to challenge the patriarchal values which keep schools of education and universities at large from taking the education of preservice teachers seriously.

CONCLUSION

This chapter has argued that feminist pedagogy is particularly well suited for those individuals interested in developing reflective teacher education programs. This compatibility is based primarily upon the fact that most teachers are women, and that teaching, as an occupation, has been socially defined as women's work. As a result, feminist pedagogy provides valuable insights into the nature of teaching, cognition, learning, and valuing in our schools and society. These insights lend themselves to helping preservice teachers and teacher educators understand the complexity of what it means to become a teacher given the current historical, social, and educational context within which teacher education programs exist. Feminist pedagogy also provides insights into the way in which reflection can be conceptualized and used in a given teacher education program.

Due to space limitations, it has not been possible to illustrate the numerous implications of using feminist pedagogy as a foundation for reflective teacher education. However, one final thought is worth noting. Teacher educators, such as the ones in this book, would do well to situate their practices and ideas within the discourse of feminist pedagogy now going on among colleagues within women's studies programs and departments. From this author's perspective, this mixing of discourses would provide for a more fully developed language and creation of practices within teacher education than would be possible if we merely "talk to ourselves." One of the difficulties of creating substantive changes in professional schools is their relative isolation from other schools, colleges, and programs; that is, their isolation from other discourses. One can only hope that the interaction between feminist discourse and teacher education discourse will continue to grow in the coming years.

ANNA E. RICHERT

12

Voice and Power in Teaching and Learning to Teach

When we think about teaching we usually think about learning as well. And learning always suggests something about the process of coming to know. I often ask my students at the beginning of their teacher education experience, "What do you think it means to know? and "How do you think teachers help students come to know?" Of course, as a teacher myself, I too must grapple with the same tough questions. As a teacher of teachers, my doing so is all the more important. In her article "Teaching as Research," Eleanor Duckworth (1986) provides a starting place for thinking about teaching and learning and learning to teach. Believing that knowledge is constructed by the learner rather than given from some outside source, Duckworth argues that to learn, or to come to know, students must engage in or with a phenomenon and then try to explain that phenomenon as they work to make sense of it. The role of the teacher in this model is to introduce learners to phenomena they would not otherwise encounter and motivate them to engage in the process of coming to know.

Learning to teach is just like learning anything else that is difficult, uncertain, complex, and infinitely challenging. As novice teachers engage in the phenomenon of teaching, and then explain what they are doing, as well as how and why, they are learning about teaching while they are learning to teach. They are constructing their own personal knowledge of teaching. Experienced teachers engage in a similar process as they continue to learn about teaching throughout their careers. For newcomers to the profession, the starting point from which they make sense of the complexity of classroom life typically comes from their prior experience as students. For both the novice and the experienced teacher, knowledge is constructed and reconstructed over time; ideas and beliefs about teaching once held to be "true" are rejected and reframed as new information becomes available and circumstances change.

Two central assumptions form the basis for my consideration of learning to teach as conceptualized in the teacher education programs included in this volume. The first is that teachers are learners. While we require that teachers begin their professional lives through a formalized preparation and credentialling system and thus assume they are necessarily learners, at least at that point, we often lose sight of the critical importance of learning as an ongoing part of professional practice. Formal teacher education is merely a launching pad for the life-long process of learning to teach described by Dewey (1933) decades ago. Dewey's (1933) notion of reflective teaching and teaching as learning emphasizes the intellectual demands of work, which is action based in thought. According to Dewey, teachers determine the purposes and consequences of their work so that what they do represents what they believe and know. In the process of reflective practice teachers become "students of education" who can act with intent as they responsibly examine the many complex aspects of their classroom practice. As teachers examine their practice and thus learn about themselves and their work, they construct knowledge about teaching and their work as teachers.

A second assumption of the analysis in this chapter, therefore, is that teacher-learners, by definition, are, and ought to be, constructors and definers of knowledge as well as dispensers of it. As thoughtful teachers do their work—all the while thinking about what they are doing or what they have done—they create knowledge about their practice which they then draw upon (and revise) as they continue to teach. The processes of learning about teaching and constructing knowledge about the task involve engaging in the phenomenon, as the Duckworth model cited earlier suggests, and then conversing about it as a way of sense making. Engaging in the phenomenon of teaching is relatively easy for teachers who typically describe their work as captivating, demanding, challenging. To not engage, their comments suggest, is considerably more difficult. "Conversing" or speaking about their work, on the other hand, is more problematic. Most frequently, the conversing teachers do occurs in conversations they have with themselves—"in the shower," "on the freeway," "while walking down the hallways to the classroom." The culture of teaching and the organization of schooling both mitigate against teachers sharing with one another their thoughts about the dilemmas of practice (Little, 1990; Rosenholtz and Kyle, 1984; Lortie, 1975; Sarason, 1972).

The idea of teacher conversation has embedded within it the concept of "voice"—the use of language to explain, describe, question, explore, or challenge. As this mechanism of conversation and explanation, voice is critical to teacher education. Considering and cultivating it are especially important in this arena given the vital connection between voice and learning, and given the prohibitive and isolating structure of schools and schooling that limits its expression. Let us turn our attention more closely to this notion of the teacher's voice in learning to teach.

While the concept of voice has long been a part of the discourse of the academy and can be found in the literature of literary criticism and psychology, for example, it has also reemerged in recent years as a central construct in feminist theory. For this chapter I am drawing on the work of feminist scholars as both a motivation for my concern and a basis for my conceptualization. I am, however, defining voice more narrowly than it typically is defined in the feminist work. Voice in this context refers to the literal speaking of experience by teachers. For the analysis in this chapter I am using the term teachers' voices to mean their descriptions of what they do, how they think, what they feel, and what they believe. Because of its centrality in the processes of learning and constructing teacher knowledge, I am concerned with the cultivation of the teacher's voice in teacher education.

The discussion in the following pages focuses on this issue of voice and its relevance to teaching and learning to teach. The discussion takes place along two separate lines: (1) voice and speaking one's truth; and (2) voice and being heard. This chapter argues for drawing novice teachers into a conversation that causes them to articulate their points of view and thus reveal what they know and believe about teaching and learning. Reflective practice requires that teachers engage in this conversation. Therefore, programs preparing teachers for reflective teaching must include the opportunity for the development of the knowledge and skills for such a conversation. The programs of teacher education considered in this volume are examined in light of these premises.

VOICE AND SPEAKING ONE'S TRUTH

Voice is a necessary part of reflective teaching as it is an instrument of self consciousness that allows teachers to examine their beliefs and experiences. By talking about what they do, believe, feel, or think, teachers raise to a level of consciousness the complex matters of their work. Just as in the women's movement when women began to speak for themselves and define their own lives and experiences through the critical process of consciousness raising, teachers talking about their lives and work is a critical methodology for teachers. The process of consciousness raising gives teachers the opportunity to claim their work as their own and the responsibility to define their reality from their own historical experience. By giving voice to their experience, teachers speak their own truths.

Consciousness raising for reflective self-examination and identification as suggested here is reminiscent of the methodology of the second wave of feminism or the women's movement of the 1960s when women began to talk with one another about their lives. Through these conversations women began to define for themselves the circumstances of their work and other experiences rather than having those circumstances defined for them. A similar process of self definition and identification is important for teachers. By giving voice to their experience, teachers can claim what they do and what they know. They can examine the historical precedents of their work just as they can construct new images of what might be in the world of schooling. Seen in this light, talking about teaching is an important part of both doing it, and learning about it.

Teachers who talk about what they do and why, are able to know what they do and why, and to question themselves as well. The process of reflection in which teachers think about their work in order to question its purpose, examine its consequences, and therefore learn about it, involves talking or a conversation of some sort. "In order for reflection to occur," the authors of *Women's Ways of Knowing* (1986), explain:

> the oral and written forms of language must pass back and forth between persons who both speak and listen, or read and write—sharing, expanding, and reflecting on each other's experiences. Such interchanges lead to ways of knowing that enable individu-

als to enter into the social and intellectual life of their community. Without them, individuals remain isolated from others; and with out the tools for representing their experiences, people also remain isolated from the self. (p. 26)

For student-teachers, the opportunity to talk about their actions, their thinking, their beliefs, and their feelings, is part of the process of learning to be a reflective teacher. In the formulation of explanations and the critical examination of those explanations novice teachers can "come to know" in ways that enable them to enter and participate in both the social and intellectual lives of their new profession. While the act of talking and that of learning overlap in many ways, there are several points of juncture that are especially noteworthy when considering the process of learning to teach.

The first concerns the examination of preconceptions that is essential as one enters the profession of teaching. Unlike in other professions, novices enter teaching with considerable experience and knowledge about what they are learning to do, and what their beliefs are about it as well. Most beginning teachers have more than sixteen thousand hours of classroom experience before they enter their formal professional preparation. They arrive with clear images of what schools are like and what teachers do. One place where "giving voice" is essential in teacher education, therefore, is in the articulation of ideas and beliefs about teaching as one enters the field.

We have learned from research, and we know from practice, that preconceptions affect learning for all learners, including teacher-learners (Feiman-Nemser and Buchmann, 1985). Determining student teacher preconceptions about teaching is an important first step in planning for their learning to teach. Having novice teachers articulate their ideas and beliefs about teaching is a factor in preparing reflective teachers that is addressed by all seven programs of teacher education described in this volume. "Entering perspectives of students exert a strong influence on their experiences within teacher education," they claim at the University of Florida. It is imperative, therefore, to "help students reveal and confront their perspectives about teaching" (p.10). And at the University of New Hampshire the faculty explain that as student teachers talk about their teaching or the teaching of others, they

start to become better acquainted with their own, often unarticulated, perhaps inconsistent and muddled, but nonetheless powerful, beliefs and assumptions about education. (p. 8)

Having student-teachers articulate their entering beliefs about teaching and learning is only a beginning step in preparing novice teachers to speak what they know as they learn to teach. Talking about their current experiences in classrooms gives teachers a chance to examine classroom practice from the point of view of what they already know, and what they are coming to know. Voice is a vehicle for reflective practice which results in ongoing learning in teaching. Knowing how to speak, including how to frame questions, how to grapple with answers, how to identify problems and focus solutions, how to use theory to inform practice, and so on, is as important as knowing what to speak about. Programs of teacher education must have a structured expectation of voice; they must provide ample opportunity and a safe and supportive environment for the voiced conversations to be exercised.

The conversations student-teachers need to have take many forms. Some of them occur alone and become conversations students have with themselves. In those instances student teachers are free to explore on their own the complexities of their feelings including some of the more difficult to express such as the fear of failure, perceived inadequacy, and disappointment or even unexplainable joy. They are also able to think about what they know and believe about teaching and learning. Writing in journals is one way for teachers to converse with themselves. Journal writing was mentioned as a program element in all seven programs described here. As a vehicle for cultivating the teacher's voice journals create an especially powerful means for novices to explore teaching and their personal experiences of the learning process (Richert, 1987; Yinger and Clark, 1981). The writing process lets you "know what you know, know what you feel, know what you do and how you do it, and know why" (Yinger and Clark, 1981). It increases "awareness of values and implicit theories through which one processes experience," the authors of the Catholic University program add (p. 104)—an awareness which is essential to the definition of self as both teacher and learner.

Talking with oneself as cultivated by such activities as journal writing, is one way to cultivate voice in teacher education. Talking with others is equally important. "Reflective dialogue," as it is described by the Kent State authors—between the student-teachers themselves, and/or the student-teachers and faculty, master teachers, university supervisors, and so forth, is also essential for novices to make sense of what they know and what they are coming to know. Talking with others is a key structural component in each of the programs of reflective teacher education presented in this volume. At the University of New

Hampshire the program is organized around the idea of learning communities in which teachers of varying experience and perspective come together as "co-explorers" in a reflective dialogue that takes many forms from "think aloud" sessions with faculty, to oral presentation with written responses in class assignments. The cohort structure at Catholic University, Kent State, and the University of Maryland similarly stress teachers talking and learning together.

Student-teachers learn to think as they talk, and they become conscious of what they know and believe as they hear themselves speak (and examine what they've spoken). Anne, a student-teacher at the University of New Hampshire, strikes at the core of why speaking is so powerfully connected to learning. Reflecting on the "co-equal" supervising structure at her university she notes that while supervisors keep careful ethnographic notes on the students while they teach, they do not make inferences from their notes until after the student teacher herself is able to examine and think through her own analysis of the classroom happenings. Anne describes her reaction to this process:

> They let me do the thinking and feeling from what they see. I like that. I am able to make inferences about my lesson. If they just told me how they felt I did, I wouldn't have to think, I'd just listen. (p. 14)

VOICE AND BEING HEARD

Listening to yourself as an authority on your own experience, as Anne was asked to do by her university faculty, is an important part of learning. In fact listening to your own words and attempted explanations is fundamental to reflective practice that results in learning to teach. While the power of speaking lies in part in the fact of being heard, being heard is not something that can be taken for granted in teaching. For one thing, being heard implies that someone is listening and there is no norm for listening to teachers within the professional community of schools. Beyond the norms of the profession, the demands on teachers' time preclude much reciprocal conversation among colleagues; teachers are too busy to listen to themselves let alone listen to one another.

Additionally, teachers aren't heard because they don't speak. And they don't speak because they are part of a culture that silences them by a set of oppressive mechanisms such as overwork, low status, and an externally defined standard for performance—a similar set, incidentally, which has oppressed women for generations. Education locates expertise in teaching outside the teacher. Curriculum guidelines, state mandates, university-based research, school and district policies and hierarchies, all contribute to a consistent message to teachers that the primary source of knowledge for their work comes not from them, but from a source outside of them. "Being heard" as a description of teachers' experience in the work environment, represents a relatively revolutionary position rather than a position that is normative in the profession.

But to learn in teaching, and to know one's self, teachers need to be heard. As teachers are heard, they move towards claiming their place, as Belenky and her colleagues suggest above, in "both the social and intellectual worlds" of their profession. Teachers need to talk and be heard as they figure out who they are and what they know. A student-teacher whom I interviewed for another project explained:

> Sometimes there are things that I need to deal with that I don't know if I can deal with or not without articulating them. Sometimes I just need to be heard; I think that's important. ("John" in Richert, 1987, p. 183)

The socialization teachers receive as students before entering the profession is a process better characterized by a goal of remaining quiet rather than speaking out. This factor combined with that of school organizations which typically silences teachers rather than encouraging them to speak and be heard, renders reflective teacher education critical if we are to create new norms for teaching and teacher learning.

Being heard and hearing others, therefore, must be central to the curriculum in teacher education. Learning to hear oneself, or "honoring one's own voice" as it is sometimes described in the feminist literature, is an important part of the process of coming to know. Students must be asked to speak what they know, and hear what they speak. They must be asked to speak what they feel and hear that as well. The program at Catholic University integrates many opportunities for the teacher-learners to listen to themselves and notice what they think or feel. For example, in the Reading, Language, and Literature class the

> students are asked to be alert to statements in the readings that give them an "Aha!" feeling, i.e., a new insight that changes or enlightens their thinking. (p. 103)

They are asked to hear themselves. Similarly, the framework that guides University of New Hampshire's academic component on "philosophic inquiry," considers safety and risk taking in learning to speak and practicing being heard. The course sequence in philosophic inquiry is planned in four phases which move the students from a place of noticing, speaking, and listening to one another freely, to an equally respectful but increasingly critical, sophisticated, and professional speaking-and-hearing nearer the end of the course of study. At the early phase of "acquaintance," for example, students are asked to notice their reactions to readings and experiences just as they are in the Catholic University course cited above. In this instance the faculty ask students to hear themselves by naming and tracking their responses to the readings. These heard responses then become data for an emergent philosophy. The University of New Hampshire document explains:

> Students begin to notice their own responses, their spontaneous "gut reactions" to what's being read, studied, and said—and they keep track of (i.e., write down) these responses as important "clues" to their own embryonic position. (p. 9)

Just as teachers learn to listen to themselves, they must also learn to listen to, and hear, one another. "This means each person makes a methodological commitment not only to listen to others," they explain at the University of New Hampshire, "but to endeavor to understand them on their own terms" (p. 4). Hearing one another "on their own terms" creates the condition for a caring relationship which is predicated on apprehending the reality of the other according to Noddings (1984). In such relationships teachers come to hear one another and consequently share their experiences in trusting and authentic ways.

Hearing one another and being heard open many doors for the teacher who is otherwise isolated in a school structure that prohibits the exchange of ideas. In terms of teacher learning and the construction of knowledge, conversation is essential. As teachers share their experiences and their understandings, their knowledge of their work grows, as does their knowledge of themselves—an outcome of consciousness raising already discussed. Teachers, like any learners, are bounded in their ability to be rational (Carey and Shulman, 1984). By talking together, teachers can overcome the limits of bounded rationality and become better able to process the infinite complexity of teaching and learning to teach. Part of the process involves listening to the ideas of their colleagues and comparing those ideas with their own.

In teacher education novices need a variety of chances to meet together and listen to one another think aloud. Oral presentations provide one example of how this might occur. As students present their work orally they have the opportunity to speak and be heard, and their colleagues have the opportunity to listen and to hear. Hearing someone else's ideas, just as in hearing one's own, provides a powerful learning opportunity.

> (I)t often happens that as one student expresses and embodies their own version of a tradition we have been studying, it will suddenly come alive for other students who had not hither to been able to envision this possibility. (University of New Hampshire, p. 13)

The group processes at all seven institutions are based on this notion of teachers learning together by talking and listening to one another. The organization of the groups varies from the cohort structure at Maryland, Kent State, Florida, Michigan State, and Catholic University, to the communities of support and inquiry at the University of New Hampshire. Students can work together on such projects as action research (Florida and Catholic University), or engage in formal discussions of fieldwork experiences such as those described at the University of Houston and Michigan State. In all instances the groups and assignments need to be organized in ways which ensure that the speaker is heard, and that the listener as well as the speaker are learning from the critical examination of the explanation of experience shared in the process.

CONCLUDING THOUGHTS

The notion of power, which until this point appears explicitly only in the title of this chapter, can be considered now as the chapter draws to a close. In the feminist literature, voice and power are often linked by a conceptualization that either explicitly states, or implicitly implies, that claiming, experiencing, and/or honoring one's voice empowers the individual by putting her in contact with her own intelligence. This also is the argument of this chapter. As teachers talk about their work and "name" their experiences, they learn about what they know and what they believe. They also learn what they do not know. Such knowledge empowers the individual by providing a source for action that is generated from within rather than imposed from without. In Dewey's (1933) terms, teachers who know in this way can act with intent; they are empowered to draw from the center of their own knowing and act as critics and creators of their world rather than solely respondents to it, or worse, victims of it. Agency, as it is described in this model, casts voice as the connection between reflection and action. Power is thus linked with agency or intentionality. People who are empowered— teachers in this case—are those who are able to act in accordance with what they know and believe.

There is, however, a caveat in this argument. The caveat concerns the contexts of teacher learning and teacher action in which this voice-claiming is to occur. Educational institutions, like the larger contexts of which they are a part, are not neutral environments which welcome diverse voices and honor them equally. Instead, voice is attached to authority in educational institutions, and authority is connected with power that is typically zero/sum based and operates according to a "if-you-have-more-I-have-less" principle. Empowerment is rendered problematic in these settings where power is viewed as a scarce resource rather than a shared one that holds potential for institutional and personal change.

Given the reality of the typical school context, therefore, it may not be so that teachers empowered through the mechanism of voice described in this chapter can act in accordance with what they know and believe. It is so, however, that with no voice, teachers will not be able to act with intent. If we are to envision a world of schooling that better meets the needs of our changing society, it is essential that we change our conception of power to be inclusive rather than exclusive. It is also essential that we prepare teachers to claim their voice and in so doing, claim access to their own power and consequently the potential for change. Through claiming and exercising voice, teachers can learn to draw on what they know and believe as they enter the world of schools. Similarly they can prepare themselves for responsible work that is responsive to the increasingly complex demands of teaching in the twenty-first century. Beyond affecting their ability to work effectively, however, is the issue of voice and living powerfully. Preparing teachers to exercise their voices prepares them to act with agency in their own lives. It is with an eye towards empowerment of that magnitude that I believe we must examine our work in teacher education. For it is towards the teacher who lives and works with agency that we will look for leadership and hope in the coming years of school change.

13

The Essentialist Tension in Reflective Teacher Education

*Essentialist thought is at work in every social universe
and especially in the field of cultural production—the
religious, scientific, and legal fields, etc.—where games
in which the universal is at stake are being played out.*
                                        Bourdieu

Above, French culture critic and educational theorist, Pierre Bourdieu[1] names the philosophic topic of this critique chapter. This is the
matter, indeed the debate, over essentialism in late modern institutions
and social practices. The purpose is to explore the meaning of essentialism for reflective teacher education. This will be undertaken in several steps: defining essentialism, conceptualizing it in light of the teacher
education programs of this book, and offering a non-essentialist coun-
terpart in a reflection about teaching. What should emerge is recognition of the importance for the work of teacher professionals of the primary intellectual debate of the present epoch. As will be seen, this is
between modernist essentialism and postmodernist non-essentialism.

For introductory purposes, "essentialism" is defined as any belief,
practice or theory that exemplifies "the will to truth," that is, that there
is one belief, explanation, action, practice, and so forth, that is the best
possible.[2] Such a life-orientation is relevant to reflective teaching and
teacher education for several reasons: First, teachers, as all persons,

have a set of beliefs which deeply undergird their actions in the world (Quine and Ullian, 1970). In the language of philosophy, these concern such matters as the nature of reality, persons, knowledge, and goodness. They are beliefs that premise all other "theorizations" about teaching and thus descriptions of teacher preparatory programs. Second, like many others, those concerned about teaching are often essentialist in their thinking, even as they struggle with non-essentialist intuitions. This is because essentialism hegemonically dominates the commonsense lives of those who live in late twentieth century, western, capitalist, liberal democracies (Rorty, 1989a). Third and finally, because they are reformist in intent, reflective teacher education programs may indeed offer possibilities of non-essentialism in theory and practice. They may suggest, as does this author, that changing teaching practice relies on changing teacher thinking and teacher beliefs (Fenstermacher, 1986), and that "foundational" changes are necessary. Whether these possibilities are present is the point of the central section of this chapter. Prior are sections that establish the definitional frame for analysis; subsequent are ones that offer both a conceptualization of postmodern teaching and a reconsideration of the chapter's relevance.

INTRODUCING THE ESSENTIAL TENSION

In what follows, various forms of the terms "essential" and essentialism are used and clarification is vital. To begin, philosopher of science, Thomas Kuhn (1959, 1977) poses an *essential tension* in scientific practice as between tradition and innovation, between its doing with "tools at hand" or with "divergent approaches," by "traditionalists or iconoclasts" (p. 227). In science, one might suggest that worthwhile practice requires and worthwhile practitioners possess both orientations.

A similar tension exists in teacher education, between convention and innovation—between typical and alternative conceptions and processes in the education of new teachers. The point of alternative programs is that they seek to fulfill enduring conventional aims of preparing good teachers but in new ways. These new ways center on the concept of reflective teaching, a concept that is part of a late-century, educational reform effort. As exemplars of this book demonstrate, reflective reforms are played out in various programmatic aspects that include the awareness and assessment of the multiple contexts of teaching (University of Houston), the enhancement of teacher judgment (University of Florida), and the establishment of inquiry as support for all persons involved in the preparation process (University of New Hampshire).[3]

This chapter takes up what Richard Bernstein (1983) calls an "uneasiness" (p. 1) that underlies these particular reforms, the education reform effort, and indeed all intellectual and practical action today. This is the *essential tension between modernism and postmodernism* that is encapsulated in the phrase "essentialist tension." The *essentialist tension* expands Kuhn's notion from the practical realm of micro-scientific practice to the more abstract realm of macro-theory (in which practices take place). Here is the needed clarification: (1) Explanations of life in the post-industrial world center on the terms modernism and post-modernism. These explanations are located in a time of transition and perhaps of change unlike any of historical precedent (Lyotard, 1984). (2) The tension between these worldviews is itself a continual tug toward modernism because the latter is both historically antecedent and dominant. (3) As indicated previously, the dominant pull of western modernism is toward essentialism. Richard Rorty writes about it this way:

> Essentialism has been fruitful in many areas—most notably in helping us see elegant mathematical relationships behind complex motions, and perspicuous micro-structures behind confusing macro-structures. But we have gradually became suspicious of essentialism as applied to human affairs, in areas such as history, sociology and anthropology. The attempt to find laws of history or essences of cultures—to substitute theory for narrative as an aid to understanding ourselves, others, and the opinions which we present to one another—has been notoriously unfruitful. (Rorty, 1989b, p. 2)[4]

As Rorty indicates, the essential tension between modernism and postmodernism is presently being played out in all social arenas, such as education, in the tensive interrogation of postmodernist critique on modernist life. What has ensued is "a contest between an entrenched vocabulary which has become a nuisance [read modernism] and a half-formed new vocabulary which vaguely promises great things [read postmodernism]" (Rorty, 1989a, p. 9). Moreover, as the new vocabulary is parasitic on the old for its own existence and practice (see Hutcheon, 1988), there is present the constant flux of accommodation and contradiction that creates the uneasiness referred to above.

A caveat about the present debate. Within it, all thoughtful participants are in some agreement about the nature of the relation between theory and persons' knowledge of the world. Three common ideas are that all beliefs, practices, institutions (etc.) are historically evolving and socially constructed and are available through mediated language (Taylor, 1985). Together these mean that there are no absolute, neutral, objective, transcendental ways of being, understanding and acting. However, as indicated, debate still continues over the extent to which individual scholars are willing to give up theoretical essentials—as sources, as beginning and ending points, as processes, as rationales. Even more significantly, the everyday lives of most persons continue conventionally without much thought given to the essentialisms that underpin modernity and its "search for certainty."[5]

DEFINITIONAL ELABORATION

Since essentialism is endemic to modernity and for several hundred years historically evolving, it is not surprising that it has taken on several subtle theoretical forms. Some recognition of them is useful for what follows as critique, since while essentialism in teacher education is to be conceptualized at a level of functional theory, these theories are themselves underpinned by more pervasive essentialist theoretical-worldviews. One notes to begin that the term essentialism has several historic and present usages that relate to but are not the same as those employed herein. Two examples are found in proposals and rejections for linguistic essentialism (Quine, 1953), that there is "truth" to the meaning of terms, and gender essentialism (de Lauretis, 1986), that there is a "nature" to females and males.[6] As well, there have been and are proposed theories of cultural essentialism. Related to the latter, and dating from the 1950s, a philosophical, educational essentialism promotes

> the established beliefs and institutions of our modern heritage not only as real but true, and not only true but good. It recognizes . . . that this heritage is marred by flaws . . . but it insists that these are usually if not always the results of mistakes in human judgment, not evils inherent in the universe or in man. (Brameld, 1971, p. 182)

One form of essentialist educational philosophy is perennialism, an advocacy for the tenets of classical education from such thinkers as Plato, Aristotle, and Thomas Aquinas. In his explication and critique, Theodore Brameld (1971) explains that "medieval theory and practice . . . [in] education have remained influential down through the centuries," (p. 291) and particularly in an American revival beginning in the twenties. Adherents of perennialism include Robert Hutchins (and his great books) and more recently, Mortimer Adler (and his paideia). It is noted that E. D. Hirsch (1987) with his cultural literacy is also essentialist.[7] These and other occasional uses of the term are more narrowly construed than the formulations that now follow, yet they exhibit the same spirit.

A starting point is to return to and refine the introductory definition as characterized in "the will to truth." Proposals of one best belief, explanation, action, practice, and so on, are all instances of a more general, stipulated definition: *Essentialism is any expression of totality, singularity, sameness or oneness.* In the chart that follows, essentialism is found in more traditional metaphysics as in the first four categories as well as in the last four from social-political theory.

A final word about this list of modernist essential-isms. Several decades ago (and still present in some foundations textbooks), philosophers of education taught the "isms" in which educators learned to see themselves as realists or existentialists, and so forth. To name an essentialism for identification and adoption by reflective teacher educators and others is precisely the opposite purpose of this chapter. To do this is *essentialist* and accounts poorly for what philosophic insight can give to educational thought and practice. In presenting the tensions in the next section and subsequently in offering a postmodern illustration, the hope is for reformulation of founding beliefs away from modernist essentials.

EXEMPLIFYING TENSIONS

For theorization about essentialism to have significance for teacher education, it must be connected to the world of practice and in this book to the program descriptions of particular reformist teacher education programs. Analysis that follows is somewhat generalizable as other proponents and programs in reflective teaching and in like reform efforts are subject to similar reflection.[16] The analysis is undertaken through exemplification of a series of tension indicators, of concepts that allow for modernist and postmodernist interpretation—and precisely do not reify and essentialize as do the theoretical formulations just presented.[17] They are as philosophers describe them "open concepts." Importantly, each can be considered in each program context and many others are also relevant. In addition to reification, other dangers are

CHART 13.1
Forms of Essentialism

Theoretical Form	Definition
Foundationalism	This is the philosopher's quest to search for an Archimedian point upon which to ground knowledge. Examples are the two foundations of Man(sic) and God written about by Descartes.[8]
Objectivism	This is the basic conviction that there is or must be some permanent, ahistorical matrix or framework that can be appealed to in determining the nature of rationality, knowledge, truth, goodness, or rightness.[9] Some like Plato's forms are unchanging and others like Hegel's *Geist* (spirit) are dynamic.
Rationalism	This is to pose an inherent order in reality of unchangeable principles that are uncoverable only through reason. Reason has various characteristics as logos or logic, telos or aim, or as transcendence to perfection. The Scholastics are rationalists in their pursuit of God's word through reason.[10]
Formalism	This is the idea that the world is best understood as given forms or essences and man's task is to uncover and represent them.[11] Relatively recent manifestations of formalism are found in attempts to define art by essential elements or concepts as in the writings of Clive Bell and Frank Sibley.[12]
Structuralism	This is the theory that social life can be defined in terms of essences with internal coherence, systematicity, and completeness. Many are regenerating, reproducing, and changing.[13] Among structuralists are Claude Levi-Strauss, Piaget, and Chomsky.
Functionalism	This is understanding social life through a biological metaphor, as explanation of human "processes" such as selection, socialization, and training necessary for survival. Each functional aspect contributes to the whole, as Talcott Parsons writes.[14]
Universalism	This is to theorize social essentialism at the level of culture in sameness of beliefs, institutions, and practices by everyone. Common examples are marriage and burial customs. A recent account is Nancy Chodorow's (1978) claim for the universal role of mothering.
Relativism	This is the theoretical stance taken by some opponents of other essentialisms that there is no belief, practice, or theory that is transhistorical or universal. This is essentialist if taken as absolute. More recent theorizing in anthropology has promoted cultural relativism over universalism. The work of Clifford Geertz is one example[15]

potentially present that must be avoided. Clearly, program descriptions are always partial and may be misconstrued, and program statements cannot be reduced to the beliefs of participants in them.

University of Florida, PROTEACH.[18] A *tension of language* is exemplified in the tug-of-war between program linguistic formulations that close dawn and fix meaning (read modernism) and that open up and make meanings fluid (read postmodernism). Examples are prevalent in the PROTEACH description. Consider firstly modernist language form: in claiming *common* principles and definitions—that is, of reflection itself, in needing "a unified view of teaching" and programmatic coherence, in desiring consensus and resolution of conflict aver program purposes and development processes, (even more subtlety) in naming "*a* theory of learning" as required for the program and as an aim unresolved. Consider as contrast, postmodernist language form: in raising questions rather than answers, in emphasizing dialogue and "continual revision," in "viewing learning as socially constructed," in noting elements of theoryladenness and perspective, in recognizing the strong influence of societal context in defining reflective teaching, and in proposing continual formative rather than summative evaluation. Overall impressions emerge. First, the pull of modernist knowing is so strong that postmodernist intuition is devalued and often offered apologetically. Second, language reflects this in its own striving for fixed clarity. Adequate words are not available for all that postmodern insight suggests precisely because the words themselves come out of modernism.

Michigan State University, multiple perspectives. A *tension of diversity* is exemplified in both a pull toward plurality that is undergirded by modernist sameness and desire for certainty and, as counterpull, a tendency toward plurality that is undergirded by postmodernist acknowledgement and respect for internal difference. Subtlety of analysis is required since multiple perspectives answers the American ideological need for individualism. Some indication of postmodern differentiation is present in program description: in opposing superficial knowledge, in organizing curriculum around complex concepts, in believing that teacher education is more than "one-size-fits-all." However, modernism is asserted in even stronger claims for singularity: in calling for "a coherent program" based on "the knowledge base of teaching and learning," and in desiring direct correspondences of schooling functions and student outcomes. Reification is also present, for instance in naming only "four functions of schooling." Another impression is encapsulated in two fictional phrases, the first (modernist) which seems pervasive in this and most other programs with multiple elements and contrasts significantly with the second (postmodernist): "We agree on the same multiple elements and on their same, singular composition," or "in our multiple elements, we agree to disagree about their composition and value their own diversity."

University of New Hampshire, communities of inquiry and support. A *tension of voice* is exemplified in mutually-held desires both for "safe space" for individuals and for community, founded on the premise that "something of value—social, personal, intellectual, ethical" arises out of mutually reinforcing exchange. This is the tension (present in modernism and reformulated in postmodernism) between personal autonomy and group solidarity. The tension exists not only at the level of discourse as in the first two exemplars, but also at the level of the continual interplay of process. In this description gone are absolutes replaced instead by relativities. However, these relativities are also construable in modernist and postmodernist formulations. Suggestive of postmodern voice(s) is a questioning of assumptions of both the program and teaching practice, establishing inquiry situations with no "win or lose," and valuing the particularity of each teaching community. Modernist voice is present in constraints of "traditional" theoretical formulations as in promotion of established views of human development and learning and of "standard ethical criteria to judge the morality of practices." One impression concerns the limitation of possible divergent voices due to initiating modernist frames since they strongly bound the possibility of postmodern conceptions for those who are theoretically uninitiated.

University of Maryland, reflection, research, and repertoire. Also an aspect of process is a *tension of edifice* exemplified in competing desires for program operation that are both stable and flexible. The tension "kicks in" when organization precludes a wide degree of flexibility that participants intuitively desire. Edifices are both institutional and programmatic and in modernist terms, reflective of a relatively-fixed theoretical basis. In the Maryland program an example is found in the initial description that begins and thus frames the rest of the organization in precise terms (seemingly unchanging) of criteria for student selection and cohort formation, and as well, curriculum and program structure. All of a piece, this descriptive frame is coupled with modernist theories of education that include models of teaching, and research on effective teaching and school effects. While these modernist discourses are easy to locate, their postmodern counterparts are more difficult to find. However, indications are present in particular ritualization by cohorts and in incorporation of curriculum from different paradigms such as the "radical social critique of schooling." This last serves as a significant illustration: while most radical, critical theory is modernist (Hassan, 1986), its inclusion opens possibility for other new theory and concommitant changed organizational structure.

University of Houston, RITE. A *tension of change* is itself illustrative of a change in tension location—from discourse and process to conception. From the Houston program the key exemplification of a changing conception of change is this disclosure: "Our reluctance to present. . .[the program] as a completed product is that we have come to realize that programs in teacher education are not static entities, but are continually modified." Tensive as modern/postmodern, program indicators include how modification is defined, how negotiation for control of modification is defined, and how negotiated and modified theories of understanding uncertainty are themselves defined. Gone here is not only a technical orientation but a positivist one as well: there are no simple answers to continually changing conditions of teaching and teacher education. However, some modernist elements are retained as in the Tylerian approach to considerations of the social and political context of the program (albeit modified), in discipline-boundary cohesion (the educational psychologists) and in valuing the correspondence (and its linearity) between the intended and operationalized curriculum. In addition to the conception of change, postmodern indicators include the strong presence and value for unanswerable questions. Postmodern impression is thus to take change rather than stasis as natural.

Kent State University, ATTEP. A *tension of power* is present in the Kent State program that is implicit rather than explicit. This is operationalized in a dualistic system of social relations that is perpetuated by a program for academically able students. Any program that advocates curriculum for some students that is "intellectually demanding and sufficiently stimulating" implies in its separation that other curriculum for other students is not demanding or sufficient. This is modernist if conceived as part of a "given" social order. This becomes postmodernist if the society, the program with its differentiated curriculum, and so on, and the cultural narrative or worldview that underpins it are all criticized. In the modern form, the societal status quo is defined in monolithic terms and is affirmed as continuing. In the postmodern form it is challenged. In the first, student categorization that is able and not able is placed in a neutral society: there is just "student." In the second, not only are the students defined by the social constructions of race, class, and gender but these categories are also reconceptualized in particular figurations of place and time. In the first, a modernist "meritocracy" is promoted and in the second a dangerous elitism is recognized. A general impression is that unintended consequences result from unexamined assumptions about societal order and power.

The Catholic University of America, reflective problem solving. A *tension of theory* is found in the Catholic University program; here conception of tension is extended to the level of theory. Once again, the problematic is hidden and even more difficult to uncover than the power relations above. Significantly, working through this tension requires a positioning within a postmodern frame. Precisely because it is "critical," the program demonstrates an awareness of power and relative theoretical frameworks. Illustrative is a definition of reflection as "viewing a situation from multiple perspectives, seeing alternatives to and consequences of one's actions, and understanding the broad social and moral embeddedness of teaching." Another indication is the application of a notion of situation in the transfer of all elements of educational theories to practices. However there still are modernist remnants. These are found in a one-way concept of transfer, a precise "think out loud" model of lesson critique, and a structured problem-solving guide. Impressions are important: first in the obvious attention paid to teacher education as "theoretical" and in placing theories inherent to the program in a broader conception. Again, just as in several tensions above, possibility exists for postmodern formulation. One important aspect for further consideration is to understand the ethical dimensions of theories themselves (Stone, 1991a).

A POSTMODERN EXAMPLE

In the preceding section, through a consideration of modernist and postmodernist discourse, process, and conception, indications of postmodern non-essentialism are suggested in the reflective teaching program descriptions. As now understood, these exist in tension with the strong pull of essentialist, modernist practices. Over and against typical, modernist "teaching," some sense is given for what postmodern teaching might look like, as difficult as that is to conceive in the late modern world. This difficulty exists, as mentioned previously, because of the dominance of modernist language. In this section, a purposeful break is attempted with that language and its practices. The reader will bear with the author (with me) as the postmodern reflection seems a bit fantastic for conventional teacher education literature and this is to be expected. It is unfamiliar and precisely offered to create dissonance

(Stone, 1991b). It is postmodern is spirit, form, and content.

In beginning this reflection, I am ordered by the task at hand: to frame myself and the world as I envision it, and as these elements relate to action in the world and specifically to teaching. Four concepts are momentarily significant; these are multiplicity, remaking, identity, and contextuality. These too evolve in what emerges as text. Initially they are formed into a reflective statement: continually in the process of remaking are my multiple identities as they exist in continually remade and multiple contexts. This is my own recognition of a postmodern world.

I begin by envisioning myselves, never as single self any longer but always as many persons related to and constrained to some degree in a body. My identity is identities, some of which I and others know and some which we do not. I am always the same and more than woman, daughter, friend, teacher. I am always the same and more than female, white, middle-class, heterosexual, western, North American, well-educated, and feminist. I am always more than a single person, "the" college professor, drinking coffee and sitting before a word processor in Honolulu, Hawaii on a winter(!) Sunday morning in the decade of the nineties.

Part of this multiplicity of identities arises from their continual remaking. "Re"-making is not redoing in the old way given my recognition of the multiplicity. It is rather a continual interruption of the "old" me(s) and a discordant emerging of the "new" me(s). There is no way to separate the new from the old and this contributes. Of course I am confused, conflicted, and contradictory in this reforming, reconstituting. This now is natural and indeed welcomed by me(s) in the presently constituted world.

Multiple, remaking identities are not without orderliness but this too is a new conception. Order is momentary and contingent, recognized and utilized for a time and then transformed into new order. There are thus "orders" that are evident as fragments of time but which possess some degree of temporal continuity. Postmodern life and identity are not insanity, chaos or anarchy; rather "life" is transcient (and of course tenuous and ambiguous).

Moreover, all momentary, continually changing selves are themselves contextualized. I(s) am not cut off from all others in some narcissistic, abstracted individualism. I am not defined in contexts of existentialist angst, psychologized "individual difference" or liberal autonomy. Context counts, in the historicized present, in what a situation and its participants "is" precisely because of a particular configuration of historical, socio-cultural factors. Context connects my identities to those of others, because we are male and female, working and upper class, Hispanic/Chicano and Hawaiian/part Hawaiian, over and under forty (etc.). Our differences are those differences that matter, and that remake us in relation to each other, what we all are.

These continually remade multiple identities that I am, interact with those of all other persons as we act in the world. The world is socially constructed, itself contingent if enduring. How I am able to act—the frames I use, the purposes I set, the results I evaluate—are all themselves analogues to who I am. That is, they are identifiable, multiple, remade, and contextualized. I envision my actions in their remaking quality. They remake me and other persons, our actions, our continually new situations. Among actions we undertake are those of teaching.

Needless to say since I as teacher am remade, my concept of teaching is remade as well. Teaching is a flexible language game, a post-"modern" dance, a conversation. I envision it as a freeform, malleable, plastic sculpture. I see it hanging like Eco's pendulum. It too is continually reforming, in its various aspects and dimensions. There is, however, still a shape, a contextualized situation. Teaching incorporates multiple persons with multiple identities, engaged in multiple tasks of multiple knowings and learnings with multiple possibilities of what is created. Herein "teaching certainties" are given up; there is no "model" of teaching, no behavioral objectives, no founding set of knowledge. But, of course there is still an entity, a concept called "teaching" that continues to exist.

Lastly, like every other worldly interaction, the multiple "we" in teaching know it when we see it—and in all of its particularity. Amid reflection, now I ponder: teaching too has postmodern identities. Its conception is never static, absolute, or totally lucid. Its practice is the messiness of us working our way through it—through educations. It is an analogue to us and our world, and its present embodiment (as in this reflection) is just all there is.

Any postmodern reflection is reminiscent of the self-portrait just presented. Its presentation is humble (Ferguson, 1991) and cannot be taken *too seriously* given its contingent form. It has no privileged status either as one's own statement or as a statement for others. It cannot make definitional claims since such claims are themselves always tentative. It exists only in the sense that some persons find it useful and then only for a time. As just presented, it is historicized at a particular place and time, and written by someone with a continuously fluid positioning. Its textual meaning is in motion also as it is read by others in their own postmodern positions.[19]

SUMMATION

The foundational question of essentialism interrogates all aspects of late twentieth-century practical and theoretical life. This means that it influences education and teaching and the particular reflective teacher education programs described in this book. In this critique chapter, essentialism is defined as any expression of totality, singularity, sameness, or oneness. Essentialism is also defined as constitutive of modernity with its continual need for and pull toward certainty. As the chapter has indicated, parasitic on, yet disruptive of, modernist essentialism is postmodern non-essentialism. Kathy Ferguson (1991) characterizes it as the "subversion toward fixed meaning claims," and in its poststructural form as the idea to "force open a space for the emergence of counter-meanings" (p. 324).

At the chapter's outset, a rationale was offered for those concerned about teaching and particularly for "reflective practitioners" (Schön, 1983) to consider the essentialism of their beliefs about the world and about their work. At this point of summary, something else needs to be said about this. There are several reasons for "giving up certainty" in teaching, not the least because its practice *is* always so contingent (Stone, 1990). Significantly, reforms of teaching and teacher education must be unpinned by changed beliefs—about procedures, contexts, theories, and their historical places in the present day. As any competent observer clearly knows, many problems exist in educational life, and piecemeal, band-aid reforms are largely unsuccessful. One possible avenue to reform is to follow the intellectual "revolution" of the epoch to see where it leads. This then is the more general message of the chapter in its look at a set of particular reformist teacher education programs. One can propose that their values lie in the presence of postmodern intuitions. Overall and in sum, a first step toward reform for these programs and all others is to gain some understanding of the essential tension of the age with its essentialist leanings toward modernism. While the latter is to be expected, efforts can be made toward displacement of the modernist, conventional forms of life that are taken for granted.

The concluding and most important point is this: to fail to take account of postmodernist insights is to retain the educational status quo with its modern-shortcomings. This is unethical. It is unethical because present life does not offer the possibility of social and educational equality for all persons promulgated as the overarching societal aim of the late twentieth-century, democratic west. Finally, it is unethical because the worldview of modernism, as essentialist, promotes sameness, oneness, and the desire for certainty. As a worldview it has been and is still constructed and controlled by some few for most others. It is their view, their sameness, and their oneness that is promoted. Difference is not foundationally valued. Thus a modernist position is elitist, harmful, and unethical. Surely, teachers and their teacher educators, who are personally reflective about their work as are the contributors to the present volume, desire something more.[20]

Afterword

The introduction to this volume raised the question of whether or not reflection was indeed a distinct orientation to teacher preparation or whether conceptions of reflection differed on such fundamental criteria as to preclude that possibility. Various typologies were offered as a basis for the reader's judgment. In addition, two of the critics, Sparks-Langer (chapter 9) and Zeichner (chapter 10) have analyzed the different dimensions or conceptions of reflection within each of the programs. While Sparks-Langer accepts diversity within programs, Zeichner sees overly generic approaches to reflection with little common commitment to a specific conception of good teaching. In his critique, Goodman (chapter 11) makes an observation similar to Zeichner's. But irrespective of their differences, the critics accept the basic premise that reflection is a conceptual orientation, albeit with quite distinct variations within it. That is a position with which I agree.

THE PARADIGM QUESTION REVISITED

The reader will remember that Feiman-Nemser (1990) takes an opposing view. But her contention that reflection is not a conceptual framework is grounded in a misinterpretation of van Manen's (1977) "ways of knowing" concept.[1] Equating ways of knowing with foci for reflection, Feiman-Nemser claims that each way of knowing warrants a distinct conceptual orientation to teaching: the technical level warrants the technological or behavioral orientation with its focus on efficient means to achieve predetermined objectives, and so forth.

The problem with this interpretation is that ways of knowing better describe the process of reflection than its content. Based on the main traditions of the social sciences (empirical-analytic, hermeneutic-phenomenological, and critical-dialectical), van Manen's levels of reflectivity make explicit different ways of and reasons for examining educational phenomena. He illustrates with his own undergraduate experience of studying the human hand from scientific and humanistic perspectives. And although he admits that "moving from one orientation to another is usually experienced as a transition between two worlds—a shift from one reality to another" (p. 212), he argues that the limitations of each way of knowing for practical action *require* movement to a higher level of reflectivity (i.e., from the technical to the interpretive; from the interpretive to the critical). Thus, for van Manen, teacher educators would be ill-advised to construct program goals around only one level of reflection: treated in isolation, they seriously distort understanding and limit ways of being practical.

Since many of the programs described in this volume depend on combined levels to develop students' reflective judgment, it would be difficult to subsume their program goals under the academic, practical, technological, personal, or critical orientations. The Catholic University program, for example, encourages students to structure problem analysis using van Manen's three levels. ATTEP's core seminars are built around different content and modes of inquiry (i.e., learning/psychological; teaching/sociological; schooling/critical). The RITE program is structured on the concept of five levels of awareness. Multiple Perspectives draws upon the notion of technical, clinical, personal, and critical competencies. And faculty in the Maryland program are seeking ways to incorporate more of a critical-dialectical knowing. Moreover, the goals of these programs are not primarily content oriented. Quality of reflection is equally as important. PROTEACH, for example, explicitly lays out expectations for reflective content, attitudes, and processes.

A separate but related problem in omitting reflection as a conceptual orientation is that nothing within the other orientations requires its inclusion. Although many teacher educators might be disposed to developing reflective capabilities in students, others are not. Scholarly debates as well as descriptions of teacher education programs indicate strong adherence to prescribed skill development (technical rationality) in the preservice years (Berliner, 1988; Howey and Zimpher, 1989; NET-WORK, 1987).

Berliner, for instance, suggests that the "struggle to develop reflective practitioners, sensible decision makers, and proficient problem solvers" is a more proper goal "for teachers who are more experienced than the novices" in preservice programs (p. 26). Warning against expecting too much of preservice teachers, he recommends narrowing expectations to following scripted lessons, observing and classifying classroom phenomenon, and practicing classroom routines. Teaching skills like decision making and priority setting, Berliner argues, are better left until beginners acquire more competence—somewhere around the third year of teaching.

There are at least two benefits, then, in viewing reflection as a conceptual orientation. The first is that limiting program goals to one way of knowing or one type of content seriously distorts, as van Manen would say, the practical reality of teaching. Reflection has the capacity to bring together aspects of teaching which the other orientations separate, leaving teacher preparation unnecessarily and impractically restrictive. Do we really want teachers to be expert only in (or even primarily in) the subject areas they teach, as in the academic paradigm? Or do we want them to draw solely, or primarily, from personal experience in their reflection, ignoring other forms of potentially useful knowledge, as in the practical paradigm? Only a reflective paradigm, it seems to me, has the power to integrate essential components of teaching. As Doyle (1990) recognizes in his typology, reflective teachers draw upon personal, craft, propositional, and theoretical knowledge.

The second benefit in viewing reflection as a conceptual orientation is that reflective capacities in teacher candidates might not be addressed at all in the other orientations. Given the difficulties involved in facilitating and sustaining reflection documented by the contributors to this volume and other authors (Wildman and Niles, 1987; Zeichner and Liston, 1987), proposing that reflection is a "natural disposition" seems foolhardy. Such a proposal suggests that left to their own devises, prospective teachers will spontaneously develop into reflective practitioners or that faculty will spontaneously construct programs which develop reflective orientations. And yet we know that even many experienced teachers operate too often out of tradition, habit, and prescription rather than reflective judgment. We also know that many teacher educators are themselves poor models of what they teach. Without an explicit commitment to reflection in program goals, and faculty dialogue about achieving those goals, a "disposition toward reflection" is not likely to be more than sporadic or superficial.

Given everything that teacher education programs are asked to accomplish, reflection could too easily be relegated to the non-essential or taken-for-granted outcomes list if it is not specified as the underlying paradigm or primary goal. Teacher education programs will not encourage reflection by default. As several cases presented here suggest, even when reflection is the operating paradigm, inconsistencies occur between the official and the enacted curriculum. Both the Multiple Perspectives and PROTEACH programs report supervisors inadvertently focusing on easily recorded effective teaching behaviors rather than prompting reflection on more critical and complex issues. If reflective teaching is a goal to which teacher education programs subscribe, this goal must be explicitly structured into programs and evaluated, and faculty must discuss the content, processes, and attitudes of reflection they regard as important.

In the long run, debate about whether reflection is a distinct conceptual orientation may not be as important as clearly specifying the type, purpose, and nature of reflective inquiry expected of prospective teachers. This specificity becomes increasingly urgent as institutions struggling to gain accreditation latch on to models of teacher education which appear to have currency without appreciating the variations which exist and the problems involved in defining and fostering reflection. Perhaps reflection has now become so common that we need different terms or more specific descriptors for program orientations.

Because of the need for clarity and commitment, Feiman-Nemser's argument that reflection is not a conceptual orientation may do a great service for reflective teacher educators. We need to ask ourselves, as she does: Does this orientation promote a particular vision of teaching? Does it have a theory of learning to teach? Do faculty hold goals and means of achieving those goals in common? Do programs articulate content for reflection?

CONCEPTIONS OF GOOD TEACHING

Assuming that reflection is a distinct conceptual orientation, Kennedy's (1989) contrast with a professional standards (or technical rationality) model provides a particularly useful framework in which to envision contrasting images of good teaching. The basic distinction between technical rationality and reflective practice allows for differentiation within the two approaches.

From my reading of the case studies, the critique chapters, and the various typologies described in the introduction, I would propose that there are at least six different ways in which knowledge is used to guide practice. These different relations between knowledge and practice also have implications for what type of knowledge, and ultimately what type of teaching, is valued. Since all but the first type, which is strictly behavioral, involve some form of reflection, I will refer to the way knowledge is used to guide practice as *quality* of reflection and the type of knowledge valued as *content* for reflection. The first two categories are types of technical rationality while the last four are versions of reflective practice.

Technical Rationality

In this approach to teaching, students are encouraged to conform their practice to generalizations about relationships among variables which result from empirical research (Grimmett, MacKinnon, Erickson, and Riecken, 1990; Tom and Valli, 1990). Because of the quest for certainty and generalizable relationships, Stone (chapter 13) would characterize this approach as essentialist.

Behavioral. This is the only image of good teaching which excludes any form of reflection. As indicated in the introduction, concern here is strictly with skill acquisition, "with fostering the development of skill in an actual performance of a predetermined task" (Zeichner, 1983, p. 4). In behavioristic teacher education programs, candidates would need to demonstrate adequate teaching competency based primarily on effective teaching research. External authorities would judge both the types of behaviors viewed as appropriate and the candidate's adequacy in demonstrating those behaviors. Though not intentional, some supervisors at Michigan State University and the University of Florida found themselves slipping into this mode of teacher preparation.

Technical decision making. This image of good teaching also emphasizes the adequate performance of prescribed teaching behaviors. However, in this case, prospective teachers are trained to judge their own performance. "Propositional knowledge is reflected upon and then applied to practice in an instrumental manner" (Grimmett, MacKinnon, Erickson, and Riecken, 1990, p. 25). This knowledge is not open to judgment or debate. Instead, reflective decision making is limited to the technical determination about whether or not one's own performance conforms to this knowledge.

While Stone found pulls toward essentialism in each of the case studies, none essentially advocates either of these first two approaches to teacher preparation. Using research knowledge in such a straightforward way to determine practice is seen as overly restrictive. With Schön, program designers reject the adequacy of "instrumental problem solving made rigorous by the application of scientific theory and technique" (Schön, 1983, p. 21). Instead, they emphasize the tentativeness and tenuousness of the theory/practice relation. As the University of New Hampshire authors put it, "Our vision of teacher as decision maker challenges the orthodoxy of a single knowledge base where ends are undisputed and means are empirically revealed" (p. 6).

Reflective Practitioner

In this general approach to good teaching, the theory/practice relation is problematized. The reflective question is not "Did I employ such and such aspect of research," but "Is that theory or finding relevant to this situation, and do I accept the value assumptions implicit in that strand of research?" Distinction is made between research findings—the way things work in general—and practice—the uniqueness of each classroom event (University of Maryland). Students are asked to formulate for themselves an answer to the question, "What is the role of research in teaching practice?" (University of Florida). Unreflective conformity to even authoritative knowledge is strongly discouraged. Because of this, and because of its emphasis on contextuality and multiplicity, this approach would be characterized by Stone as non-essentialist.

Reflection-in-action. This is, of course, Schön's preferred image of the reflective practitioner, one who realizes that the "complexity, uncertainty, instability, uniqueness, and value-conflict" inherent in teaching situations limit the usefulness of technical rationality (Schön, 1983, p. 39). In this type of reflection, external knowledge only tangentially guides practice. The situation itself is viewed as an important source of knowledge. Reflective practitioners must read their unique contexts to determine how to proceed; they must be versed in conditional as well as propositional and procedural knowledge (Brophy, 1987). For the first time, craft knowledge derived from one's own practice is valued. Like the previous two levels, however, focus is still primarily on pedagogical activity. The main difference is that contextual factors are now considered. Problematizing or inquiring about the broader goals and purposes of schooling is not yet central.

Deliberative. The reflection-in-action approach to teaching implies the possibility of conflicting guides to practice. The deliberative approach[2] to teaching makes reflection on competing explanations, perspectives, and theories a central component of teacher preparation— almost a precondition for reflective action. In this approach, knowledge does not directly guide practice but, rather, indirectly informs it (Grimmett et al., 1990). A vivid example of deliberative reflection is found in the University of New Hampshire program (chapter 1). In constructing their own philosophies of education, students are asked to make competing positions on specific issues explicit. In the case of Sally, this involved examining how collaborative, utilitarian, and individual rights positions would inform home/school relations. The notion of dilemmas of teaching, used in a number of programs, also prompts this type of reflection.

Personalistic. Sparks-Langer (chapter 9) refers to his as the narrative approach to teaching while Zeichner (chapter 10) labels it the developmental. Teacher's voice, personal growth, and professional relations are of primary concern. The concept of a teacher's appreciation system (used in the PROTEACH program) tends to displace or supercede the more technical and limited concept of knowledge base. Richert's critique chapter best exemplifies this approach. Assuming that teachers must be constructors and definers of their own knowledge, Richert uses the feminist concept of voice to argue that experiences in hearing one's own voice and the voices of others must be an essential part of the teacher education curriculum. Though she finds examples of these experiences across all seven cases the University of New Hampshire most centrally structures their program around developmental experiences.

Critical. The last approach to teaching is the critical, which evolved from the social reconstructionist tradition in educational reform. Only at this level are social and political implications of teaching and schooling central to the reflective preparation of teachers. However, as Zeichner (chapter 10) cautions, study of the social and political aspects of schooling does not necessarily constitute a critical perspective. This perspective must emphasize the real possibility that schools are implicated in perpetuating an unjust social order. Further, it should help teachers act at classroom, school, and system levels to correct these injustices. While Richert's feminist analysis is part of a personal or narrative tradition, Goodman's feminist perspective (chapter 11) extends this critical tradition. He notes the lack of attention to critically-oriented aspects of feminist pedagogy: the relation between the powerlessness of women and the powerlessness of teachers; the legitimation of masculine rationality; and the need to take women students seriously. The absence of these

TABLE 1
Models of Teacher Preparation

	Technical Rationality		Reflective Practice			
	Behavioral	Technical Decision Making	Reflection in Action	Deliberative	Personalistic	Critical
Quality of Reflection	not applicable	matching performance to external guidelines	contextualizing craft and propositional knowledge	weighing competing claims and viewpoints	hearing one's own voice	problematizing the goals and purposes of schooling in light of justice and other ethical criteria
Content for Reflection	*generic instruction and management behaviors derived from research on teaching	generic instruction and management behaviors derived from research on teaching	personal teaching performance	a range of teaching concerns	personal growth and relational issues	social and political dimensions of schooling

*In the behavioral model, this is *prescribed*, not reflective content.

TABLE 2
Levels of Reflective Teacher Preparation

	Level	Quality of Reflection	Content for Reflection
Reflective Practice	6. critical (social reconstructionist)	problematizing the goals and purposes of schooling in light of justice and other ethical criteria	social and political dimensions of schooling
	5. personalistic (developmental, narrative)	hearing one's own voice	personal growth and relational issues
	4. deliberative (social efficiency, cognitive)	weighing competing claims and viewpoints	a range of teaching concerns
	3. reflection-in-action	contextualizing craft and propositional knowledge	personal teaching performance
Technical Rationality	2. technical decision making	matching performance to external guidelines	generic instruction and management behaviors derived from research on teaching
	1. behavioral	not applicable	*generic instruction and management behaviors derived from research on teaching

*At the behavioral level, this is *prescribed*, not reflective content.

themes supports Zeichner's and Sparks-Langer's conclusions that the critical perspective receives relatively limited attention across the seven programs.[3]

LEVELS VERSUS MODELS OF
REFLECTIVE TEACHER PREPARATION

These six approaches to good teaching and teacher preparation can be viewed in two ways: either as mutually exclusive visions of good teaching or as hierarchical qualities of good teachers. Table 1 captures the notion of opposing ideal types; table 2 portrays the approaches as levels within a taxonomy with behavioral as the first and lowest level of teaching competence, and critical as the sixth and highest. My own preference would be for reflective teaching models to adopt the latter perspective. This synthesis of levels is consistent with the practice of many of the programs in this volume. It is also in keeping with van Manen's advice that practitioners use all three ways of knowing and with the perspectives of numerous other scholars—including Schon.

Oddly, as much as he casts technical rationality as the foil to his reflective practitioner model, Schön himself discusses technical training as an essential base for reflective practice and draws upon technical information in his own problem-solving examples (Richardson, 1990; Gillis, 1988). Friendly critics have also questioned the technical rationality/reflective practitioner dichotomy, arguing that it does not adequately portray the world of practice (Shulman, 1988); that knowledge-in-action must be informed by technical rationality; and that "the results of scientific-inquiry can be and have been of great help in the indeterminate zones of practice." (Fenstermacher, 1988, p. 45)

Shulman (1988) claims that "most teachers are capable of teaching in a manner that combines the technical with the reflective, the theoretical and practical, the universal and the concrete" and that "we need a continuous interplay between the two principles of technical rationality and reflection-in-action" (pp. 33-35). Fenstermacher (1988) further argues that no bifurcation exists between science and practice and that knowledge from each should inform the other.

In a related discussion, Tom (1991) has argued that technical rationality (and specifically research on teaching effectiveness) portrays teaching in a "dangerously" simplistic light. Comprising isolated bits of information about individual variables, this reflective tradition ignores the complexity of teachers' work, indeterminate aspects of teaching, tradeoffs teachers must make between competing goals, and the professional judgment they must exercise. But instead of advocating an alternative approach, Tom calls for a synthesis of traditions which would include social efficiency (or technical rationality). Separately, he says, the different traditions "are grounded on a myopic vision of what constitutes an adequate rationale" for a professional curriculum. But since each "holds the promise of throwing light on a different domain of the riddle of teacher education," taken together they offer a balanced and comprehensive view of the teacher education curriculum.

Though Tom opposes giving equal rank to each tradition, I see them as a hierarchical taxonomy (illustrated in table 2). This type of ordering is similar to van Manen's and to one proposed by Prakash and Waks (1985) regarding conceptions of educational excellence. Claiming that excellence is described by competing advocates as mental proficiency, disciplinary initiation, self-actualization, and social responsibility, the authors "view each of the last three conceptions as at least potentially more inclusive of relevant educational values than the one preceding it" (p. 79). They argue that these different conceptions are compatible if shaped and given meaning by the most inclusive conception of excellence—social responsibility.

A similar case can be made for the conceptions of teacher education outlined in tables 1 and 2. They are compatible if interpreted within the broader and higher conceptions. Such an ordering suggests that certain levels might be prerequisite to others (e.g., a basic grasp of technical knowledge and skill is needed for deliberative reflection) and that certain educational issues or questions are more important than others (e.g., how to make schools more just and democratic is more important than maximizing time on task). Thus, I would second Zeichner's caution against programs having a "generic" emphasis toward reflection, where the content of reflection is immaterial and the only purpose it serves is to make teachers' actions more conscious and intentional. Instead, a reflective orientation to teacher preparation should clearly address the content, processes, and attitudes valued in reflective practice.[4]

This discussion is not meant to imply that designing such programs is an easy task. The chapters in this volume attest to both developmental and institutional problems in constructing reflective programs. As a critic and learning-to-teach researcher, Calderhead (chapter 8) also reminds us of several factors which impede the implementation of reflective programs: lack of coherent theories about the learning-to-teach process; lack of agreement on program goals; the different ideas and expectations with which teaching candidates approach their preparation; and the ambitious (but perhaps unrealistic) goals programs set for themselves—a factor which echoes Berliner's (1988) concern.

Kennedy (1989) voices additional concerns about the developmental process of fostering reflective practice. Calling the reflective process "chaotic and slippery," she conjures up this scenario:

> Imagine a practitioner who does a bad job of interpreting a new situation. Such a practitioner can draw faulty conclusions from this new experience and consequently alter her working knowledge in faulty ways. This same practitioner will then use this faulty working knowledge to interpret other new situations in the future, and may, through this inappropriate interpretive lens, find still more 'evidence' that confirms the original bad idea. (p. 3)

Reflection is obviously not synonymous with wise judgment; experience can teach wrong lessons.

Too often, Kennedy (1987, 1989) reminds us, we induce false principles from experience. We use new knowledge to confirm rather than disconfirm or challenge our thinking; a priori assumptions about what constitutes good teaching are particularly difficult to dislodge. We overestimate the relationship among various events on the one hand and, on the other, fail to recognize similar problem structures from one event to another. Further complicating the matter is that we as yet know little about the way teachers organize their working knowledge (Kennedy, 1987). What, for example, would prompt Teacher A to use personal experience as a justification for a particular action while Teacher B might draw upon empirical research as justification for a different course of action? The line between reflection and rationalization seems to be easy to cross—but not always easy to detect. As Ross, Johnson, and Smith (chapter 2) ask, how can we tell the difference between reflection and procedural display?

CONCLUSION

With schools, colleges, and departments of education looking for models of teacher preparation to guide their programs, often with the threat of accreditation denial looming, there is the continued risk that "reflection" will become more and more of a slogan and carry less and less meaning. Reflection is endangered if it becomes merely one more goal or objective uncritically thrown into the hopper of desirable outcomes. Reflection evolved in different ways in the programs described in this volume. In some places it was the central, guiding concept. In others it emerged over time with other program goals. However, the institutions do share one important thing in common: program faculty collaboratively designed and redesigned their programs in a thoughtful, deliberative manner. While total agreement will remain an elusive goal, continued inquiry and negotiation about the meaning and purpose of reflection must remain on the agenda if teacher educators are ever to

> identify clearly the educational and political commitments that stand behind their own and others' proposals regarding reflective teaching so that we can move beyond the current situation where important differences in our motives and passions are hidden from view by the use of popular slogans. (Tabachnick and Zeichner, 1991, p. 2)

Notes and References

FOREWORD

References

Good, T. L. 1990. Building the knowledge base of teaching. In D. D. Dill & Associates, eds., *What teachers need to know: The knowledge, skills, and values essential to good teaching* (pp. 17-75). San Francisco: Jossey-Bass.

National Council for Accreditation of Teacher Education. 1990. *Standards, procedures, and policies for the accreditation of professional education units.* Washington, DC: Author.

Schön, D. A. 1983. *The reflective practitioner: How professionals think in action.* New York: Basic Books.

Tom, A. R. 1985. Inquiring into inquiry-oriented teacher education. *Journal of Teacher Education*, 36(5):35-44.

Zeichner, K. M. 1991. Reflections on reflective teaching. In K. M. Zeichner and B. R. Tabachnick, eds., *Issues and practices in inquiry-oriented teacher education* (pp. 1-21). London: Falmer Press.

INTRODUCTION

Notes

I would like to thank Alan Tom, Series Editor, and Lois Patton, SUNY Press Editor-in-Chief, for encouraging and supporting this project.

1. Many of these factors are part of the more pervasive social skepticism toward scientific certainty, social engineering, and hierarchical management. I deal here only with the more proximate influences on teacher education.

2. Action research has a long history of use in in-service teacher education. Although its initial application tended to fit a technical, applied science, quasi-experimental model, later versions have stressed critical inquiry and

interpretive paradigms. (See Tom, 1985; Carr and Kemmis, 1986; and Noffke, 1990).

3. Other such cases the reader might want to pursue are Beyer (1984), Tom (1988); and Noordhoof and Kleinfeld (1990).

References

Barnes, H. 1987. The conceptual basis for thematic teacher education programs. *Journal of Teacher Education*, 38(4):13-18.

Beyer, L. 1984. Field experience, ideology, and the development of critical reflectivity. *Journal of Teacher Education*, 35(3):36-41.

Carr, W., and S. Kemmis. 1986. *Becoming critical: Education, knowledge and action research*. London: Falmer.

Clark, C., and P. Peterson. 1986. Teachers' thought processes. In M. C. Wittrock, ed., *Handbook of research on teaching* (pp. 255-296). New York: MacMillan.

Clift, R., W. R. Houston, and M. Pugach, eds. 1990. *Encouraging reflective practice in education: An analysis of issues and programs*. New York: Teachers College Press.

Doyle, W. 1990. Themes in teacher education research. In W. R. Houston, ed., *Handbook for research on teacher education* (pp. 3-24). New York: MacMillan.

Elbaz, F. 1983. *Teacher thinking*. New York: Nichols Publishing Co.

Feimen-Nemser, S. 1990. Teacher preparation: Structural and conceptual alternatives. In W. R. Houston, ed., *Handbook of research on teacher education* (pp. 212-233). New York: MacMillan.

Goodlad, J. 1990. Better teachers for our nation's schools. *Phi Delta Kappan*, 72(3):185-194.

Grimmett, P., and G. Erickson, eds. 1988. *Reflection in teacher education*. New York: Teachers College Press.

Grimmett, P. et al. 1990. Reflective practice in teacher education. In R. Clift, W. R. Houston, and M. Pugach, eds., *Encouraging reflective practice in education* (pp. 20-38). New York: Teachers College Press.

Grossman, P. 1990. *The making of a teacher*. New York: Teachers College Press.

Kennedy, M. 1989. Reflection and the problem of professional standards. *Colloquy*, 2(2):1-6.

LaBoskey, V. 1991. A conceptual framework for reflection in preservice teacher education. Paper presented at the Conceptualizing Reflection in Teacher

Development Conference, Bath, England.

Lanier, J., and J. Little. 1986. Research on teacher education. In W. C. Wittrock, ed., *Handbook of research on teaching* (pp. 527-569). New York: MacMillan.

Noffke, S. 1990. Action research and the work of teachers. A paper presented at the Annual Meeting of the American Educational Research Association.

Noordhoff, K., and J. Kleinfeld. 1990. Shaping the rhetoric of reflection for multicultural settings. In R. Clift, W. R. Houston, and M. Pugach, eds., *Encouraging reflective practice in education* (pp. 163-185). New York: Teachers College Press.

Richardson, V. 1990. The evolution of reflective teaching and teacher education. In R. Clift, W. R. Houston, and M. Pugach, eds., *Encouraging reflective practice in education* (pp. 3-19). New York: Teachers College Press.

Ross, D. 1990. Programmatic structures for the preparation of reflective teachers. In R. Clift, W. R. Houston, and M. Pugach, eds., *Encouraging reflective practice in education* (pp. 97-118). New York: Teachers College Press.

Schön, D. 1987. *Educating the reflective practitioner.* San Francisco: Jossey-Bass.

Shulman, L. 1987. Knowledge and teaching: Foundations of the new reform. *Harvard Educational Review*, 57(1):1-21.

Tabachnick, B., and K. Zeichner, eds. 1991. *Issues and practices in inquiry-oriented teacher education.* New York: Falmer.

Tom, A. R. 1985. Inquiring into inquiry-oriented teacher education. *Journal of Teacher Education*, 36(5):35-44.

————. 1986. What are the fundamental problems in the professional education of teachers? Paper delivered at the Conference on Excellence in Teacher Education through the Liberal Arts, Chicago.

————. 1988. The practical art of redesigning teacher education: Teacher education reform at Washington University, 1970-1975. *Peabody Journal of Education*, 65(2):158-179. (Published in 1990).

Tom, A. R., and L. Valli. 1990. Professional knowledge for teachers. In W. R. Houston, ed., *Handbook of research on teacher education* (pp. 373-392). New York: MacMillan.

Valli, L. 1990. Moral approaches to reflective practice. In R. Clift, W. R. Houston, and M. Pugach, eds., *Encouraging reflective practice in education* (pp. 39-56). New York: Teachers College Press.

van Manen, M. 1977. Linking ways of knowing with ways of being practical. *Curriculum Inquiry*, 6(3):205-228.

Zeichner, K. 1983. Alternative paradigms of teacher education. *Journal of Teacher Education*, 34(3):3-9.

————. 1987. Preparing reflective teachers: An overview of instructional strategies which have been employed in preservice teacher education. *International Journal of Educational Research*, 11(5):565-575.

CHAPTER 1

Notes

1. Approximately 15 percent of graduates begin the program at the post-baccalaureate level. These students may take fifteen months to two years to complete the program. Extended descriptions of the five year program can be found in Andrew (1981), Andrew (1986), and Andrew in DeVitis and Sola (1989). For detailed information on the full year internship, see Corcoran and Andrew (1987). For research on graduates, see Andrew (1990).

2. We recruit and select people who share the following characteristics:

- they are committed to teaching.
- They are competent and knowledgeable in the subject areas that they will teach.
- They are able thinkers and perceptive observers.
- They communicate well; they are good speakers, listeners and writers.
- They are open, flexible and caring in interpersonal relationships.

3. The middle 50 percent of students admitted to the Master's degree programs in Teacher Education have the following profile: (1) GPA, 2.75-3.30; (2) GRE Verbal, 500-590, GRE Quantitative, 460-610, GRE Analytical, 510-640; (3) three strongly supportive letters of recommendation; (4) an undergraduate preparation appropriate for the intended area of certification; (5) a grade of B- or better in required Education courses and a positive recommendation from school and university personnel from the semester of clinical experience. Currently, approximately 25 percent of applicants are denied admission to the final phase of the program.

4. The collaborative supervisory team context became a "temporary system" (Oja and Pine, 1987) in the school that differed from the permanent system of the school context in a number of significant ways which provided crucial facilitative conditions for collaborative inquiry. For example, the collaborative supervisory team context was characterized by the following conditions: non-hierarchical, self-managed; norms of collegiality and experimentation; power diffused among the team; teachers develop their own agendas and flexibly take on a variety of roles and responsibilities; a setting of pause, reflective thinking, cognitive expansion, participatory and collaboratively shared decision making.

References

Andrew, M. D. 1974. *Teacher leadership: A model for change.* Washington, D.C.: Association of Teacher Educators. Bulletin 37.

————. 1981. A five-year teacher education program: Successes and challenges. *Journal of Teacher Education,* 32(3):40-43.

————. 1986. Restructuring teacher education: The University of New Hampshire's five year program. In Lasley, T. J., ed., *The dynamics of change in teacher education* (pp. 59-87). Washington, D.C.: AACTE.

————. 1989. Subject-field depth and professional preparation: New Hampshire's teacher education program. In DeVitis, J. L., and P. A. Sola, eds., *Building bridges for educational reform: New approaches to teacher education* (pp. 44-62). Ames, IA: Iowa State University Press.

————. 1990. Differences between graduates of four- and five-year teacher preparation programs. *Journal of Teacher Education,* 45(2):45-51.

Corcoran, E., and M. D. Andrew. 1987. A full year internship: An example of school-university collaboration. *Journal of Teacher Education,* May-June, 17-22.

Diller, A. 1991. What happens when an ethics of care faces pluralism: Some implications for education. In Power, F. C., and D. K. Lapsley, eds., *Moral education in a pluralistic society.* Notre Dame, IN: Notre Dame Press. (In Press)

Greene, M. 1988. *The dialectic of freedom.* New York: Teachers College Press.

James, W. 1899. *Talks to teachers on psychology: And to students on some of life's ideals.* New York: Norton Library Edition, 1958.

Lugones, M. C., and E. V. Spelman. 1983. Have we got a theory for you! Feminist theory, cultural imperialism and the demand for "The woman's voice." *Women's Studies International Forum,* 6:19-31. (Reprinted in Pearsall, 1986).

Oja, S. N. 1988. *Program assessment report: A collaborative approach to leadership in supervision.* Part B of the Final Report to the U.S. Office of Education, Office of Educational Research and Improvement. Durham, NH: Collaborative Research Projects.

Oja, S. N., and G. J. Pine. 1987. Collaborative action research: Teachers' stages of development and school contexts. *Peabody Journal of Education,* 64:96-115.

Oja, S. N., and L. Smulyan. 1989. *Collaborative action research: A developmental process.* London: Falmer Press.

Sanders, J. T. (1972). Good teaching—A disjunctive concept? *Teacher Education,* 5:14-19.

CHAPTER 2

Notes

1. In this chapter the term student is used interchangeably with the term preservice teacher. The term, children, is used to refer to elementary age pupils.

2. It is important to note that PROTEACH is a college-wide program that includes three teacher preparation programs: elementary, secondary and special education. The three programs share a core set of underlying principles, several common courses, and some common faculty. However, they are, in reality, three distinct programs with individual identities. This chapter describes ongoing work from elementary PROTEACH.

3. Examples are drawn from the experiences of one of the three instructors teaching the course during Fall 1989. However, description of general practices refers to "instructors" because the assignment and strategies for approaching it were collaboratively developed by the three instructors and implemented within all three sections.

4. This conference has been renamed because a number of our graduates wanted to continue coming after their first few years of teaching. The conference is now called "Revisiting PROTEACH: A Professional Development Conference."

References

Ashton, P., J. Comas, and D. D. Ross. 1989. Examining the relationship between perceptions of efficacy and reflection. Paper presented at the annual meeting of the American Educational Research Association, San Francisco, CA.

Barnes, H. L. 1987. The conceptual basis for thematic teacher education programs. *Journal of Teacher Education*, 38(4):13-18.

Bondy, E. 1989. What is good teaching? Views of "Experienced" preservice teachers. Paper presented at the annual meeting of the American Educational Research Association, San Francisco.

Bullough, R., and A. Gitlin. 1989. Toward educative communities. *Qualitative Studies in Education*, 2(4):285-298.

Butt, R. L., and D. Raymond. 1989. Teacher development using collaborative autobiography. A paper presented at an international/invitational Conference on Teacher Development, Toronto: Ontario Institute for Studies in Education.

Clandinin, D. J. 1986. *Classroom practice: Teacher images in action*. Philadelphia: The Falmer Press.

Combs, A. W. et al. 1974. *The professional education of teachers.* Boston: Allyn and Bacon.

Dewey, J. 1933. *How we think.* Chicago: Henry Regnery Co.

Goodman, J. 1984. Reflection and teacher education: A case study and theoretical analysis. *Interchange,* 15(3):9-26.

Hayes, L. F., and D. D. Ross. 1989. Trust versus control: The impact of school leadership on reflection. *Qualitative Studies in Education,* 2(4):335-350.

Hoover, N. L., and L. J. O'Shea. 1987. The influence of a criterion checklist on supervisors and interns conceptions of teaching. Paper presented at the annual meeting of the American Educational Research Association, Washington, D.C.

Kilgore, K., D. D. Ross, and J. Zbikowski. 1990. Understanding the teaching perspectives of first year teachers. *Journal of Teacher Education,* 41(1):28-38.

Kitchener, K., and P. King. 1981. Reflective judgment concepts of justification and their relationship to age and education. *Journal of Applied Developmental Psychology,* 2:89-116.

Krogh, S. L., and R. Crews. 1989. Determinants of reflectivity in student teachers' reflective reports. (Occasional paper no. 4) Gainesville: University of Florida Department of Instruction and Curriculum.

Lanier, J. E., and J. W. Little. 1986. Research on teacher education. In M. Wittrock, ed., *Third handbook of research on teaching* (pp. 527-569). New York: Macmillan.

Posner, G. 1985. *Field experience: A guide to reflective teaching.* New York: Longman.

Roland, C. 1990. Redefining preservice education of art teachers in Florida: A response to Shargel. Invited paper presented at the Conference on Preservice Education in the Arts, Tallahassee, Florida.

Ross, D. D. 1987. Reflective teaching: Meaning and implications for preservice teacher educators. Paper prepared for the Reflective Inquiry Conference, Houston, Texas.

————. 1989a. Programmatic structures for the preparation of reflective teachers. In Clift, R., W. R. Houston, and M. Pugach, eds., *Encouraging reflective practice: An examination of issues and exemplars* (pp. 98-118). New York: Teachers College Press.

————. 1989b. First steps in developing a reflective approach to teaching. *Journal of Teacher Education,* 40(2):22-30.

Ross, D. D., P. Ashton, and C. Mentonelli. 1989. Developing reflective teachers:

The connections between university coursework and elementary class-rooms. Paper presented at the annual meeting of the American Educational Research Association, San Francisco.

Ross, D. D., and E. Bondy. 1990. Teacher self-empowerment: Developing a knowledge base for teachers and teacher educators. Paper presented at the annual meeting of the American Educational Research Association, Boston, MA.

Ross, D. D., and S. L. Krogh. 1988. From paper to program: A story from elementary PROTEACH. *Peabody Journal of Education,* 65(2):19-34 (published in 1990).

Schön, D. A. 1983. *The reflective practitioner.* New York: Basic Books.

———. 1987. *Educating the Reflective Practitioner.* San Francisco: Jossey-Bass.

Smith, D. C., R. G. Carroll, and B. Fry. 1984. PROTEACH: Professional teacher preparation at the University of Florida. *Phi Delta Kappan,* 66(2):134-135.

Tabachnick, B., and K. Zeichner. 1984. The impact of student teaching experience on the development of teacher perspectives. *Journal of Teacher Education,* 35(6):28-36.

Valli, L., and N. E. Taylor. 1987. Reflective teacher education: Preferred characteristics for a content and process model. Paper prepared for the Reflective Inquiry Conference, Houston, Texas.

van Manen, M. 1977. Linking ways of knowing with ways of being practical. *Curriculum Inquiry,* 6:205-228.

Weade, R. 1987. Negotiating a culture: The preservice teachers' socialization into reflective teaching practice. Paper presented at the annual meeting of the American Educational Research Association, Washington, D.C.

Weade, R. 1989. The development of student perspectives about teaching. Paper presented at the annual meeting of the American Educational Research Association, San Francisco.

Zeichner, K. M. 1988. University of Florida, Gainesville: Elementary PROTEACH and secondary english PROTEACH, a site report. In *Dialogues in teacher education,* East Lansing, Michigan: National Center for Research on Teaching, 55-81.

Zeichner, K. M., and D. P. Liston. 1987. Teaching student teachers to reflect. *Harvard Educational Review,* 38(6):23-48.

CHAPTER 3

References

Applegate, J. 1987. Early field experience: Three viewpoints. In M. Haberman and J. Backus, eds., *Advances in teacher education.* Vol. 3 (pp. 75-93).

Norwood, NJ: Ablex.

Arends, R. 1988. *Learning to teach.* New York: Random House.

Berliner, D. 1979. Tempus educare. In P. Peterson and H. Walberg, eds., *Research on teaching: Concepts, findings, and implications* (pp. 120-135). Berkeley: McCutchan.

Berliner, D. 1985. Laboratory settings and the study of teacher education. *Journal of Teacher Education,* 36(6):2-8.

Borko, H. 1988. Research on learning to teach: Implications for graduate teacher preparation programs. In A. Woolfolk, ed., *Research perspectives on the graduate preparation of teachers* (pp. 69-87). Englewood Cliffs, NJ: Prentice-Hall.

Borko, H. et al. 1979. Teachers' decision making. In P. Peterson and H. Walberg, eds., *Research on teaching: Concepts, findings, and implications* (pp. 136-160). Berkeley: McCutchan.

Borko, H., and C. Livingston. 1989. Cognition and improvisation: Differences in mathematics instruction by expert and novice teachers. *American Educational Research Journal,* 26(4):473-498.

Borko, H. et al. 1988. Student teachers' planning and post-lesson reflections: Patterns and implications for teacher preparation. In J. Calderhead, ed., *Teachers' professional learning* (pp. 65-83). London: The Falmer Press.

Borko, H., and R. Shavelson. 1990. Teachers' decision making. In B. Jones and L. Idol, eds., *Dimensions of thinking and cognitive instruction* (pp. 311-346). New Jersey: Erlbaum.

Brookover, W. et al. 1979. *School social systems and student achievement: Schools can make a difference.* New York: Praeger.

Emmer, E., C. Evertson, and L. Anderson. 1980. Effective classroom management at the beginning of the school year. *Elementary School Journal,* 80(5):219-231.

Evertson, C., and E. Emmer. 1982. Effective management at the beginning of the school year in junior high classes. *Journal of Educational Psychology,* 74:485-498.

Evertson, C. et al. 1983. Improving classroom management: An experimental study in elementary classrooms. *Elementary School Journal,* 84(2):173-188.

Evertson, C., W. Hawley, and M. Zlotnik. 1985. Making a difference in education quality through teacher education. *Journal of Teacher Education,* 36(3):2-12.

Feiman-Nemser, S. 1983. Learning to teach. In L. Shulman and G. Sykes, eds.,

Handbook of teaching and policy (pp. 150-170). New York: Longman.

Feiman-Nemser, S., and M. Buchmann. 1983. Pitfalls of experience in teacher education. *Teachers College Record*, 87(1):53-65.

Fenstermacher, G. 1980. On learning to teach effectively from research on teacher effectiveness. In C. Denham and A. Lieberman, eds., *Time to learn* (pp. 127-137). Washington, D.C.: National Institute of Education.

Fenstermacher, G., and J. Soltis. 1986. *Approaches to teaching*. New York: Teachers College Press.

Fullan, M. 1991. *The meaning of educational change*. 2d ed. New York: Teachers College Press.

Gagne, H. 1985. *The cognitive psychology of school learning*. Boston: Little, Brown, and Co.

Garner, R. 1987. *Metacognition and reading comprehension*. Norwood, NJ: Ablex Publishing Corporation.

Giroux, H. 1983. *Theory and resistance in education: A pedagogy for the opposition*. South Hadley, MA: Bergin and Garvey.

Good, T., and J. Brophy. 1987. *Looking in classrooms*. 4th ed. New York: Harper and Row.

Good, T., and J. Brophy. 1986. School effects. In M. Wittrock, ed., *Handbook of research on teaching*. 3d ed. (pp. 570-602). New York: Macmillan.

Good, T., and D. Grouws. 1977. Teaching effects: A process-product study in fourth-grade mathematics classrooms. *Journal of Teacher Education*, 28(3):49-54.

Good, T., D. Grouws, and M. Ebmeier. 1983. *Active mathematics teaching*. New York: Longman.

Goodlad, J. 1984. *A place called school*. New York: McGraw Hill.

Holmes Group. 1986. *Tomorrow's teachers*. East Lansing, MI: Author.

Hopkins, D. 1982. Doing research in classrooms. *Phi Delta Kappan*, 64:274-275.

———. 1985. *A teacher's guide to classroom research*. Milton Keynes, England: Open University Press.

Joyce, B., and R. Clift. 1984. The Phoenix agenda: Needed reform in teacher education. *Educational Researcher*, 13(4):5-18.

Joyce, B., and B. Showers. 1985. The search for validated skills of teaching: Four lines of inquiry. Paper presented at the annual meeting of American Educational Research Association, Chicago.

Joyce, B., and M. Weil. 1980. *Models of teaching*. 2d ed. Englewood Cliffs, NJ: Prentice Hall.

Leinhardt, G., and J. Greeno. 1986. The cognitive skill of teaching. *Journal of Educational Psychology*, 78:75-95.

Leinhardt, G., and R. Putnam. 1987. The skill of learning from classroom lessons. *American Educational Research Journal*, 24(4):556-588.

Lieberman, A., and L. Miller. 1984. *Teachers, their world and their work*. Alexandria, VA: Association for Supervision and Curriculum Development.

Lortie, D. 1975. *Schoolteacher: A sociological study*. Chicago: University of Chicago Press.

McCaleb, J. 1985. *Follow-up evaluation of beginning teachers*. College Park, MD: University of Maryland.

McCaleb, J. et al. 1987. Innovation in teacher education: The evolution of a program. *Journal of Teacher Education*, 37(4):57-64.

Rutter, M. et al. 1979. *Fifteen thousand hours: Secondary schools and their effects on children*. Cambridge, MA: Harvard University Press.

Shor, I., and P. Freire. 1987. *A Pedagogy for Liberation*. South Hadley, MA: Bergin and Garvey.

Stallings, J. 1976. *Implementation and child effects of teaching practice in follow through classrooms*. Menlo Park, CA: SRI International.

Yinger, R., and C. Clark. 1981. *Reflective journal writing: Theory and practice*. East Lansing, MI: Institute of Research on Teaching, Michigan State University.

CHAPTER 4

References

Applegate, J., and B. Shaklee. 1990. Some observations about recruiting bright students for teacher preparation. *Peabody Journal of Education*, 65(2):52-65.

Applegate, J., B. Shaklee, and L. Hutchinson. 1989. Stimulating reflection about learning to teach. Paper presented at the Annual Meeting of the American Educational Research Association, San Francisco, CA.

Benbow, C. P., and J. Stanley. 1983. *Academic precocity: Aspects of its development*. Baltimore, MD: Johns Hopkins University Press.

Cruickshank, D. R. 1984. Toward a model to guide inquiry in preservice teacher education. *Journal of Teacher Education*, 35(6):43-48.

Feldhusen, J., J. Van Tassel-Baska, and K. Seeley. 1989. *Excellence in educating the gifted*. Denver, CO: Love Publishing.

Gowan, J., and G. D. Demos. 1964. *The education of the ablest*. Springfield, IL: Charles C. Thomas.

Guba, E., and Y. Lincoln. 1981. *Effective evaluation*. San Francisco, CA: Jossey-Bass Publishers.

Harvey, O. J., D. Hunt, and H. Schroeder. 1961. *Conceptual systems and personality organization*. New York: Wiley.

Holly, M. L. 1989. *Writing to grow: Keeping a personal-professional journal*. Portsmouth, NH: Heinemann.

Hutchinson, L. M. 1989. Interactive styles in traditional and reflective teacher education seminars. Paper presented at the Annual Meeting of the American Educational Research Association, San Francisco: CA.

Kulik, C., and J. A. Kulik. 1982. Effects of ability grouping on secondary school students: A meta-analysis of evaluation findings. *American Educational Research Journal*, 19(3):415-428.

Lortie, D. C. 1975. *Schoolteacher*. Chicago: University of Chicago Press.

Noffke, S., and K. Zeichner. 1987. Action research and teacher thinking: The first phase of the action research on action research at the University of Wisconsin-Madison. Paper presented at the Annual meeting of the American Educational Research Association. Washington, D.C.

Perry, W. G. 1970. *Forms of intellectual and ethical development in the college years: A new scheme*. New York: Holt, Rinehart and Winston.

Ryan, K. et al. 1977. *The first year teacher study*. Columbus, OH: The Ohio State University. (ERIC Document Reproduction Service no. ED 135-766).

Schlechty, P. C., and V. S. Vance. 1983. Recruitment, selection and retention: The shape of the teaching force. *The Elementary School Journal*, 84(4):467-487.

Stuck, A. 1984. Cognitive development: A perspective for teacher development. Paper presented at the Annual Meeting of American Association of College of Teacher Education. San Antonio, TX.

Tannenbaum, A. 1983. *Gifted children*. New York: McMillian.

Taylor, M. B. 1983. The development of the measure of epistemological reflection. *Dissertation Abstracts International*, 44(1065A). University Microfilms no. DA83-18, 441.

Tom, A. 1985. Inquiring into inquiry-oriented teacher education. *Journal of Teacher Education*, 35(5):35-44.

Van Tassel-Baska, J. 1985. The talent search model: Implications for secondary school reform. *National Association of Secondary School Principals Journal*, 69(482):39-47.

CHAPTER 5

Notes

1. In the Multiple Perspectives program, students are referred to as "teacher candidates" during their initial terms in the program. They become "student teachers" during their last term when they are engaged in full day on-site teaching practice and research.

2. The field instructor role in the Multiple Perspectives program differs from that found in many teacher education programs. As will be developed in this chapter, the nature and function of field instruction is unlike that of the traditional field supervisor.

3. To date, applicants have been almost entirely undergraduates. Recently, however, we have seen some growth in the number of applicants already possessing baccalaureate degrees.

4. Michigan State University operates on a quarter/term schedule. Students normally take courses during the fall, winter, and spring terms which last for ten weeks. The MSU faculty recently voted to ratify the conversion of the schedule to fifteen week semesters. This change will coincide with the redesign of the teacher education programs described later in this chapter.

5. Unit plans are structured around the following components: (1) assessment (students, classroom environment, curriculum, and self); (2) goal (real life application of the content); (3) terminal objective(s) (classroom-based applications which reflect a condition and student behavior); (4) enabling objective(s) (support the terminal objective and reflect condition, behavior, and criteria); (5) evaluation (both formative and summative); (6) daily calendar (intended/proposed sequence of activities); and (7) management plan (explication of classroom norms and expectations).

Daily lesson plans, while more streamlined, follow essentially the same format: (1) assessment (of previous lesson); (2) special needs (for the particular lesson); (3) enabling objective (for the particular lesson, related to terminal objective); (4) instructional plan (description of sequence of instructional activities); (5) evaluation (of students); and (6) reflection (assessment of lesson).

6. All field experiences in the Multiple Perspectives program are arranged in urban schools. In the first term of field experience, teacher candidates teach one period two times a week.

7. The course sequence described is that for the secondary cohort. The elementary cohort follows the same general pattern. The additional methods

courses that are part of their program necessitate the extension of their program to six quarters.

8. Most field instructors are doctoral students in the Department of Teacher Education. Recently, classroom teachers from affiliated Professional Development Schools have begun to take on the role of field instructor. As the Professional Development Schools initiative develops, we anticipate even more involvement by classroom teachers in this role.

9. Teacher candidate/field instructor pairings are reviewed and adjusted each term. Though it is rare for a teacher candidate/field instructor combination to remain intact throughout the teacher candidate's program, assignments are not routinely changed.

10. At the time this chapter was being written, few details of the new programmatic structure were in place. One note that can be shared, however, is that all new programs will incorporate all four of the functions of schooling as outlined in this paper.

References

Cohen, D. (1988). *Teaching practice: Plus ca change . . .* Issue paper 88-3. East Lansing, MI: Michigan State University, National Center for Research on Teacher Education.

Department of Teacher Education. 1990. *Task Force Report.* College of Education, Michigan State University.

The Holmes Group. 1986. *Tomorrow's teachers: A report of the Holmes Group.* East Lansing, MI: Author.

Hoerr, W. and J. Putnam. 1989. *The relationship of field instructor and teacher candidate experience levels to the quality of field conferences.* Paper presented at the meeting of the American Educational Research Association, San Francisco, CA.

Hoerr, W. and J. Putnam. 1990. *Correlations between teacher candidate entry characteristics and the focus of field conferences.* Paper presented the meeting of the American Educational Research Association, Boston, MA.

Kennedy, M. 1987. *Inexact sciences: Professional education and the development of expertise.* Issue paper 87-2. East Lansing, MI: National Center for Research on Teacher Education.

LaForce, B., J. Putnam, and B. Johns. 1986. *Substance of teacher candidate-field instructor conferences.* Paper presented at the meeting of the Association of Teacher Educators, Atlanta, GA.

Lortie, D. 1975. *Schoolteacher: A sociological study.* Chicago: University of Chicago Press.

Polin, R. and J. Putnam. 1987. *The use of a professional knowledge exam in teacher education as a measure of program effectiveness.* Paper presented at the meeting of the American Association of Teacher Educators, Houston, TX.

Putnam, J. 1988. *Long-term program evaluation: Three case studies.* Presented to College Level Program Evaluation Committee in the College of Education at Michigan State University.

————. 1987. *Program evaluation reports.* Presented to College Program Evaluation and Program Level Committees in the College of Education at Michigan State University.

————. 1985a. Perceived benefits and limitations of teacher educator's demonstration lessons. *The Journal of Teacher Education*, 36(6):36-41.

————. 1985b. Applications of classroom management research findings. *Journal of Education for Teaching*, 11(2):145-164.

————. 1984. *Program guide for operations, Multiple Perspectives teacher education program.* Department of Teacher Education, Michigan State University, East Lansing, Michigan.

Putnam, J. and H. Barnes. 1984. *Applications of classroom management research findings.* Research series no. 154. East Lansing, MI: Institute for Research on Teaching.

Putnam, J. and J. Burke. (In press). *Classroom learning community.* Chappaqua, NY: Lane Akers.

Putnam, J. et al. 1989. *Field instructors perceptions about their role, it's implementation, and their growth related to their conferences with teacher candidates.* Paper presented at the meeting of the American Educational Research Association, San Francisco, CA.

Putnam, J. and B. Johns. 1987a. *What preservice teachers learn from observing demonstration lessons taught by teacher educators.* Paper presented at meeting of the American Educational Research Association, Washington, D.C.

————. 1987b. *Preservice teachers' perceptions and misconceptions of classroom management, organization, and descriptive tasks confronted during two years of field experience.* Paper presented at the meeting of the American Educational Research Association, Washington, D.C.

————. 1987c. *New frontiers: The role of evaluation in design, initial implementation, refinement, and ongoing programmatic development and implementation of a teacher education program.* Paper presented at the meeting of the Association of Teacher Educators, Houston, TX.

————. 1987d. The potential of demonstration teaching as a component for teacher preparation and staff development programs. *International Journal of Education*, 11(5):577-588.

Putnam, J., B. Johns, and S. Oja. 1987. *A Multiple Perspectives teacher training program: New roles for faculty.* Unpublished manuscript, Michigan State University

Sarason, S. 1982. *The culture of the school and the problem of change.* 2d ed. Boston: Allyn and Bacon, Inc.

Schön, D. 1983. *The reflective practitioner.* New York: Basic Books.

————. 1987. *Educating the reflective practitioner.* San Francisco: Jossey-Bass.

Schwab, J. 1974. The concept of the structure of a discipline. In E. Eisner and E. Vallance, eds., *Conflicting Conceptions of Curriculum.* Berkeley, CA: McCutchan.

————. 1978. *Science, curriculum, and liberal education: Selected essays.* I. Westbury and N. Wilkof, eds. Chicago: University of Chicago Press.

Zimpher, N., and K. Howey. 1987. Adapting supervisory practices to different orientations of teaching competence. *Journal of Curriculum and Supervision*, 2(2):101-127.

CHAPTER 6

Notes

1. The authors would like to thank Peter Grimmett for helping us develop Figure 6.1.

References

Berlak, A., and H. Berlak. 1981. *Dilemmas of schooling.* London: Methuen.

Blum, I. H., and L. Valli. 1988. Using research knowledge to improve teacher education: A problem solving approach. Final Report-Project Portrayal. OERI/NIE Contract #400-85-1062. November.

Cohn, M. 1981. A new supervision model for linking theory to practice. *Journal of Teacher Education*, 32(3):26-30.

Elliot, J. 1980. The implications of classroom research for the professional development of teachers. *World yearbook in education.* London: Kogan Page.

Feiman-Nemser, S., and M. Buchmann. 1985. Pitfalls of experience in teacher preparation. *Teacher College Record*, 86(1):53-65.

Glickman, C. D. 1990. *Supervision of instruction: A developmental approach.* 2d ed. Boston: Allyn and Bacon.

Goldhammer, R., R. H. Anderson, and R. J. Krajewski. 1980. *Clinical supervision: Special methods for the supervision of teachers.* 2d ed. New York: Holt, Rhinehart, and Winston.

Grant, C. A., and K. M. Zeichner. 1984. On becoming a reflective teacher. In C. A. Grant, ed., *Preparing for Reflective Teaching* (1-18). Boston: Allyn and Bacon.

Holly, M. L. 1984. *Keeping a personal-professional journal.* Greelong, Australia: Deakin University Press.

Hook, S. 1966. John Dewey: His philosophy of education. In R. D. Archambault, ed., *Dewey on Education: Appraisals* (pp. 127-129). New York: Random House.

Koehler, V. 1985. Research on preservice teacher education. *Journal of Teacher Education,* 36(1):23-30.

Perkins, D. N. 1987. Thinking frames: An integrative perspective on teaching cognitive skills. In R. B. Baron and R. J. Sternberg, eds., *Teaching thinking skills: Theory and practice* (pp. 41-61). New York: Freeman.

Posner, G. J. 1988. *Field experience: methods of reflective teaching.* New York: Longman.

Schwab, J. J. 1973. The practical 3: Translation into curriculum. *School Review,* 81(4):501-522.

Valli, L. 1989a. Assessing the reflective practice of student teachers. In J. J. Denton and D. G. Armstrong, eds., *Shaping Policy in Teacher Education Through Program Evaluation* (pp. 21-35). (Instructional Research Laboratory College of Education, Texas A & M University) Texas: College Station.

————. 1989b. Collaboration for transfer of learning: Preparing preservice teachers. *Teacher Education Quarterly,* 16(1):85-95.

————. 1990. Moral approaches to reflective practice. In R. T. Clift, W. R. Houston, and M. Pugach, eds., *Encouraging reflective practice in education: An analysis of issues and programs* (pp. 39-56). New York: Teachers College Press.

Valli, L., and I. Blum. 1987. Using research knowledge to improve teacher education: A problem solving approach. Progress Report and Implementation Plan. OERI/NIE Contract #400-85-1062. June.

————. 1989. Evaluating a reflective teacher education model. Paper presented at the annual meeting of the American Educational Research Association. San Francisco, CA.

————. 1988. Reflective teacher education: Preferred characteristics for a content and process model. In H. C. Waxman, ed., *Images on Reflection in Teacher Education* (pp. 20-21). Reston, VA: Association of Teacher Educators.

van Manen, M. 1977. Linking ways of knowing with ways of being practical. *Curriculum Inquiry*, 6(3): 205-228.

Wildman, T. M., and J. A. Niles. 1987. Reflective teachers: Tensions between abstractions and realities. *Journal of Teacher Education*, 38(4):25-31.

Yinger, R., and C. Clark. 1981. *Reflective journal writing: Theory and practice*. East Lansing, MI: Institute for Research on Teaching. Occasional paper no. 50.

Zeichner, K. M. 1987. Preparing reflective teachers: An overview of instructional strategies which have been employed in preservice teacher education. *International Journal of Educational Research*, 11(5):565-575.

CHAPTER 7

We would like to thank Faith Marshall and Charles Nichols for their perceptions concerning the early years of program implementation and their help with references for this chapter.

References

Bloom, A. 1987. *The closing of the American mind: How higher education has failed democracy and impoverished the souls of today's students*. New York: Simon and Schuster.

Borrowman, M. 1956. *The liberal and technical in teacher education: A documentary history*. New York: Teachers College Press.

Brace, D. 1984. *Negotiating the curriculum: Tutors and students* (Coombe Lodge Working Paper). Blagdan, England: Further Education Staff College.

Clifford, G., and J. Guthrie. 1988. *Ed school*. Chicago: University of Chicago Press.

Clift, R. T., W. R. Houston, and M. C. Pugach, eds. 1990. *Encouraging reflective practice in teacher education: An analysis of issues and programs*. New York: Teachers College Press.

Dewey, J. 1904. The relation of theory to practice in education. In C. A. McMurry, ed., *Third yearbook of the National Society for the Scientific Study of Education* (pp. 9-30). Chicago: University of Chicago Press.

Eisner, E. W. 1985. *The educational imagination*. 2d ed. New York: Macmillan.

Grimmett, P. P., and G. L. Erickson, eds. 1989. *Reflection in teacher education*. New York: Teachers College Press.

Hall, G. E., and H. L. Jones. 1976. *Competency-based education: A process for the improvement of education.* Englewood Cliffs, NJ: Prentice-Hall.

Holmes Group. 1986. *Tomorrow's teachers.* East Lansing, MI: Author.

Howey, K. R., N. L. Zimpher. 1989. *Profiles of preservice teacher education: Inquiry into the nature of programs.* Albany, NY: State University of New York Press.

Jones, T. B. 1982. Educational self-determinism and degree planning: The Metro U Experience. *Alternative Higher Education,* 6(4):203-213.

Kagan, N. 1980. *Interpersonal process recall: A method of influencing human interaction.* Lansing, MI: Michigan State University.

Kridel, C. 1983. Student participation in general education reform: A retrospective glance at the Harvard Redbook. *The Journal of General Education,* 35(3):154-164.

McCarthy, J. et al. 1989, March. *Reflective Inquiry Teacher Education: Faculty perceptions of change.* Paper presented to the annual meeting of the American Educational Research Association, San Francisco, CA.

Niemi, J. A. 1985. Fostering participation in learning. In S. H. Rosenblum, ed., *Involves adults in the educational process.* (pp. 3-12). San Francisco: Jossey Bass.

Redesign Task Force. 1985, April. *A proposal for the redesign of the University of Houston-University Park College of Education teacher education program.* Houston: College of Education, University of Houston.

Rooker, R. A. 1981. "Participatory democracy" doesn't belong in academe. *Journalism Educator,* 35:50-52.

Schön, D. A. 1991. *The reflective turn.* New York: Teachers College Press.

Sparrow, B. 1986. Communication: A negotiated curriculum theme. *English in Australia,* 75:13-22.

Stallings, J. 1986. *The Stallings observation system.* Training manual. Houston: University of Houston.

Tyler, R. W. 1949. *Basic principles of curriculum and instruction.* Chicago: University of Chicago Press.

van Manen, M. 1977. Linking ways of knowing with ways of being practical. *Curriculum Inquiry,* 6(3):205-228.

Walker, D. F. 1987. Curriculum theory is many things to many people. *Theory into Practice,* 21(1):62-65.

Walker, D. F. 1990. *Fundamentals of curriculum.* San Diego, CA: Harcourt Brace.

Waxman, H. C. et al. 1989. In Jon J. Denton and David G. Armstrong, eds., *Concerns, motivations, and concepts of teaching by prospective teachers at two points in their program.* (pp. 13-20). College Station, TX: Instructional Research Laboratory, Texas A&M University.

Zeichner, K. M. 1981-82. Reflective teaching and field-based experience in teacher education. *Interchange,* 12(4):1-22.

Zeichner, K. and Liston, D. 1987. Teaching student teachers to reflect. *Harvard Educational Review,* 57(1):23-48.

CHAPTER 8

References

Book, C., J. Byers, and D. Freeman. 1983. Student expectations and teacher education traditions with which we can and cannot live. *Journal of Teacher Education,* 34(1):9-13.

Brickhouse, N. W. 1990. Teachers' beliefs about the nature of science and their relationship to classroom practice. *Journal of Teacher Education,* 41(3):53-62.

Calderhead, J. 1988. Learning from introductory school experience. *Journal of Education for Teaching,* 14(1):75-83.

Goodlad, J. 1983. *A place called school: prospects for the future.* New York: McGraw Hill.

Handal, G., and P. Lauvas. 1987. *Promoting reflective teaching: Supervision in action.* Milton Keynes: Open University Press.

Korthagen, F. A. J. 1988. The influence of learning orientations on the development of reflective teaching. In J. Calderhead, ed., *Teachers' professional learning* (pp. 35-50). Lewes: Falmer Press.

Lacey, C. 1977. *The socialization of teachers.* London: Methuen.

Lanier, J. E., and J. W. Little. 1986. Research on teacher education. In M. C. Wittrock, ed., *Handbook of research on teaching.* 3d ed. (pp. 527-569). New York: Macmillan.

Tabachnick, B. R., and K. M. Zeichner. 1984. The impact of the student teaching experience on the development of teacher perspectives. *Journal of Teacher Education,* 35(6):28-36.

Wilson, S. M., and S. S. Wineburg. 1988. Peering at history through different lenses: The role of disciplinary perspectives in teaching history. *Teachers' College Record,* 89(4):525-539.

CHAPTER 9

References

Anderson, R. C. 1984. Some reflections on the acquisition of knowledge. *Educational Researcher*, 13(5):5-10.

Berliner, D. C. 1986. In pursuit of the expert pedagogue. *Educational Researcher*, 15(7):5-13.

Carter, K. et al. 1988. Expert-novice differences in perceiving and processing visual classroom information. *Journal of Teacher Education*, 39(3):25-31.

Clark, C. M., and P. L. Peterson. 1986. Teachers' thought processes. In M. C. Wittrock, ed., *Handbook of research on teaching* (pp. 255-296). New York: Macmillan.

Cochran-Smith, M., and S. L. Lytle. 1990. Research on teaching and teacher research: The issues that divide. *Educational Researcher*, 19(2):2-11.

Connelly, F. M., and D. J. Clandinin. 1990. Stories of experience and narrative inquiry. *Educational Researcher*, 19(4):2-14.

Eisner, E. W. 1982. An artistic approach to supervision. In T. J. Sergiovanni, ed., *Supervision of Teaching* (pp. 53-66). Alexandria, VA: Association for Supervision and Curriculum Development.

Hollingsworth, S. 1990. Teacher educator as researcher: An epistemological analysis of learning to teach reading. Paper presented at the annual meeting of the American Educational Research Association, Boston, MA.

Huberman, M. 1990. Linkage between researchers and practitioners: A qualitative study. *American Educational Research Journal*, 27(2):363-392.

Kagan, D. M. 1988. Teaching as critical problem solving: A critical examination of the analogy and its implications. *Review of Educational Research*, 58(4):482-505.

Lampert, M., and C. M. Clark. 1990. Expert knowledge and expert thinking in teaching: A response to Floden and Klinzing. *Educational Researcher*, 19(4):21-23.

Leinhardt, G. 1990. Capturing craft knowledge in teaching. *Educational Researcher*, 19(2):18-25.

Leinhardt, G., and J. G. Greeno. 1986. The cognitive skill of teaching. *Journal of Educational Psychology*, 78(2):75-95.

McLaren, P. 1989. *Life in schools*. New York: Longman.

Piaget, J. 1978. *Success and understanding*. Cambridge, MA: Harvard University Press.

Ross, D. D. 1990. Programmatic structures for the preparation of reflective teachers. In R. Clift, W. R. Houston, and M. D. Pugach, eds., *Encouraging reflective practice in education* (pp. 97-118). New York, NY: Teachers College Press.

Schön, D. A. 1983. *The reflective practitioner*. New York: Basic Books.

————. 1987. *Educating the reflective practitioner*. San Francisco: Jossey-Bass.

Shulman, L. S. 1987. Knowledge and teaching: Foundations of the new reform. *Harvard Educational Review*, 57(1): February, 31.

Smyth, J. 1989. Developing and sustaining critical reflection in teacher education. *Journal of Teacher Education*, 40(2):2-9.

Sparks, G. M. 1988. Teachers' attitudes toward change and subsequent improvements in classroom teaching. *Journal of Educational Psychology*, 80(1):111-117.

Sparks, G. M., and J. M. Simmons. 1989. Inquiry-oriented staff development: Using research as a source of tools, not rules. In S. Caldwell, ed., *Handbook of Staff Development* (pp. 126-139). Oxford, OH: National Staff Development Council.

Sparks-Langer, G. M. et al. 1990. Reflective pedagogical thinking: How do we promote it and measure it? *Journal of Teacher Education*, 41(5):23-32.

Sparks-Langer, G. M., and A. B. Coltron. 1991. Synthesis of research on teachers' reflective thinking. *Educational Leadership*, 48(6):35-44.

Tom, A. R. 1985. Inquiry into inquiry-oriented teacher education. *Journal of Teacher Education*, 36(5):35-44.

van Manen, M. 1977. Linking ways of knowing with ways of being practical. *Curriculum Inquiry*, 6(3):205-228.

Zeichner, K., and D. Liston. 1987. Teaching student teachers to reflect. *Harvard Educational Review*, 57(1):23-48.

CHAPTER 10

Notes

1. Richardson's (1990) analysis of the evolution of Reflective Teaching and Teacher Education in the United States is one such exception.

2. These include Joyce, 1975; Hartnett and Naish, 1980; Zeichner, 1983; Kirk, 1986; and Feiman-Nemser, 1990.

3. In a dialogic relationship, theory and practice inform each other. See

Britzman (1991) pp. 49-55 for a discussion of various views of the theory-practice relationship that transcend the artificial dichotomy that is posited in a technical rationality.

4. These recent shifts in Elementary PROTEACH are discussed in Ross and Krogh (1988). This shift away from a social efficiency emphasis and toward a developmentalist focus are not surprising given the history of teacher education at this institution that was discussed earlier.

References

Altrichter, H. 1988. Enquiry-based learning in initial teacher education. In J. Nias and S. Groundwater-Smith, eds., *The Enquiring Teacher* (pp. 121-134). London: Falmer Press.

Ashcroft, K. and M. Griffiths. 1989. Reflective teachers and reflective tutors: School experience in an initial teacher education course. *Journal of Education for Teaching*, 15(1):35-52.

Atkin, J. M. and J. D. Raths. 1974. *Changing patterns of teacher education in the U.S.* Paris: Organization for Economic Co-operation and development.

Beyer, L. 1989. *Critical reflection and the culture of schooling: Empowering teachers.* Geelong, Australia: Deakin University Press.

Borrowman, M. 1965. Liberal education and the professional preparation of teachers. In M. L. Borrowman, ed., *Teacher education in America: A documentary history* (pp. 1-53). New York: Teachers College Press.

Britzman, D. 1991. *Practice makes practice: A critical study of learning to teach.* Albany, NY: State University of New York Press.

Buchmann, M. 1984. The priority of knowledge and understanding in teaching. In L. Katz and J. Raths, eds., *Advances in teacher education* (pp. 29-50). Norwood, NJ: Ablex.

Bullough, R. and A. Gitlin. 1991. Toward educative communities: Teacher education and the development of the reflective practitioner. In B. R. Tabachnick and K. Zeichner, eds., *Issues and practices in inquiry-oriented teacher education* (pp. 35-55). London: Falmer Press.

Calderhead, J. 1989. Reflective teaching and teacher education. *Teaching and Teacher Education*, 5(1):43-51.

Clandinin, J. and F. M. Connelly. 1986. The reflective practitioner and the practitioners' narrative unities. *Canadian Journal of Education*, 11(2):184-198.

Clark, C. 1988. Asking the right questions about teacher preparation: Contributions of research on teacher thinking. *Educational Researcher*, 17(2):5-12.

Clift, R., W. R. Houston, and M. Pugach. 1990. *Encouraging reflective practice: An examination of issues and examples.* New York: Teachers College Press.

Cruickshank, D. 1987. *Reflective teaching.* Reston, VA: Association of Teacher Educators.

Dewey, J. 1933. *How we think.* Chicago: Henry Regnery.

Duckworth, E. 1987. *The having of wonderful ideas.* New York: Teachers College Press.

Elbaz, F. 1983. *Teacher thinking: A study of practical knowledge.* London: Croom Helm.

Erickson, F. 1986. Qualitative methods in research on teaching. In M. Wittrock, ed., *Handbook of research on teaching.* 3d ed. (pp. 119-161). New York: Macmillan.

Feiman-Nemser, S. 1990. Teacher preparation: Structural and conceptual alternatives. In W. R. Houston, ed., *Handbook of research on teacher education* (pp. 212-233). New York: Macmillan.

Freedman, S., J. Jackson, and K. Boles. 1983. Teaching: An imperiled profession. In L. Shulman and G. Sykes, eds., *Handbook of teaching and policy* (pp. 261-299). New York: Longman.

Gentile, J. R. 1988. *Instructional improvement: Summary and analysis of Madeline Hunter's essential elements of instruction and supervision.* Oxford, OH: National Staff Development Council.

Good, T. 1990. Building the knowledge base of teaching. In D. Dill, ed., *What teachers need to know* (pp. 17-75). San Francisco: Jossey Bass.

Gore, J. 1987. Reflecting on reflective teaching. *Journal of Teacher Education,* 38(2):22-39.

Grimmett, P. et al. 1990. Reflective practice in teacher education. In R. Clift, W. R. Houston, and M. Pugach, eds., *Encouraging reflective practice in education* (pp. 20-38). New York: Teachers College Press.

Handal, G. and P. Lauvas. 1987. *Promoting reflective teaching.* Milton Keynes, United Kingdom: Open University Press.

Hartnett, A. and M. Naish. 1980. Technicians or social bandits? Some moral and political issues in the education of teachers. In P. Woods, ed., *Teacher strategies* (pp. 254-274). London: Croom Helm.

Joyce, B. 1975. Conceptions of man and their implications for teacher education. In K. Ryan, ed., *Teacher education.* Chicago: University of Chicago Press.

Kemmis, S. 1985. Action research and the politics of reflection. In D. Boud, R.

Keogh, and D. Walker, eds., *Reflection: Turning experience into learning* (pp. 139-164). London: Croom Helm.

Kirk, D. 1986. Beyond the limits of theoretical discourse in teacher education: Towards a critical pedagogy. *Teaching and Teacher Education,* 2(2):155-167.

Kitchner, K. and P. King. 1990. The reflective judgement model: Transforming assumptions about knowing. In J. Mezirow, ed., *Fostering critical reflection in adulthood* (pp. 159-176). San Francisco: Jossey Bass.

Kliebard, H. 1986. *The struggle for the American curriculum, 1893-1958.* Boston: Routledge and Kegan Paul.

Koerner, J. 1963. *The miseducation of American teachers.* Boston: Houghton Mifflin.

Korthagen, F. 1985. Reflective teaching and preservice teacher education. *Journal of Teacher Education,* 36(5):11-15.

Korthagen, F. 1988. The influence of learning orientations on the development of reflective teaching. In J. Calderhead, ed., *Teachers professional learning* (pp. 35-50). London: Falmer Press.

Liston, D. and K. Zeichner. 1987. Reflective teacher education and moral deliberation. *Journal of Teacher Education,* 38(6):2-8.

Liston, D., and K. Zeichner. 1991. *Teacher education and the social conditions of schooling.* New York: Routledge.

Lucas, P. 1988. An approach to research-based teacher education through collaborative inquiry. *Journal of Education for Teaching,* 14(1):55-73.

MacKinnon, A., and G. Erickson. 1988. Taking Schön's ideas to a science teaching practicum. In P. Grimmett and G. Erickson, eds., *Reflection in teacher education* (pp. 113-138). New York: Teachers College Press.

MacIntyre, A. 1988. *Whose justice? which rationality?* Notre Dame, IN: University of Notre Dame Press.

Martinez, K. 1989. *Critical reflections on critical reflection in teacher education.* Paper presented at the Fourth National Conference on the Practicum in Teacher Education, Rockhampton, Australia.

Mitchell, L. S. 1931. Cooperative schools for student teachers. *Progressive Education,* 8:251-255.

Perrone, V. 1989. Teacher education and progressivism: A historical perspective. In Author, *Working Papers: Reflections on teachers, schools and communities.* New York: Teachers College Press.

Perry, W. G. 1970. *Forms of intellectual and ethical development in the college years.* New York: Holt, Rinehart, and Winston.

Pollard, A., and S. Tann. 1987. *Reflective teaching in the primary school*. London: Cassell.

Reilly, D. 1989. A knowledge base for teacher education: Cognitive science. *Journal of Teacher Education*, 40(3):9-13.

Richardson, V. 1990. The evolution of reflective teaching and teacher education. In R. Clift, W. R. Houston, and M. Pugach, eds., *Encouraging reflective practice in education* (pp. 3-19). New York: Teachers College Press.

Robottom, I. 1988. A research-based course in science education. In J. Nias and S. Groundwater-Smith, eds., *The enquiring teacher: Supporting and sustaining teacher research* (pp. 106-120). London: Falmer Press.

Ross, D. and S. Krogh. 1988. From paper to program: A story from elementary PROTEACH. *Peabody Journal of Education*, 65(2):19-34.

Shulman, L. 1986. Those who understand: Knowledge growth in teaching. *Educational Researcher*, 15(2):4-14.

————. 1987. Knowledge and teaching: Foundations of the new reform. *Harvard Educational Review*, 57(1):1-22.

Tabachnick, B. R., and K. Zeichner. 1991. *Issues and practices in inquiry-oriented teacher education*. London: Falmer Press.

Tickle, L. 1987. *Learning teaching, teaching learning*. London: Falmer Press.

Tom, A. 1985. Inquiring into inquiry-oriented teacher education. *Journal of Teacher Education*, 36(5):35-44.

Valli, L. 1990a. Moral approaches to reflective practice. In R. Clift, W. R. Houston, and M. Pugach, eds., *Encouraging reflective practice in education* (pp. 39-56). New York: Teachers College Press.

————. 1990b. *The question of quality and content in reflective teaching*. Paper presented at the annual meeting of the American Educational Research Association, Boston.

Waxman, H. J. et al., eds., *Images of reflection in teacher education*. Reston, VA: Association of Teacher Educators.

Wildman, T. and J. Niles. 1987. Reflective teachers: Tensions between abstractions and realities. *Journal of Teacher Education*, 38(4):25-31.

Wilson, S., L. Shulman, and A. Richert. 1987. 150 different ways of knowing: Representations of knowledge in teaching. In J. Calderhead, ed., *Exploring teachers thinking* (pp. 104-124). London: Cassell.

Zeichner, K. 1983. Alternative paradigms of teacher education. *Journal of Teacher Education*, 34(3):3-9.

Zeichner, K., and D. Liston. 1990. Traditions of reform in U.S. teacher education. *Journal of Teacher Education*, 41(2):3-20.

Zeichner, K., and B. R. Tabachnick. 1991. Reflections on reflective teaching. In B. R. Tabachnick and K. Zeichner, eds., *Issues and practices in inquiry-oriented teacher education* (pp. 1-21). London: Falmer Press.

Zumwalt, K. 1982. Research on teaching: Policy implications for teacher education. In A. Lieberman and M. McLaughlin, eds., *Policy making in education* (pp. 215-248). Chicago: University of Chicago Press.

CHAPTER 11

Notes

1. Some cultural feminists suggest that patriarchy and its oppressive nature are in fact rooted in biology. For example Daly (1978) suggests that male's inability to give birth and thus "produce life" results in a form of dependence upon females and this dependence, in turn, leads to resentment and thus, the need to dominate and control the women of the world. From Daly's perspective, women need to create a new society based upon female consciousness and biology. Since men are, due to their inadequate biological composition, incapable of understanding this new world, their presence is generally regarded as unnecessary or even detrimental. Feminist pedagogy and cultural feminism as used in this chapter does not support Daly's vision. While legitimating the existence and value of a feminine versus a masculine ethos, it does not support the contention that men, due to their innate biology, are incapable of altering their socially constructed masculine consciousness. In addition, the goal is not to merely replace a masculine with a feminine consciousness, but rather to eventually synthesize these two divergent ways of thinking, valuing, and being.

References

Alcoff, L. 1988. Cultural feminism versus post-structuralism: The identity crisis in feminist theory. *Signs: Journal of Women in Culture and Society*, 13(3):405-434.

Apple, M. 1990. The politics of official knowledge in the United States. *Journal of Curriculum Studies*, 22(4):377-400.

————. 1986. *Teachers and texts: A political economy of class and gender relations in education*. London: Routledge and Kegan Paul.

Belenky, M. et al. 1986. *Women's ways of knowing: The development of self, voice, and mind*. New York: Basic Books.

Best, R. 1983. *We all have scars: What boys and girls learn in elementary schools*. Bloomington: Indiana University Press.

Beyer, L. 1988. Training and educating: A critique of technical-mindedness in teacher preparation. *Current Issues in Education*, 8(1):21-40.

——. 1984. Field experience, ideology, and the development of critical reflectivity. *Journal of Teacher Education*, 35(5):36-41.

Bunch, C., and S. Pollack. 1983. *Learning our way: Essays in feminist education*. Trumansburg, NY: Crossing Press.

Clark, D., and G. Marker. 1975. The institutionalization of teacher education. In K. Ryan, ed., *Teacher education* (pp. 53-86). Chicago: University of Chicago Press.

Cruickshank, D. R. et al. 1981. *Reflective teaching*. Bloomington, IN: Phi Delta Kappa.

Culley, M., and C. Portuges. 1985. *Gendered subjects: The dynamics of feminist teaching*. London: Routledge and Kegan Paul.

Daly, M. 1978. *Gyn/Ecology*. Boston: Beacon Press.

Dewey, J. 1933. *How we think: A restatement of the relation of reflective thinking to the educative process*. Chicago: Henry Regnery.

——. 1904. The relation of theory to practice in education. In *The relation of theory to practice in the education of teachers*, Third NSSE Yearbook, Part 1. Bloomington, IL: Public School Publishing Co.

Eder, D. 1985. The cycle of popularity: Interpersonal relations among female adolescents. *Sociology of Education*, 58(3):154-165.

Eder, D., and M. Hallinan. 1978. Sex differences in children's friendships. *American Sociological Review*, 43(2):237-250.

Elsbree, W. 1939. *The American teacher*. New York: American Book Co.

Franklin, B. 1986. *Building the American community: The school curriculum and the search for social control*. New York: Falmer Press.

Frymier, J. 1987. Bureaucracy and the neutering of teachers. *Phi Delta Kappan*, 69 (September):9-14.

Gilligan, C. 1982. *In a different voice: Psychological theory and women's development*. Cambridge, MA: Harvard University Press.

Gitlin, A. 1983. School structure and teachers' work. In M. Apple and L. Weis, eds., *Ideology and practice in schooling* (pp. 193-212). Philadelphia: Temple University Press.

Goodman, J. 1988. The disenfranchisement of elementary teachers and strategies for resistance. *Journal of Curriculum and Supervision*, 3(3):201-220.

———. 1986. University education courses and the professional preparation of teachers: A descriptive analysis. *Teaching and Teacher Education: An International Journal of Research and Studies,* 2(4):341-353.

———. 1985. Field-based experience: A study of social control and student teachers' response to institutional constraints. *Journal of Education for Teaching,* 11(1):26-49.

———. 1984. Reflection and teacher education: A case study and theoretical analysis. *Interchange,* 15(3):9-26.

Goodwin, M. 1980. Directive-response speech sequences in girls' and boys' task activities. In S. McConnell-Ginet, R. Borker, and N. Furman, eds., *Women and language in literature and society.* New York: Praeger.

Gore, J. 1987. Reflecting on reflective teaching. *Journal of Teacher Education,* 38(2):33-39.

Greene, M. 1978. *Landscapes of learning.* New York: Teachers College Press.

Grumet, M. 1981. Pedagogy for patriarchy: The feminization of teaching. *Interchange,* 12(2-3):165-184.

Guba, E., and D. Clark. 1978. Levels of R and D productivity in schools of education. *Educational Researcher,* 7(5):3-9.

Harding, S., and M. Hintikka. 1983. *Discovering reality: Feminist perspectives on epistemology, metaphysics, methodology, and philosophy of science.* Dordrecht, Holland: Reidel.

Howey, K., S. Yarger, and B. Joyce. 1978. *Improving teacher education.* Washington, D.C.: Association of Teacher Educators.

Janssen-Jurreit, M. 1980. *Sexism: The male monopoly on history and thought.* New York: Farrar.

Joyce, B., and R. Clift. 1984. The Phoenix agenda: Essential reform in teacher education. *Educational Researcher,* 13(4):5-18.

Judge, H. 1982. *American graduate schools of education: A view from abroad.* New York: Ford Foundation.

Keller, E. 1985. *Reflections on gender and science.* New Haven, CT: Yale University Press.

Kliebard, H. 1975. The rise of scientific curriculum making and its aftermath. *Curriculum Theory Network,* 5(1):27-38.

Laird, S. 1988. Reforming "women's true profession": A case for "feminist pedagogy" in teacher education? *Harvard Educational Review,* 58(4):449-463.

Lanier, J. and J. Little. 1986. Research on teacher education. In M. C. Wittrock, ed., *Handbook of research on teaching* (pp. 627-569). New York: Macmillan.

Lather, P. 1985. *The absent presence: Patriarchy, capitalism, and the nature of teacher work.* Paper presented at the annual Bergamo Curriculum Theory and Practice Conference, Dayton, OH.

Leck, G. 1987. Feminist pedagogy, liberation theory, and the traditional schooling paradigm. *Educational Theory,* 37(3):343-354.

Lesko, N. 1988. *Symbolizing society: Stories, rites, and structure in a Catholic high school.* New York: Falmer Press.

Lever, J. 1976. Sex differences in the games children play. *Social Problems,* 23(4):478-487.

Lightfoot, S. 1978. *Worlds apart: Relationships between families and schools.* New York: Basic Books.

Lortie, D. 1975. *Schoolteacher: A sociological study.* Chicago: Chicago University Press.

Maher, F. 1987. Toward a richer theory of feminist pedagogy: A comparison of "liberation" and "gender" models for teaching and learning. *Journal of Education,* 169(3):91-100.

Noddings, N. 1984. *Caring: A feminine approach to ethics and moral education.* Berkeley: University of California Press.

Peseau, B. 1982. Developing an adequate resource base for teacher education. *Journal of Teacher Education,* 33(4):13-15.

Peseau, B., and P. Orr. 1981. *The second annual academic and financial study of teacher education programs in senior state universities and land grant colleges, 1978-1979.* Montgomery: University of Alabama.

Peseau, B. 1980. The outrageous underfunding of teacher education, *Phi Delta Kappan,* 62(2):100-102.

Rich, A. 1985. Taking women students seriously. In M. Culley and C. Portuges, eds., *Gendered subjects: The dynamics of feminist teaching* (pp. 21-28). London: Routledge and Kegan Paul.

Sarason, S. 1971. *The culture of school and the problem of change.* Boston: Allyn and Bacon.

Shannon, P. 1987. Commercial reading materials, a technological ideology, and the deskilling of teachers. *Elementary School Journal,* 87(3):309-329.

Shrewsbury, C. 1987. What is feminist pedagogy? *Women's Studies Quarterly,* 15(3-4):6-13.

Shrum, W. 1988. Friendship in school: Gender and racial homophily. *Sociology of Education*, 61(4):227-239.

Spender, D. 1982. *Invisible women: The schooling scandal*. London: Writers and Readers Publishing Cooperative.

Stober, M., and D. Tyack. 1980. Why do women teach and men manage? A report on research on schools. *Signs: Journal of Women in Culture and Society*, 5(4):494-503.

Tabachnick, B., T. Popkewitz, and K. Zeichner. 1979-80. Teacher education and the professional perspectives of student teachers. *Interchange*, 19(4):12-29.

Tabachnick, B., and K. Zeichner. 1985. The development of teacher perspectives: Social strategies and institutional control in the socialization of beginning teachers. *Journal of Education for Teaching*, 11(1):1-25.

Tabakin, G., and K. Densmore. 1986. Teacher professionalization and gender analysis. *Teachers College Record*, 86(2):257-279.

Thorne, B., and Z. Luria. 1986. Sexuality and gender in children's daily worlds. *Social Problems*, 33(3):176-190.

Thorne, B. 1986. Girls and boys together . . . but mostly apart: Gender arrangements in elementary schools. In W. Hartup and Z. Rub in, eds., *Relationships and development* (pp. 167-184). Hillsdale, NJ: Lawrence Erlbaum.

Tom, A. 1984. *Teaching as a moral craft*. New York: Longman Press.

Weiler, K. 1988. *Women teaching for change: Gender, class, and power*. New York: Bergin and Garvey.

Zeichner, K. 1986. Social and ethical dimensions of reform in teacher education. In J. Hoffman and S. Edwards, eds., *Reality and reform in clinical teacher education* (pp. 87-107). New York: Random House.

Zeichner, K., and D. Liston. 1987. Teaching student teachers to reflect. *Harvard Educational Review*, 57(1):23-48.

CHAPTER 12

References

Belenky, M. et al. 1986. *Womens ways of knowing: The development of self, voice, and mind*. New York: Basic Books, Inc.

Dewey, J. 1933. *How we think: A Restatement of the relation of reflective thinking to the educative process*. Chicago: Henry Regnery Co.

Duckworth, Ed. 1986. Teaching as research. *Harvard Educational Review*, 56(4):481-495.

Feiman-Nemser, S., and M. Buchmann. 1985. Pitfalls of experience in teacher preparation. *Teachers College Record*, 87(1):53-65.

Little, J. W. 1990. The persistence of privacy: Autonomy and initiative in teachers' professional relations. *Teachers College Record*, 91(4):509-536.

Lortie, D. 1975. *Schoolteacher: A Sociological study*. Chicago: University of Chicago Press.

Noddings, N. 1984. *Caring: A Feminine approach to ethics and moral education*. Berkeley: University of California Press.

Richert, A. E. 1991. Teaching teachers to reflect: A consideration of program structure. *Journal of Curriculum Studies*, 22(6):509-527.

———. 1987. Reflex to reflection: Facilitating reflection in novice teachers. Unpublished doctoral dissertation, Stanford University.

Rosenholtz, S. J., and S. J. Kyle. 1984. Teacher isolation: Barrier to professionalism. *American Educator*. Winter:10-15.

Sarason, S. 1971. *The culture of school and the problem of change*. Boston: Allyn and Bacon.

Shulman, L. S., and N. B. Carey. 1984. Psychology and the limitations of individual rationality for the study of reasoning and civility. *Review of Education Research*. Winter:501-524.

Yinger, R., and C. Clark. 1981. *Reflective journal writing: Theory and practice*. East Lansing MI: Institute for Research on Teaching. Occasional paper no. 50.

CHAPTER 13

Notes

1. Excellent sources for an overview of Bourdieu's social and educational theory are in Bourdieu (1977) and DiMaggio (1979).

2. This definition is stipulated for the chapter; see also the section on definitional elaboration.

3. These are illustrative references representative of others in this volume.

4. See also Rorty (1979).

5. Dewey's (1929, 1960) writings are a precursor to the present debate.

6. These two examples are simply put for illustrative purposes and do not do justice either to the matter of essential language or of essential personhood.

7. In a work in progress, this author claims that the proposals of E. D. Hirsch (1987) are culturally essentialist and imperialist.

8. See Bernstein (1983), p. 16.

9. Ibid., p. 8.

10. Bernstein (1971), p. 16

11. See Rorty (1979).

12. Papers by Bell and Sibley, respectively, are in Beardsley (1966) and Tillman and Cahn, eds. (1969).

13. An introduction to structuralism is found in Kneller (1984); see also the excellent account from Cherryholmes (1988) as it applies to curriculum studies.

14. See Feinberg and Soltis (1985) for discussions of both functionalism and cultural universalism.

15. See Geertz (1983).

16. Here the general arises as analogue to the particular.

17. A dualism is established here that itself is modernist and often critiqued. Such dichotomies need not be hierarchical and harmful if they do not "exhaust meaning" (Ferguson, 1991).

18. For stylistic reasons, quotation marks are often eliminated in taking ideas directly from the descriptive chapters in the present volume. Every attempt is made to represent each program accurately, given that the analysis itself is highly interpretive. In addition, some elements are underscored for emphasis by the author.

19. Two studies in teacher education that are (at the least) postmodern in spirit are from Pagano (1990) and Britzman (1991). See also Lather (1989), Brodkey (1987), and Stone (1990), as well as Bowers (1987) and the edited collection from Giroux (1991).

20. A special thanks to Linda Valli for assistance with the chapter revisions.

References

Beardsley, M. 1966. *Aesthetics, from classical Greece to the present.* University, AL: The University of Alabama Press.

Bernstein, R. 1971. *Praxis and action.* Philadelphia: University of Pennsylvania Press.

———. 1983. *Beyond objectivism and relativism: science, hermeneutics and praxis.*

Philadelphia: University of Pennsylvania Press.

Bourdieu, P. 1977. Cultural reproduction and social reproduction. In J. Karabel and A. Halsey, eds., *Power and ideology in education* (pp. 487-511). New York: Oxford University Press.

———. 1987. The historical genesis of a pure aesthetic. *The Journal of Aesthetics and Art Criticism*, 46 (special issue):201-210.

Bowers, C. 1987. *Elements of a post-liberal theory of education.* New York: Teachers College Press.

Brameld, T. 1950, 1971. *Patterns of educational philosophy.* New York: Holt, Rinehart, and Winston.

Britzman, D. 1991. *Practice makes practice.* Albany, NY: State University of New York Press.

Brodkey, L. 1987. Postmodern pedagogy for progressive educators. *Journal of Education*, 169(3):138-143.

Cherryholmes, C. 1988. *Power and criticism.* New York: Teachers College Press.

Chodorow, N. 1978. *The reproduction of mothering.* Berkeley, CA: University of California Press.

de Lauretis, T. 1986. *Feminist studies/critical studies.* Bloomington, IN: Indiana University Press.

Dewey, J. 1929, 1960. *The quest for certainty.* New York: Capricorn Books.

DiMaggio, P. 1979. Review essay: on Pierre Bourdieu. *American Journal of Sociology*, 84(6):1460-1474.

Feinberg, W., and J. Soltis. 1985. *School and society.* New York: Teachers College Press.

Fenstermacher, G. 1986. Philosophy of research on teaching: three aspects. In M. Wittrock, ed., *Handbook of research on teaching* 3d ed. (pp. 37-49). New York: Macmillan Publishing Company.

Ferguson, K. 1991. Interpretation and genealogy in feminism. *Signs*, 16(2):322-339.

Geertz, C. 1983. *Local Knowledge.* New York: Basic Books.

Giroux, H., ed. 1991. *Postmodernism, feminism, and cultural politics.* Albany, NY: State University of New York Press.

Hassan, I. 1986. Pluralism in postmodern perspective. *Critical Inquiry*, 12(3):503-520.

Hirsch, E. 1987. *Cultural Literacy.* Boston: Houghton Mifflin.

Hutcheon, L. 1988. *A poetics of postmodernism.* New York: Routledge.

Kneller, G. 1984. *Movements of thought in modern education*. New York: John Wiley and Sons.

Kuhn, T. 1959, 1977. The essential tension: tradition and innovation in scientific research. In *The essential tension* (pp. 225-139). Chicago: The University of Chicago Press.

Lyotard, J. 1984. *The Postmodern Condition: A report on knowledge*. G. Bennington and B. Massumi, trans. Minneapolis: University of Minnesota Press.

Pagano, J. 1990. *Exiles and communities*. Albany, NY: State University of New York Press.

Quine, W., and J. Ullian. 1970. *The web of belief*. New York: Random House.

Rorty, R. 1979. *Philosophy and the mirror of nature*. Princeton: Princeton University Press.

——— . 1989a. *Contingency, irony and solidarity*. Cambridge: Cambridge University Press.

——— . 1989b. Philosophy, literature and inter-cultural comparison: Heidegger, Kundera, and Dickens. Paper presented at the Sixth East-West Philosophers' Conference, Honolulu, HI, 1989.

Schön, D. 1983. *The reflective practitioner*. New York: Basic Books.

Stone, L. 1990. Contingency in teaching: A suggestive framework. Paper presented at the annual meeting of the American Educational Research Association, Boston.

——— . 1991a. The social nature of aesthetics: Taking the notion seriously. *Arts and Learning Research*, 8(1):143-162.

——— . 1991b. Postmodern social construction: Initiating dissonance. Paper presented at the annual meeting of the American Educational Research Association, Chicago.

Taylor, C. 1985. *Human agency and language*. Cambridge: Cambridge University Press.

Tillman, F., and S. Cahn, eds. 1969. *Philosophy of art and aesthetics*. New York: Harper and Row.

AFTERWORD

Notes

1. Though not central to my argument here, it should be noted that each of Feiman-Nemser's conceptual orientations has considerable variation within

them. Thus, it seems strange to argue, as she does, against reflection as a distinct orientation on these grounds.

2. In a previous publication (Valli, 1990), I used the term deliberative to include both this category as well as the reflection-in-action category.

3. Through personal correspondence, Dorene Ross raised the interesting question of why the critical perspective is not more pervasive. Though it's beyond the scope of this book, teacher educators and researchers might want to ponder this issue. Is critical theory too insular, too esoteric, or too political for the current U.S. context? Or do other factors come into play?

4. I do not mean to imply by these hierarchical levels that the ones at the bottom are unimportant. They are simply insufficient. One could also argue that unless a teacher is well grounded in the "lower" levels, that a critical mode of reflection is an incomplete model of good teaching.

References

Berliner, D. 1988. *The development of expertise in pedagogy.* Washington, D.C.: AACTE Publications.

Brophy, J. 1987. Educating teachers about managing classrooms and students. Occasional paper no. 115. East Lansing, MI: Institute for Research on Teaching, Michigan State University.

Doyle, W. 1990. Themes in teacher education research. In W. R. Houston, ed., *Handbook of research on teacher education* (pp. 3-). New York: MacMillan.

Feimen-Nemser, S. 1990. Teacher preparation: Structural and conceptual alternatives. In W. T. Houston, ed., *Handbook of research on teacher education* (pp. 212-233). New York: MacMillan.

Fenstermacher, G. 1988. The place of science and epistemology in Schön's conception of reflective practice? In P. Grimmett and G. Erickson, eds., *Reflection in teacher education* (pp. 39-46). New York: Teachers College Press.

Gilliss, G. 1988. Schön's reflective practitioner: A model for teachers? In P. Grimmett and G. Erickson, eds., *Reflection in teacher education* (pp. 47-53). New York: Teachers College Press.

Grimmett, P. et al. 1990. Reflective practice in teacher education. In R. Clift, W. R. Houston, and M. Pugach, eds., *Encouraging reflective practice in education* (pp. 20-38). New York: Teachers College Press.

Howey, K., and N. Zimpher. 1989. *Profiles of preservice teacher education.* New York: State University of New York Press.

Kennedy, M. 1987. Inexact sciences: Professional education and the development of expertise. In E. Rothkopf, ed., *Review of research in education,* vol. 14 (pp. 133-167). Washington, D.C.: AERA.

————. 1989. Reflection and the problem of professional standards. *Colloquy*, 2(2):1-6.

NETWORK. 1987. A compendium of innovative teacher education projects. Andover, MA: The NETWORK, Inc.

Prakach, M., and L. Waks. 1985. Four conceptions of excellence. *Teachers College Record*, 87(1):79-101.

Richardson, V. 1990. The evolution for reflective teaching and teacher education. In R. Clift, W. R. Houston, and M. Pugach, eds., *Encouraging reflective practice in education* (pp. 3-19). New York: Teachers College Press.

Schön, D. 1983. *The reflective practitioner*. New York: Basic.

Shulman, L. 1988. The dangers of dichotomous thinking in education. In P. Grimmett and G. Erickson, eds., *Reflection in teacher education* (pp. 31-38). New York: Teachers College Press.

Tabachnick, B., and K. Zeichner, eds. 1991. *Issues and practices in inquiry-oriented teacher education*. New York: Falmer.

Tom, A. R. (1991). Whither the professional curriculum for teachers. *The Review of Education*, 14:21-30.

Tom, A. R., and L. Valli. 1990. Professional knowledge for teachers. In W. R. Houston, ed., *Handbook of research on teacher education* (pp. 373-392). New York: MacMillan.

Valli, L. 1990. Moral approaches to reflective practice. In R. Clift, W. R. Houston, and M. Pugach, eds., *Encouraging reflective practice in education* (pp. 39-56). New York: Teachers College Press.

van Manen, M. 1977. Linking ways of knowing with ways of being practical. *Curriculum Inquiry*, 6(3):205-228.

Wildman, T., and J. Niles. 1987. Reflective teachers: Tensions between abstractions and realities. *Journal of Teacher Education*, 38(4):25-31.

Zeichner, K. 1983. Alternative paradigms of teacher education. *Journal of Teacher Education*, 34(3):3-9.

Zeichner, K., and D. Liston. 1987. Teaching student teachers to reflect. *Harvard Educational Review*, 57(1):23-48.

Contributors

MICHAEL D. ANDREW is Professor of Education and Director of Teacher Education at the University of New Hampshire. He earned his Baccalaureate degree from Cornell University and Master of Arts in Teaching and Doctorate at Harvard University. He has taught science at the middle and high school levels and has been involved with science education, curriculum, and teacher education at the University of New Hampshire since 1966. He was principal initiator of the five year teacher education program at the University of New Hampshire and has published extensively on that program.

JANE APPLEGATE is Dean of the College of Human Resources and Education at West Virginia University. During her years in higher education she has been actively involved in local, state, and national developments related to teacher education. Her publications, conference presentations, grants, and consultant work reflect her concern for the growth, preparation, and continuing educational needs of America's teachers. Her research activities have focused especially on the kinds of learning students of teaching acquire through experience in schools.

RICHARD ARENDS is currently Dean of the School of Education at Central Connecticut State University. He received his Ph.D. in education from the University of Oregon where he was on the faculty from 1975 to 1984. A former elementary, junior high, and high school teacher, his special interests are the social psychology of education, teacher education, and organizational development and school improvement. Professor Arends has authored or contributed to over a dozen books on education and has worked widely with schools and universities throughout North America and the Pacific Rim. The recipient of numerous awards, he was selected in 1989 as the outstanding teacher educator in the state of Maryland and in 1990 received the Judith Ruskin award for outstanding research in education given by the Association for Supervision and Curriculum Development (ASCD).

HILDA BORKO is Associate Professor of Curriculum and Instruction at the University of Colorado, Boulder. At the time she wrote this chapter, she was on the faculty of The University of Maryland. Her current research interests include the process of learning to teach and expert-novice differences in teacher cognition and action. She is presently co-principal investigator (with Catherine Brown and Robert Underhill) of a longitudinal study of Learning to Teach Mathematics, funded by the National Science Foundation. She is also Editor of the Teaching, Learning, and Human Development Section of the *American Educational Research Journal*.

JAMES CALDERHEAD is Professor of Education at the University of Bath. He has taught in both primary and secondary schools in England and Scotland, and spent eleven years at the University of Lancaster lecturing in the Department of Educational Research. His research interests focus on teachers' professional development and the ways in which student teachers learn to teach. His publications include, *Teachers' Classroom Decision-Making*, and *Exploring Teachers' Thinking*, published by Cassell, and *Teachers' Professional Learning*, published by Falmer Press.

MARIA J. CIRIELLO spent eight years as a teacher in elementary school and fourteen years as an administrator in elementary and secondary schools before pursuing her doctorate at The Catholic University of America. In 1987 she joined the faculty at Catholic University as Assistant Professor working in the areas of Teacher Education and Education Administration. Her research interests include selection, commitment, and job satisfaction issues of teachers and administrators. She has an article relating to reflective teaching in *Educational Foundations*.

RENEE T. CLIFT is an Associate Professor of Curriculum and Instruction at the University of Illinois at Urbana-Champaign where she is helping to redesign graduate and undergraduate teacher preparation programs. She is also studying the process of learning to teach secondary school English, the nature of collaboration for teacher education and professional development, and the impact of school settings on opportunities for professional learning. Her recent publications include articles in *Journal of Teacher Education, Journal of Staff Development,* and an edited volume (with W. R. Houston and Marleen C. Pugach) published by Teachers College Press, *Encouraging Reflective Practice in Teacher Education: An Analysis of Issues and Programs.*

ELLEN CORCORAN is currently an Associate Professor of Education at the University of New Hampshire. After serving in the Peace Corps in West Africa, she taught in New York City while completing her Master's and Doctoral degrees at New York University. She came to the University of New Hampshire in 1972 and has been actively involved with its five year program since that time. Her major research interest focuses on the dynamics of learning to teach during the internship year.

ANN DILLER teaches Philosophy of Education at the University of New Hampshire. She does research on ethics and education. Publications include: "The Ethics of Care and Education: A New Paradigm, Its Critics, and Its Educational Significance, " *Curriculum Inquiry*, #18.3 (1988), pp. 325-342.

JESSE GOODMAN received his Ph.D. degree in 1982 from the University of Wisconsin in Madison and is now an associate professor at Indiana University. His primary interests include teacher education/socialization and the development and implementation of emancipatory pedagogy. He has had over twenty-five articles on these topics published in a variety of scholarly journals and books. Since 1986, his research on teacher socialization has received four national awards for distinguished scholarship and was selected as a finalist for a fifth award. Recently, the Indiana Association of Colleges for Teacher Education presented him with the Teacher Educator of the Year Award. He recently completed a book entitled *Elementary Schooling for Critical Democracy* published by the State University of New York Press.

S. G. GRANT is a doctoral student in the Department of Teacher Education in the College of Education at Michigan State University . He has held positions as a high school social studies teacher, a state social studies consultant, and as a director of graduate studies. His research interests include social studies education, teacher education, and curriculum development. Currently, he holds a research assistantship with the Center for Policy Research in Education which is studying the relationship between state curriculum policies and teacher practice.

W. ROBERT HOUSTON, Professor and Associate Dean for Academic Affairs, University of Houston, has been principal investigator of twenty-four major research and development projects that have explored competency-based teacher education, teacher induction, and reflective inquiry in teacher education. Among his thirty-nine edited or authored books are *Handbook of Research on Teacher Education* (Macmillan, 1990) and *Encouraging Reflective Practice in Education* with R. T. Clift and M. C. Pugach (Teachers College Press, 1990).

MARGARET JOHNSON is a graduate student of teacher education at the University of Florida. Prior to returning to graduate school, she was teacher and administrator in an international school in Mallorca, Spain. Her current work includes coordination of evaluation studies of elementary PROTEACH, co-directing the PROTEACH Beginning Teacher Conference, and research with PROTEACH students.

JOSEPH McCALEB is an Associate Professor at the University of Maryland, College Park where he has held a joint appointment in the Department of Curriculum and Instruction and in the Department of Speech Communication for fifteen years. Prior to college teaching, he taught in high school and junior high school. His graduate degrees were from the University of Texas. He is especially interested in critical literacy and at-risk youth.

JANE McCARTHY has been actively involved in the field of teacher education and research in teacher and school effectiveness since 1975. She is currently the Associate Director of the Accelerated Schools Project at Stanford University. Prior to this appointment, she served as Chairperson of the Instructional Studies and Teacher Education Program Area at the University of Houston where she coordinated the teacher certification program. Dr. McCarthy's research interests include classroom management, instructional effectiveness, and school restructuring.

SHARON NODIE OJA is Associate Professor and Director of Field Experiences in the University of New Hampshire Five-Year Teacher Education Program where she teaches courses in human development and learning. She received her Ph.D in 1978 from the University of Minnesota. Dr. Oja has been a principal investigator in two nationally funded school-university projects focusing on teachers' cognitive-developmental growth: A Collaborative Approach to Leadership in Supervision, and Teacher Stages of Development in Relation to Collaborative Action Research in Schools.

JOYCE PUTNAM is a Professor of Teacher Education at Michigan State University. She received her Ph.D. degree from Michigan State University and has directed and coordinated teacher education programs at MSU since 1973. Dr. Putnam was previously an elementary and secondary teacher. Her research interests include classroom organization and management and the process of how teachers learn to teach. She is the author of numerous journal articles and recently she completed a book with Bruce Burke titled *Organization and Management for Classroom Learning Communities*. Dr. Putnam is engaged currently with the Professional Development School movement at Michigan State and with the redesign of teacher education programs.

ANNA E. RICHERT is an Assistant Professor of Education at Mills College in Oakland, California. In both her teaching and her research she is examining notions of reflective practice. She places her research on teacher reflection into nested frames of teacher learning at one level, and the moral and ethical imperatives of teacher decision making and knowledge construction at the next. Her current work focuses on the use of case methods in teacher education to enhance teacher reflection and teacher empowerment.

DOREEN DOERRE ROSS is a Professor of Education at the University of Florida. She has published widely on issues related to teacher judgment and teacher reflection in journals such as *Contemporary Education, Educational Forum, Journal of Teacher Education,* and *Peabody Journal of Education.* She was a co-director of the Florida conference on Reflective Inquiry and has guest edited an issue of *Qualitative Studies in Education* on reflective practice.

BEVERLY SHAKLEE is an Associate Professor in Teacher Development and Curriculum Studies at Kent State University. She is currently directing two grants through the U.S. Department of Education: Early Assessment for Exceptional Potential, and the Cooperative Alliance for Gifted Education. Dr. Shaklee has been actively involved in the implementation of the Academically Talented Teacher Education Program (ATTEP). She has also co-authored several publications about reflection, most recently an article for the *Peabody Journal of Education.*

WILLIAM SMITH is a graduate student of teacher education at the University of Florida. Prior to returning to graduate school, he was an elementary principal at Bells Elementary in Ruffin, South Carolina. He has received a Graduate Council Fellowship at Florida and his current work includes supervision and research with student interns.

GEORGEA M. SPARKS-LANGER is Associate Professor of Teacher Education at Eastern Michigan University. She received her doctorate at Stanford University in Educational Psychology, with specializations in teacher effectiveness, teacher growth, and evaluation research. Her current research focuses on how novice teachers improve their teaching decisions and actions. Georgea has recently published articles in *Educational Leadership* and the *Journal of Teacher Education,* and has co-authored an undergraduate methods textbook, *Teaching as Decision Making.*

LYNDA STONE is Assistant Professor, Philosophy of Education, at the University of Hawaii. Prior to residing in Hawaii, she taught social studies in California secondary schools and earned her doctorate at Stanford University. While writing her dissertation she taught at several colleges and universities in the eastern United States. She defines herself largely as a social philosopher interested in issues of curriculum and teaching and often employs feminist and critical lenses to undertake analysis and critique. Her dissertation is in aesthetics, and a current project focuses on postmodern teaching.

NANCY E. TAYLOR is an Associate Professor in the Department of Education at the Catholic University of America She coordinates the Early Childhood Teacher Education Program and teaches the undergraduate reading and language arts course. Her research interest in teacher education centers on the way teachers' belief systems influence their goals and actions.

ALAN R. TOM is Professor of Education at the University of Arizona. He is author of *Teaching as a Moral Craft* and has published on such issues as the knowledge base for teaching, the relation of educational theory and practice, and the design of teacher education programs. Tom is currently preparing a book on his ideas for rethinking the structure and curriculum of the professional portion of initial teacher preparation.

LINDA VALLI is Associate Professor and the Director of Teacher Education at the Catholic University of America. She is the author of *Becoming Clerical Workers*, a critical social analysis of gender, schooling, and workplace relations, and edited *Curriculum Differentiation: Interpretive Studies of U.S. Secondary Schools* with Reba Page. She has co-authored articles with Alan Tom on the knowledge base for teaching and has published a number of articles on reflective teacher education.

KENNETH M. ZEICHNER is a Professor in the Department of Curriculum and Instruction at the University of Wisconsin in Madison and a Senior Researcher in the National Center for Research on Teacher Learning. He is co-director of the Elementary Student Teaching Program and teaches graduate courses in the study of teacher education. His recent publications include *Teacher Education and the Social Conditions of Schooling* (with Dan Liston) Routledge, 1991, *Issues and Practices in Inquiry-Oriented Teacher Education* (edited with B. Robert Tabachnick) Falmer Press (1991), and "Contradictions and tensions in the professionalization of teaching and the democratization of schools" *Teachers College Record*.

Subject Index

A

Academically talented students, 66, 68, 69, 76
Action research, ix, xiv, 29, 44, 49, 50, 52, 53, 58, 71, 72, 111, 142, 151, 153, 155, 156, 158, 196
Adult development, 154, 155
Apprentice teaching, 14, 41, 43
Apprenticeship of observation, 177, 182
Arena of the problematic, xvii, 68, 78
AssertiveDiscipline, 35
At risk learner, 36, 170
Autobiography, 30

B

Beginning Teacher Conference, 30, 34
Beginning years of teaching, 33, 37, 60
Behavioral psychology, ix, xiii

C

Capitalism, 176
Caring, 181, 182, 195
Case study, 56
Certainty, 209
Classroom Management, 97, 108, 176, 181, 182
Co-explorers, xix, 4, 7, 9, 11, 14, 18, 19, 193

Cognitive complexity, 67, 72, 73, 157
Cognitive psychology, viii, ix, xii, xiii, 46, 48, 147, 165
Cohort group, xx, 22, 42, 50, 52, 56, 67, 70, 77, 80, 88, 111, 193
Collaboration, xiv, 19, 102, 105, 106
Collaborative action, 26; educational experiences, 124; efforts, 77; modes of learning, 167; presumptions about, 12; problem solving, 103; reflection, 172; research/inquiry, 20; seminars/triad, 155; supervisory team, 3, 4, 14, 18, 20-22; work, xx, 11
Collaborative Action Research, 19
Collaborative Approach to Leadership in Supervision Project, 18, 19
Commonplaces of education, xxi, 90, 92, 107, 108, 110, 156
Communities of inquiry and support, xix, 3, 4, 6-8, 11, 14, 16-18, 20, 22, 23, 205
Competency-based teacher education, viii, 118, 180, 185
Conceptual framework, xxi, 101, 107, 108, 111-114, 121, 172
Conceptual Orientations (of teacher preparation), xv, xvi, xviii, xix, 213-16; academic, xv-xviii, xxiv, 163, 214, 215; behavioristic, xv, xvi, 217; cognitive, xxiii, 147; critical, xvii, xxiii, 147, 214, 219; deliberative, 218, 219, 225; developmentalist,

271

Name Index

A

Adler, M., 202
Alcoff, L., 176
Altrichter, H., 162
Anderson, R. H., 47, 148
Andrew, M. D., 4-5, 17
Apple, M., 177-9
Applegate, J., 47, 73, 75, 77, 171
Aquinas, St. Thomas, 201
Arends, R., 47, 53, 140, 169-70
Aristotle, 201
Ashcroft, K., 162
Ashton, P. J., 28, 30
Atkins, J. M., 168

B

Barnard, H., 178
Barnes, H. L., xii, 25, 97
Beecher, C., 178
Belenky, M., 181
Bell, C., 203
Benbow, C. P., 70
Berlak, A., 100, 107-8
Berlak, H., 100, 107-8
Berliner, D. C., 45, 47, 54, 148, 215, 224
Bernstein, R., 200
Best, R., 181
Beyer, L., 166, 175
Bloom, A., 117
Blum, I. H., 101, 104, 107, 113
Blume, 25

Boles, K., 167
Bondy, E., 30, 34
Book, C., 141
Borko, H., 47, 59-60, 140, 169-70
Borrowman, M., 119, 163
Bourdieu, P., 198
Brace, D., 120
Brameld, T., 201
Brickhouse, N. W., 141
Brookover, W., 47
Brophy, J., 47, 53, 218
Buchmann, M., 51, 101, 163, 191
Bullough, R., 30, 167
Bunch, C., 183
Burke, J., 86
Butt, R.L., 30
Byers, J., 141

C

Calderhead, J., xxiii, 141, 162, 223
Carey, N. B., 195
Carroll, G. R., 25
Carter, K., 148
Chodorow, N., 203
Chomsky, N., 203
Ciriello, M. J., 140
Clandinin, D. J., 30, 151, 162
Clark, C. M., xiii, 104, 148-49, 192
Clark, D., 161, 185
Clifford, G., 119
Clift, R. T., xii, 45, 118, 141, 161, 170-71, 185